PARETO

julien freund

Author of

THE SOCIOLOGY OF MAX WEBER

Edited and Translated by

SIMONA DRAGHICI

PLUTARCH   PRESS

corvallis, or

Published in the United States by
PLUTARCH PRESS
P.O. Box 195
Corvallis, OR 97339-0195

Originally published in France as
PARETO: LA THÉORIE DE L'EQUILIBRE
par Julien Freund

The Appendices originally published in Switzerland as

A. L'individuel et le social

B. L'avenir de l'Europe. Le point de vue d'un italien

C. Le phénomène du fascisme

in Vilfredo Pareto: Mythes et idéologies de la politique

For information, address the publisher:
PLUTARCH PRESS
P.O. Box 195, Corvallis, OR 97339-0195

Library of Congress Cataloging-in-Publication Data

Freund, Julien
    Pareto.

    Translation of: Pareto : la théorie de l'équilibre.
    Bibliography: p.   Includes index.
    1. Pareto, Vilfredo, 1848-1923. 2. Sociology--Italy--
History. I. Draghici, Simona, 1937-
II. Pareto, Vilfredo, 1848-1923. Selections. English.
1987. III. Title.
HM22.I56P33413 1987   301'.092'4   87-11880
ISBN 0-943045-00-2 (pbk.)

Book design by JAY
Manufactured in the United States of America

While most of the English translations of Pareto's writings are in print, not the same abundance meets the eye when it comes to books and articles about Pareto and his works. Actually, the Trade Book List for 1986-1987 features only two: one, a reprint of an essay by Franz Borkenau, originally published fifty years ago, and the other, a short monograph by Charles H. Powers, not yet available from its publisher, Sage Publications, when I tried to order it. In the years since WWII, a decreasing number of essays, introductory or on specific problems, and then mainly on the empirical use of the research tools supplied by him, chapters in books on theory, as well as a couple of doctoral dissertations, has seen the light of day in the United States. Little to justify the continuous reprinting of his works. On the other hand, I must confess that I had had a copy of Julien Freund's long essay on Pareto in my library for quite a while. Eventually, one day curious to see how he had been handling Pareto's concept of ruse, I picked it up and got so engrossed in the book that I did not put it aside until I read it through. It was there and then that I decided to help reduce the discrepancy by translating it into English for the benefit of the cogent lay reader, as well as for the anxious students who find Pareto on their lists of compulsory readings without understanding very well why.

Julien Freund is well known in this country for his book entitled THE SOCIOLOGY OF MAX WEBER, which combines the talent of live and laconic writing with a keen sense of actuality and an unabating need of clarification. The same happy combination surfaces in this presentation of Pareto's works and concerns, meant for the general reader. Moreover, Julien Freund's monograph may be easily integrated into the stream of the Paretian exegesis, made public in the United States, through the years. If Lawrence J. Henderson offered a first epistemological approach to the TREATISE, half a century ago, Julien Freund expands and refines it in the light of the achievements registered in this area of science since then and also corrects it where Henderson gave in to routine thinking and saw synthesis where there was hardly any. If Homans and Curtis understood the concept of the non-logical correctly, Professor Freund defines its place and reintegrates it in Pareto's general system of thought. He also answers Borkenau's accusations, as the latter turned Pareto into a precursor of Fascism and denied him any merit as a social scientist. True, he does it not by addressing Borkenau's remarks directly, but those of a much younger socialist thinker who, faithful to the socialist stand, has adopted Borkenau's position in his own doctoral dissertation, presented at the very University of Lausanne where Pareto had previously taught. I am talking of Guy Perrin whose PhD dissertation has been published in book-form in France. However Perrin does not seem to have appreciated Borkenau's Freudian interpretations of Pareto's personality, as he refers to none. Through his own epistemological approach and by following Pareto's intellectual evolution stage by stage, Julien Freund frees himself from the vice of apologetics and instead gives the reader some of the reasons for the treatment to which both Pareto and his works have been subjected until now.

To offer a fuller illustration of the points made by Professor Freund in his monograph, I took it upon me to append three of Pareto's own articles in translation to this book. I thank Librarie Droz of Geneva for granting me permission to do so. The first is actually the paper on the sociological concepts of the individual and the social, which Pareto read at the International Congress of Philosophy in 1904. It seems to me to be as topical as it was eighty years ago. The other two belong to the category of journalism informed by the social sciences and Pareto's own insight. They were written in the last months of his life: the second, 'The Fascist Phenomenon,' was first published in Spanish in the periodical LA NACION, on March 25, 1923, less than four months before his death. Indeed, those who crudely believe that Pareto was a Fascist would not change their minds by reading it, but the uncommitted might like to follow Pareto's own testimony of the events which he was witnessing at close range, and the relevance of which did not die with Mussolini. The other article, on the future of Europe, casts light on the importance attached by Pareto to forecasting in the social sciences and presents some instances of social behaviour that have astoundingly much in common with others that we are living nowadays. The articles make lively and rewarding reading, unlike many pages of the TREATISE. This brings me also to the problem of the quotations used by Julien Freund in his exposition. Not only does he most of the time refer to the French texts printed in the Busino edition of Pareto's collected works, but in the process he also manages to strike a stylistic balance between those quotations and his own prose. This harmony I was anxious to preserve, whence my decision to translate Pareto's excerpts anew, even where English translations were already available, although by various hands who worked at different moments in time. I have considered it my duty to signal these translations in the Notes and in the Select Bibliography at the end of the book. There is still another point I wish to make: the Index which I have attached to this translation covers Professor Freund's text only, and is meant to complement the table of Contents. Pareto's own articles have not been indexed.

Julien Freund presents us with the intellectual portrait of an intelligent individual wrestling with the reality around him and of which he was a part; a man endowed with enough acumen to realize eventually that his a priori theories would hardly work in actual life, yet never tiring of trying to understand the world and of making his findings intelligible to his fellow human beings. An experience that may sound familiar and which some of us might have been sharing.

Washington, DC   Simona Draghici
   July 1986

CONTENTS

BIOGRAPHICAL NOTE

Vilfredo Pareto was born in Paris, in 1848, the son of an Italian political refugee, Raffaele Pareto, belonging to the Ligurian nobility, and of a French mother, Marie Ménetier.

Taking advantage of an amnesty, the Pareto family returned to Italy in 1850, settled at Genoa where Vilfredo attended secondary school, and then moved to Turin where he enrolled at the local University (BSc in physics and mathematics) and afterwards, at its Polytechnical School, between 1867 and 1869. He graduated from it with the title of engineer, having submitted a thesis on the fundamental principles of the equilibrium in solid bodies.

In 1871 he embarked on a career as a railway engineer with the Società Anonima delle Strade Ferrate Romane in Florence.

Travels to Austria, Germany and England.

Pareto became member of the Adam Smith Society of Florence and published his first articles on economics.

In 1882 he became director of the Società delle Ferriere Italiane.

Defeat in the Pistoia constituency at the parliamentary elections. Joined the Società internazionale per la Pace.

In 1889 married a young Russian, Alessandrina Bakunin.

Pareto took part in various conventions for peace and free trade.

The Italian Government turned down his offer to deliver a free course of lectures on political economy. One of his lectures was interrupted by the intervention of the police.

In 1891 Pareto met Léon Walras whom he succeeded as professor of political economy at the University of Lausanne in 1893.

Between 1896 and 1897, he published his COURS D'ÉCONOMIE POLITIQUE. Extended his hospitality in Switzerland to Italian socialists fleeing the country in the aftermath of the Milan riots.

In 1898 Pareto started to teach sociology on a regular basis.

In 1901 he moved to Céligny, on the shore of the Lake of Geneva. Lectured at the École des hautes études in Paris, and became editor of a series of publications on the social sciences that included the first Italian translation of a work by Max Weber.

In 1903 he published his SYSTÈMES SOCIALISTES. In 1907, his MANUALE D'ECONOMIA POLITICA, and in 1911, LE MYTHE VERTUISTE ET LA LITTÉRATURE IMMORALE.

Gradually he relinquished his teaching of political economy to Boninsegni, in order to devote more of his time to sociology.

In 1916 he published his TRATTATO DI SOCIOLOGIA GENERALE.

In 1917 the University of Lausanne celebrated the Pareto Jubilee.

In 1920 he published FATTI E TEORIE, and in 1921, his TRASFORMAZIONE DELLA DEMOCRAZIA.

In 1922 he was asked to represent the Mussolini Government on the Economic and Financial Commission of the League of Nations. His adherence to Fascism was conditional as shown by his articles published in the review GERARCHIA. In them he demanded the safeguarding of basic freedoms.

In 1923 he was nominated senator of the Italian Kingdom, but a few months later, on August 19, 1923, he died at Céligny and was buried there.

I

AN IMPERTINENT WAY OF THINKING

Pareto is an irritating and at times quite an unbearable author. Few are the books and articles about his writings that disregard his personality and remain content to deal with his theoretical stances alone. Opinions about his works invariably include judgments about Pareto the man. Thus it seems only natural to me to follow suit and talk first about the man and only afterwards turn to his work. By the way, there is also the other trend which makes it its duty to ignore his work for the sake of the reputation attached to his person. Let us then try in all clarity to understand a personality that is allegedly unyielding to such treatment.

It cannot be said that Pareto is unknown to sociologists. Nor even that he is poorly known. After all, he had his hour of glory in America, on the eve of WWII. Whoever has been reading Talcott Parsons[1] becomes aware of Pareto even if indirectly. Rather, he has been put in quarantine, which is a roundabout way of acknowledging his importance and of paying him that kind of tribute which he himself might have relished. It has been his wish that the TREATISE OF GENERAL SOCIOLOGY[2] should not find too many readers. Ultimately his fate is that which he had foreseen for himself, though perhaps only ironically. This sort of ostracism is evident above all in France, despite the efforts of his early student, G.-H. Bousquet,[3] and the brilliant pages written about Pareto by Raymond Aron, though only recently. At the beginning, in 1937, Aron had published a very critical article on Pareto's sociology in ZEITSCHRIFT FÜR SOZIAL-FORSCHUNG.[4] Possibly he had acted then under the influence of Bouglé who, as Aron remembers, had a fit of rage every time someone dared to mention Pareto's name in his presence. If Pareto is still under ban in France, this situation should undoubtedly be attributed to the influence exerted by Gurvitch whose partialities were as arbitrary as they were unjustified. In his own ÉTUDES SUR LES CLASSES SOCIALES, Gurvitch went that far to say that Pareto's concepts should be regarded as 'an example of what one should avoid in sociology.'[5] Likewise, it would not be difficult at all to show that the book on Pareto's sociology by Guy Perrin[6] may hardly be considered a contribution to the understanding of Pareto's thinking. It is built on the premise that Pareto had only sought to discredit reason and rehabilitate the obscure forces of the irrational, which contradicts Pareto's own texts.

What are the reasons behind this denigration full of animosity against Pareto and his work? They are many, and besides, they vary with their authors, the latter's political cotteries and sociological chapels. One may go on and assume that as Pareto's work is more widely read and better known, one would find other reasons to criticise him. Nor do I claim to offer a final explanation of Pareto's ordeal.

The most benign but by no means the least important reason which keeps one away from his writings is that Pareto puts his reader off by annoying and unnerving him or her, at one and the same time. While I was an impecunious student myself, I used to spend long hours summarizing books that were not easily affordable, by such authors as Bodin, Hobbes, Husserl, Simmel, Cassirer, Jaspers and others, in copybooks of my own and accompanying my notes by illustrative quotations. The only time that I gave up that method was when I was reading Pareto's TREATISE. I went on reading hastily and with the unpleasant feeling of turning round and round, always finding the same questions raised time and again. Only the illustrations were changing. Not one moment did I experience the intellectual satisfaction of making any progress in my understanding. I have equally to confess that several weeks later I borrowed the book from the library once again, determined to read it more attentively. That very likely because at the time I was opposed to that sort of analysis of society and politics. It was only much later, when eventually I grew full of indignation at the incoherence shown by the politicians and the contradictions which I I came so see between their acts and their words, that Pareto alongside others, among whom Max Weber, helped me to overcome my dismay. After all, Pareto had been trying to explain attitudes which other sociologists, either more flattering or more tolerant, were overlooking or dissimulating. The annoying cynicism that had upset me while I had been reading the TREATISE for the first time eventually ceased to irritate me. Meanwhile I too came to experience illusion and disappointment in social and political matters. Nevertheless, I still think that Pareto's writings are indigestible and tiresome to a degree. Even his admirers are of the opinion that the structure of the TREATISE is disorderly and its reading difficult. Besides, while claiming high and loud that he had no 'didactical pretensions,' Pareto eventually consented to compile a new version of his sociological book, simpler and easier to read, in co-operation with Bousquet. The precarious state of his health, however, and his subsequent death prevented him from completing that project. Ultimately it was carried out by Bousquet alone, and published under the title PRÉCIS DE SOCIOLOGIE D'APRÈS VILFREDO PARETO in 1925. [7] As a matter of fact, there are other writings that put off the reader, Hegel's or Husserl's, for instance, yet none drives those willing to get acquainted with any of them to such dispair. That Pareto can arouse feelings of this sort is due to some other reasons besides those regarding the form of his works.

From his writings one gathers the impression that Pareto was a haughty character, ready to show his contempt and to turn easily to sarcasm in order to ridicule whatever displeased him. The ill-disposed readers (or perhaps they need not be ill-disposed after all) are tempted to describe his attitude as idle arrogance, or even as vain haughtiness. The tone is almost always aggressive, yet not because Pareto was fond of polemics or controversial debate. On the contrary, by and large he refused to lend himself to that kind of discussion. Rather, because he never ceased to express his disdain for certain people and certain things, and sometimes would give the impression that he was ignorant of the virtues of irony regarding his own person. As he was of aristocratic stock, one is tempted to link his temperament to his class origin. Such an explanation, however would be too simplistic, to say the least, because Pareto's irreverence did not spare

anybody or anything, were they people, groups or ideas of
the right or of the left. He directed his caustic shafts
against the bourgeoisie and socialism alike. With feigned
artlessness he liked to play the fool, as Raymond Aron would
say, in order to abuse the philosophers, the intellectuals
and the politicians, all together. Sometimes he poked fun
at the 'literary' economists; other times, he flayed a paragraph written by Hegel or another philosopher that was difficult to understand,with the mere purpose of openly deriding
it. Still on other occasions, he diverted himself by taking
to pieces a particular speech, delivered by a politician.
He would do it in such a way as to make the latter guilty
of contradiction. In the TRANSFORMATION [8] one finds an illustration of this kind of treatment in the way Pareto held
up to ridicule a speech made by Giolitti. Pareto wrote with
ease (Busino calls him a polygraph), and for that very reason
he no doubt increased the number of demolitions which, it
goes without saying, drew hatred and enmity upon himself.
Obviously, it is not hard to find him guilty of faulty logic,
too, as for instance when he claimed to speak in the name
of the value-neutrality of science while at the same time
mocking everything that he personally disliked. His attacks
were loaded with value-judgments and expressed patent subjective positions. Thus he turned his side to his critics in
order to baffle his contemporaries indiscriminately at times,
and quite often on petty issues. In fact the intellectuals
were not late in paying him in his own coin for his cease-
less attacks against them. They feigned to ignore him. Nevertheless, if such character traits are likely to vex, they
are not enough to explain the mistrust which his work has
been held in.

Although himself a university professor for some twenty-
five years, Pareto was never a career academic in the classical meaning of the word. He had been educated at the Turin
Polytechnic and had been a railway engineer for some twenty
years afterwards. It was only in the aftermath of a defeat
suffered in the political arena (he had been a candidate
for Pistoia at the parliamentary elections) that he accepted
to replace Walras at the University of Lausanne. Nonetheless,
he did not regard his professorship as a university career
which would have compelled him to specialize in a very narrow

field. He was so widely cultured that he did not miss the occasion to show it to his colleagues from other fields, at times revealing himself something of a pedant, too much aware as he was of his own superiority. That did not however prevent him from maintaining excellent relations with Naville, the philosopher, or with Ferdinand de Saussure, now granted a position of honour by present-day structuralism. Pareto felt at ease discussing a question of mathematics, physics, or technology, and equally so when he tackled a problem of political economy (at Lausanne he was professor of political economy). Besides, one must also point to his learning in the fields of literature and philosophy: he could read classical Greek, as well as Latin; he had extensive and detailed knowledge of the literatures of various lands and times. One may become aware of that simply by reading his MYTHE VERTUISTE.[9] He even authored several articles in which he clarified certain philological problems. It is natural that Pareto's vast erudition, his broad and varied knowledge might have seemed overbearing to his colleagues. Notwithstanding, his worldliness as an interlocutor and as a lecturer saved him from imperiousness. There is a sizeable discrepancy between the tediousness of some of his writings, on the one hand, and the brilliance which his contemporaries acknowledged as his own, on the other. His superiority in the most varied subject-matters might have upset some of his fellow academics, but need not be held any longer against him, unless one is afflicted by intellectual envy. A nincompoop always finds himself at ease only among nincompoops.

Pareto is also reproached his alleged approval of Fascism and his acceptance of the honours it conferred on him after he had turned down those of the previous régime. He consented to the idea of representing Mussolini's Government at the League of Nations. Gurvitch, on his part, went so far to claim that the speeches made by Il Duce and his acolytes reflected Pareto's ideas. He did not flinch from depicting Pareto as a headspring of 'fascist and nazi propagandists.'[10] In this way, the French sociologist only showed a greater taste for hyperbole than Pareto himself. After the act, when events have receded into the past, it is quite easy to confuse the end of the political movement with its beginnings. History is full of such paralogisms, generated by resurging passion. These exaggerations aside, there is enough room left to wonder how Pareto, who made himself known as a champion of liberalism throughout his life, could discredit himself in the end by flirting with Fascism. The circumstances prevalent in Italy at the time may make the answer easier. They had led other Italian writers, such as Croce, for instance, who later on became one of the strongest opponents of the régime, to rally provisionally to the Fascist movement, in the same way as writers and politicians like a Theodor Heuss, for example, would cast their vote in favour of Hitler's government at the beginning of Hitlerism. It was in the same way that French writers, who had first supported Pétain and the Vichy régime, came eventually to join the resistance. Actually, Pareto's adherence seems to have been quite cautious, because he never went back on his liberal convictions however much he approved of the prospect of re-established order in Italy. His correspondence during that period and his article entitled 'Liberta,' which was printed in the Fascist monthly GERARCHIA, testify to that.[11] In them he defended his life-long principles and demanded the observance of every freedom, that of the press, as well as that of education, the freedom of confessional school included, though he himself was an ardent defender of lay thinking. Pareto died in 1923, before Mussolini could have had the time to embark upon his political adventures. Consequently one may only speculate whether he would have supported Mussolini's régime later on. Whenever one looks at the discriminations made after 1945, and discovers the leniency shown to certain authors and the severity to which others have been subjected, though their involvement was less than that of the former, one cannot help seeing in the criticism hurled at Pareto a pretext (or, to use his own words, a derivation) that conceals a latent yet deeper antagonism.

One of the main original features of the researchwork in the human sciences, that is in philosophy as well as in psychology and sociology, consists in debunking the designs and the so-called genuine ends of human action and of human thinking. One tries to find out the real motive and the structural trends behind the apparent and the avowed values and superstructures. Hence the attraction exerted by Marx, Nietzsche and Freund, but also by Heidegger (thanks to his unveiling theory), as well as the fad of explanations in terms of ideology. The latter passes for false-consciousness which in turn masks real intentions. More than any other subject-matter in our times, sociology participated in this vast inquisition which, under the pretext of detecting and supressing all lies, illusions, hypocrisy and mystification, condemns every human society that has ever existed. It hopes to build up a counter-society in an indefinite future, that would be transparent to itself, while its inhabitants would be fully aware of all their acts and desires. In this way, debunking has been turned into a permanent indictment of mankind, and sociology, into an enterprise that offers con-tinuous revelations which are indiscriminately assimilated to a revolutionary will. Without doubt the great social scientists at the beginning of this century, particularly Max Weber and Pareto, helped considerably to direct sociology along this path. The Paretian distinction between residues and derivations is only one of the methods of debunking. What surprises is that Pareto does not find the same favour as Marx, Freund and Weber do, with present-day sociologists and philosophers. To say nothing of the fact that Freudian thinking needed to be processed Marcuse-style in order to meet the tastes of the day. After a passing eclipse, Nietzsche is in fashion anew, thanks to additional clarifications brought to bear upon his writings. One is still wary of Max Weber to a certain extent, but the discrepancies in the interpretation of his writings are blamed on the poor performance of his translators. In brief, one thinks that all these authors can be rescued in order to make them join Marx in the empyrean inhabited by the philosophers of indis-cretion and demystification. Pareto alone is denied the privilege. The excommunication seems to be due to Pareto's very peculiar method of debunking. I am inclined to suspect that it is in this highly idiosyncratic method that one can find the main but by no means the only reason why his works have been wrapped up in relative silence.

As it will be seen further on, through his distinction between residues and derivations, Pareto tried to show that all systems of thought, whatever they might be, were only mere attempts to apply a coat of logic and rationality to actions that were actually devoid of them. These attempts

were made by intellectuals and people, in general, in their
need of justification. Those systems appeared to Pareto
as many disguises (at the level of consciousness) of deeper
residues, invariably inherent in human nature. That is why
he paid no tribute to the myth of progress or to the belief
in the possibility of setting up a better social system.
Utopia is only one kind of derivation and of camouflage.
Pareto did not spare philosophy, not for that matter did
he morality, religion or science. His devastating analysis
was extended to all ends and values, either traditional
or merely defined by various political, economic or religious
doctrines in circulation. As Pareto saw it, Marx's criticism,
for instance, was carried out in the name of unattainable
values: it had an aspiration and a normative system built
in it. Moreover, Marx's own system was endowed with an end
to be achieved, and consequently with a future. He, Marx,
criticized value-systems in the name of another value-system.
With his dry, ravaging sarcasm, Pareto cast all such attempts
into the hell of illusions. Through the sieve of censorship
he put all the fashionable vocabulary which served to edify
the intellectuals: socialism, peace, equality, justice,
and so on. In short, he took debunking to its limit without
discriminating in favour of any one philosophical system,
without flattery or hesitation, and without any warmth either.
He did not spare any idea, any social class, or at least
that is the impression one is left with, after reading his
works. That is his so-called cynicism. It will be seen later
on whether he actually walled up all the openings and burnt
all the bridges. Nonetheless, the general impression is
that by his manner of debunking he hurled us all into the
desert of non-philosophy about which Raymond Aron writes:
'The tone of this non-philosophy is unbearable to philosophers
in a way unlike the philosophy of Marx or Nietzsche. The
latter two take philosophers seriously. Neither pokes fun
at them. They both lend a pathetic garb to the split with
tradition. On the other hand, sticking to his decision to
play the fool, Pareto treats philosophers in the manner
in which Voltaire was treating Leibniz, without however
the charm and above all the laconism of the story-teller. In
the last instance, a philosopher may tolerate non-philosophy,
but not the idea that philosophy is unimportant.'[12] Pareto's

criticism remained indifferent to the tragic; without fail it turned to void everything around, sometimes leaving behind a dreary landscape of ruins and rubble.

Intellectuals are suspicious by nature, and the various debunking systems have deepened this tendency in the last fifty years. They are determined never to be taken in. On the other hand, Pareto has shown them that by taking precautions against deceit they haste to court it, nay, they come to deceive themselves. Such a lesson is very unpleasant, obviously. An author may be forgiven for warning his readers against the tricks of other people. Nonetheless, one hardly puts up with a writer who shatters all illusions, shows that all the words in use pertain to the realm of fiction, and eventually concedes the slim consolation that gullibility is a vital necessity. 'Skepticism,' he wrote, 'yields theory, faith incites to action and it is actions that practical life is made of. The ideal ends may all be both absurd and useful to society at one and the same time. It is this we have to remember here and now, and all the more because we tend to forget it too easily.'[13] Naturally, one may wonder whether the worst illusion is not that which sees illusions everywhere. Pareto never asked himself that question. Here is how he defined his method: 'We consider things exclusively and not the feelings which their names arouse in us. We study these sentiments as simple, objective facts. Hence we refuse, for example, to argue whether an action A is just, moral or immoral, unless the things referred to by these terms have already been clarified. Notwithstanding, we regard as objective fact what the people of a particular land, belonging to a particular class, at a particular time meant when they said that A was a just or moral action.'[14] Then he went on: 'I beg the reader always to remember that whenever I point to the absurdity of a doctrine, I do not intend in the least to imply that it is also detrimental to society; on the contrary, it may be very beneficial. Likewise, whenever I talk of the utility of a theory for society, I do not wish at all to insinuate that it is also experimentally true.'[15] In order to avoid the intrusion of any affective element and the slightest trace of value-judgment, as many sources of illusion and deceit, Pareto even thought of the extreme possibility of giving up the use of common, empirical notions, and of replacing them by simple letters of the alphabet, as in algebra. It is true that such a theoretical project is impracticable even from Pareto's point of view, to the extent he acknowledged that the object of sociological analysis was the role of the sentiment in the social conduct of human beings.

Such dryness is in no way compatible with the tumultuous aspirations of a certain type of sociology, more anxious to find a haven in utopia than to subject reality to sound analysis. Pareto could not help appearing to the dreamers of the future society as a killjoy. For better or for worse, one might have let him mock the revolutionaries personally, but not at all to deride the revolution and the ultimate ideal goals which it claims to promote. Thus the image one gets of Pareto is that of a sociologist that went against the stream, though he too made use of the method of ideological debunking. Ah! Had he only been content to point to the role of ideology in people's behaviour! Then he would have become one of the literary heroes of our times, for sure. Instead, Pareto followed his own logic to its very end, and so became the killjoy. Actually, he showed that explanation in terms of ideology is equally ideological and that after all, it falls victim to its own gullibility. The disenchant-ment is complete.

Nevertheless, it would be a mistake to confine Pareto to this extreme position, because, on the one hand, it is more theoretical than the one he actually adopted, and on the other, it disregards his own overall intellectual development. The position just described corresponds to a precise stage in the evolution of his thinking, namely that of the TREATISE, his best known work. In fact, as he had once believed in the feasibility of pure economics, he also came later on to believe in the feasibility of pure science that deals exclusively with facts and keeps away from any valuation and interpretation. It was a point of principle which perhaps represented an ideal yet to be attained, or better still, a model which Pareto never achieved in practice. Not only did he end by employing the vocabulary used by everybody, and in consequence terms that were inevitably multivocal, but eventually he also gave up his intentions of substituting letters of the alphabet for everyday words for fear his reasoning might become too obscure and cumbersome, as he himself admitted. Besides, he too did not miss the opportunity to deliver value-judgments and to take sides personally. How could he have done otherwise when the aim of sociology is to study the non-logical actions, ruled by sentiments and passions, and so by value-judgments? Pareto was faced by a question which he could not answer: given the non-logical action which is intrinsically valuation, is the scientist not bound to estimate the importance of the valuation within the action itself? Feelings after all elude quantification easily and so are unyielding to objective measurement and strict proportions. How is one to determine the part of faith, or aspiration, in the unfolding of an action, if not by valuation? It remains a valuation even in the case of a system of analysis that proceeds by successive approximations. Thus when Pareto wrote: 'As the ancient divinities succeeded one another, duplicated and competed among themselves, so nowadays alongside the divinity of socialism, we have got those of "social reform" or "social laws"; the lesser gods are there, too, as "social art", "social hygene", "social medicine," and so many other things which thanks to the epithet "social" come to share in the divine essence,'[16] his identification of the processes with deities does not convey genuine factual observation at all. Rather it is a valuation, a value-loaded interpretation, undoubtedly graphic, but empirically questionable. Whence it is important not to take all of Pareto's statements literally and instead, to distinguish between the theoretical model of a rigorously logical, experimental method, on the one hand, and the implementation of those intentions, on the other. The discrepancy is obvious.

Indeed, the idea of building up a sociology as rigorous and neutral as physics had preoccupied Pareto since his youth, as shown by one of his early writings: 'The development of human society takes place according to fixed and determined laws like those which have already been brought to light by physics.'[17] Nonetheless, his so-called cynicism, his disdain for reason, is the result of a slow evolution and a great many disappointments. In the first place, by limiting Pareto's thinking to the outlook expounded in the TREATISE, one ignores the fact that towards the end of his life Pareto became interested in political action above everything else and somehow neglected his sociology but for some clarifications here and there, and particularly with regard to the undulatory shape assumed by social phenomena. Likewise, one tends to belittle all the tribulations which had brought him to this allegedly pessimistic outlook. What he had thought as a young man he wrote it down in his letter of the 7th December, 1907, addressed to Antonucci: 'In 1868 I was twenty years old and capable of putting reason and sentiments together. It seemed to me then, as it seemed to everybody else, that my convictions were the fruit of reasoning, and I could not see that my reasoning was but an attempt to lend a logical appearance to what my convictions were after all compelling me to believe. Then I read Buckle and it was like a lightning-flash. It appeared to me as the ultimate in reasoning with application to the social sciences; I was rediscovering the methods employed in physics, a science that I was then reading at the University, and wondering how there could still be people left so ignorant and superstitious not to understand that doctrine. My creeed then was more or less the following: political economy as conceived by the so-called classical economists was a perfect science, or almost perfect; it remained only to put those principles into practice. In order to do that one had to imitate Cobden's coalition which was mankind's most sublime and useful achievement for centuries. In politics, sovereignty was a self-evident truth and liberty was a universal remedy. History was showing the people as good, honest, intelligent and oppressed by the upper classes and its own superstitions. Militarism and religion were the great calamities of mankind. Caesar, among the Ancients, and Napoleon I and Napoleon III, among the moderns, seemed to me the types of evil-doers. I was denying, or at least explaining away, the evils of democracy. The Terror had been no more than a faint stain on the bright record of the French Revolution.'[18]

In those early years Pareto had been an ardent liberal (and remained one for the rest of his life), an intransigent free-trader in economics, a pacifist in politics and a positivist in science. He had been admiring Bastiat, J.S. Mill and Darwin. While an engineer in Florence, he became an active member of the Adam Smith Society and an uncompromising opponent of protectionism and militarism. Impressed by the latent decline of the bourgeoisie and foreseeing a social revolution, he kept dreaming of reform. This is what he was writing in an article on the new tarrifs of the Italian customs at the time: 'Were the farmers fair, they would demand freedom of trade for everybody, instead of asking for their share of privileges alone...When landlords and industrialists agree to rob their fellow citizens, they do not dream of a third bandit lying in wait for them and to whom sooner or later they would have to give his share, and indeed not a small one. This third thief is the industrial and the agricultural worker. Today he asks, in the future he will exact, that his wages be determined by law in the way his masters have set the example, with regard to the price of manufactured goods.'[19] Pareto paid attention to the advancement of socialism: 'Slowly but surely the social tide is rising over the European continent.'[20] He was calling in question private property which, he thought, persisted because one had not yet come with something better to replace it. For a while, he even looked approvingly upon socialism, provided it would observe the basic freedoms, and regarded it as capable of taking over from the sickly bourgeoisie, unscrupulous and corrupt as the latter was. None of the ideas for which he had been fighting did materialize. He experienced another disappointment when he was defeated at the parliamentary elections; one of his public lectures in Milan was interrupted by the police and the Italian Government forbade him to teach political economy.

The desillusions multiplied. Pareto became increasingly bitter and gloomy. Economic protection and militarism were winning in Italy. Socialism was making itself known as a centralizing force that favoured state intervention above everything else. Pareto fought this new form of etatism. He brooded over the weaknesses of democracy, of the parliamentary system, aware that both were concerned with building up an 'Ethical State' that was but a 'Police State.' Without renouncing his secularism, Pareto felt irritated by the sight of the exactions called for by the Italian Government regarding freedom of religion. He came to realize that emotions and sentiments represented a force against which reason was impotent. His letters from Italy, which he started publishing in the JOURNAL DES ÉCONOMISTES in 1890, are proof of the slow germination of the ideas which he was going to develop and refine later on: 'History teaches us that it is not reason that rallies and moves the broad human masses; rather it is the emotion that takes the upper hand, influenced by certain circumstances and in a favourable milieu.'[21] In the conclusion to an essay on income tax in Saxony, and in which among other things he showed that it was in vain to hope for a solution of the social problems through a redistribution of wealth, Pareto set forth the principles of what was to become his dialectic: 'In Italy at present the government of Sr Crispi throws the socialists into prison on pretext that they speak evil of private property. It seems to us that when spoliation is practised in the form of trade protection, and in the banking institutions the principles of "mine" and "yours" are forgotten, one has no right to pose as defender of private property. On the one hand, a certain amount of money is exacted from the people in order to distribute it to the honest jobbers who enjoy the benefits of protectionism, or in order to scatter it in useless expenditures. On the other hand, the socialists want to take away an amount of almost equal size from the rich in order to distribute it to the poor. One thing is as good as the other. It is a matter of people and not of principles.'[22]

Disappointed, Pareto looked for a way out and found it in study. Passionately he turned to economic research and to mathematical economics, in particular. In 1891 he met Walras, who together with the Austrian Menger and the Briton Jevons, was one of the first theoreticians of marginalism. In 1893 Pareto succeeded him at the University of Lausanne. In spite of all that, he devoted himself entirely to research and the coherent and systematic elaboration of the ever deepening insights which he had gathered from his experience of the economic and the political worlds. The evolution of his ideas can be closely followed by reading his notes and articles gathered in book-form under the titles MYTHES ET IDÉOLOGIES and SCRITTI SOCIOLOGICI, respectively.[23]   From then on, sociology could be found at the centre of his preoccupations alongside economics. One also learns that as early as 1900 he stated clearly what was to become one of the basic traits of his sociology. In his essay entitled 'Une application des théories sociologiques,' which was published that year, one may read the following: 'Although impelled to act by non-logical motives, the human being likes to relate his actions to certain principles in a logical manner. Consequently, he comes to work out the connections later, in order to justify his actions. The individual who beguiled the other in this way by his own affirmations started by deceiving himself and ended by firmly believing his own words.'[24] During the same period, other key themes of his future thinking began to emerge, among them the idea that history evolves by successions of aristocracies, and the distinction between the truth-value of a given theory, on the one hand, and its social utility, on the other.

Unlike other authors, Pareto had not been in the possession of the groundwork of his later ideas from the start. In his case, that groundwork took shape progressively, across actual experiences and practical activities, and as a result of his own mature pondering on personal disappointments and on the ways people act effectively. Thus it would also be a great mistake to reduce Pareto's thinking to his statements in the TREATISE, because it outgrew the framework of that particular writing, the fruit of his maturity. It would be an even greater mistake to say that his outlook is impertinent as a result of his arbitrariness or sheer whim as a writer. Actually that outlook is the end-product of a long process of maturation and of his research that was always open to the real and the experienced. Everybody lives through failures and disappointments, but few people can turn them into food for thought. The choice is between naïveté and perspicacity. Pareto knew how to transform the naïveté of his youth into perspicacity in a way that made his impertinence richer with pertinences than the naïveté which remains closed to experience. Perhaps Pareto's alleged cynicism lies in his demonstration of the fact that some kinds of naïveté are false, because they conceal a hypocritical playgame under their idealistic cover.

This picture of Pareto would be defficient in more than one way if that other side of his personality, which may be described as hedonistic, is omitted. A taste of it may be had by reading his MYTHE VERTUISTE ET LA LITTÉRATURE IMMORALE. In it he lashes the moralistic rigidity of Protestant and Anglo-Saxon origin, which insists on censoring not only whatever passes for libidinous, but also everything that is simply lax and frivolous. Nowhere else did he make use with so much zest of the wealth of his erudition and his satirical verve and humour, a cross between a keen sense of ridiculousness and rhetorical ease. One has the feeling that while completing this book, Pareto was anticipating the row the well-wishers were going to kick up and he was enjoying it fully. Without doubt the topic must have been originally meant for inclusion in the TREATISE, but the great amount of notes accumulated must have induced him to change his mind. In it he deplores the extension of that rigidity to the Romance nations and especially the influence it was exerting upon the state: 'Wherever it enjoyed the support of the secular arm, the Catholic Church could, but did not, hunt for or destroy the DECAMERON. Nevertheless, in its serious writings, the Church did not allow the inclusion of attacks against religion, the monks and the priests, of the kind found in the DECAMERON. On the other hand, Bayle and Voltaire employed obscenity as cover, in order to reduce the danger of their attacks against the prevailing religion. Nowadays the roles have been reversed. One may subject the taboos of religion to ridicule at will, but must respect the taboos of chastity. The State has no longer an orthodox doctrine regarding the social organization, but it does have one where sexual feelings are concerned. Any newsstand may display an anarchist paper which writes that "the proletarians should slit the bourgeois bellies;" on the other hand, it is forbidden to display the picture of a naked woman.'[25]

Things have changed much since Pareto wrote that book. Admittedly it is not just a piece of occasional writing. In it Pareto shows that virtuousness is of all times. By insisting on the manner the 'virtuists' deflect morality for political purposes, he confirmed his thesis on derivations. Besides, the book offers an opportunity to know Pareto as a person better. Although present in his other writings, too, some of his characteristic traits stand out in bolder relief in this book: a deliberately anarchical temperament, climbing the slope of extreme liberalism, a spirit of the eighteenth century still struggling for enlightment and against obscurantism, and seeking compensation for the love of an exacting science in a certain frivolity, and finally a taste for paganism and the polytheism which allows the offering of sacrifices to several deities successively.

I I

THE ECONOMIST

At first Pareto became known as an economist. His early research and publications were in fact about financial and commercial political economy, about free trade and the rent. If later he turned to sociology, it happened because he realized that the practical application of an economic theory encountered social obstacles in the form of prejudices, and also difficulties originating in the contingent political situation. Hence the need of taking into account factors other than the economic. Initially those obstacles irritated Pareto who had been prone to think that a good theory was likely to win general acceptance and be applied into practice without delay. The disappointment, which he experienced as a result of his failures, was overcome by an ever increasing concentration on problems related to human action and sociology, in general. He was determined to find the explanation of those hindrances. Nonetheless, his earliest economic writings will not be discussed here, because they are mainly occasional pieces and calls to arms in favour of the introduction of a policy of free trade in Italy.

It was his meeting with Walras and his appointment as professor at the University of Lausanne that decided his new orientation. Very soon afterwards he asserted himself as an original theoretician in the field of political economy along the line of marginalist thinking. Pareto was not content simply to discharge the task of expounding theories and systems, which was incumbent on a professor. Rather he was a researcher and a creator, that is, a pioneer in certain areas of his subject-matter, and particularly in econometrics. For obvious reasons this is not the place to analyse all of Pareto's economic thinking, in other words, to examine his MANUAL,[1] the COURS[2] and his SYSTÈMES SOCIALISTES[3] in detail, summarize them and present his views on capital, revenue, currency, savings, the banking system, the phenomena of production and distribution, and moreover to interpret his virtual silence on investment. Certain economists may find fault with the fact that I do not insist on any of the points which might be important to them. Given the dimensions of this essay, I shall resign myself to directing one's attention to what Pareto the economist regarded as the core of his concerns, and that as clearly as possible.

1. PURE ECONOMICS

Quoting Perroux's inspired formulation,[4] one may say that Pareto was the architect of a systematization in economics pioneered by Walras in his work on the elements of pure economics. Actually it was the younger man who worked out the concept of pure economics in the most lucid and articulate way, while extending it to the whole field of economics, whereas Walras had been confining it to the market economy alone. By pure economics it should be understood the analysis of the economic process as such, independent of any psychological postulate and of social, political, moral or esthetic factors, and disregarding any external finality. On the basis of this definition, Pareto went on to exclude some other approaches, not because he considered them worthless, but for the simple reason that they were outside this particular field of research in economics, which he made his own.

a) He turned down any discussion on the psychological or philosophical nature of want or desire, retaining the notion of preference as an objective fact. For him the question was not to know why a human being desired one thing or another. Rather he started with the objective presence of desire and from it drew the economic consequences. In a letter addressed to Adrien Naville and dated the 11th January, 1897, Pareto wrote: 'From the point of view of pure economics, the question seems to me to have been solved. If a man has got some wine and wants to exchange it for chickens, there is indeed a group of forces that compel him to drink wine and another group that egg him to eat chickens. *Homo oeconomicus* is more or less a perfect pair of scales to weigh those forces. I can assume the existence of the perfect scales and build up a theory which closely resembles rational mechanics. I do not pursue any idle inquiry about the nature of those forces. Neither do I need to submit to discussion the implicit determinism,

the free choice and so on and so forth. I have cleared all
the difficulties, leaving it to psychology to solve them.'[5]

b) He turned away from any kind of combination of events, the
analysis of which was meant to provide practical solutions to
a concrete and contingent situation, what he called the pre-
scriptions useful to private persons and public bodies.

c) He refrained from any pronostication and valuation,
in the sense of putting forth an economic and social doctrine
which would claim to bring happiness to humankind, for instance, as Marxism was doing. On the contrary, the idea
of pure economics implied the isolation of the economic
activity from other human activities, the definition of
its own premises, the investigation of the uniformities
and the constants bearing upon any kind of economic system
and the logical conclusion drawn from it. He described his
project in a letter to a friend of his, the Italian economist
Maffeo Pantaleoni, as follows: 'I call pure economics all the
doctrines that can be deduced from the hedonist postulate,
with few or none of the other qualities of the human psyche.
Pure economics deal with *homo oeconomicus* who is guided solely
by the desire to obtain maximum utility with the least effort.
Applied economics add to this main characteristic feature of
homo oeconomicus all the other traits that are familiar
to us. But I am not particularly keen on this classification.
Any other would do, provided the relations between things are
not overlooked.'[6]

Thus pure economics rest on the sole premise, reached by
abstraction, namely that in order to achieve a given end, the
human being acting economically as *homo oeconomicus* employs
the means that are adapted to it, regardless of any determinant, moral or otherwise, which may intervene in a concrete
action. As a consequence, this *homo oeconomicus* is limited to
the choice made by an agent in order to secure maximum satisfaction for himself.[7] In other words, pure economics, as
Pareto saw them, were concerned with any individual to the
extent he was expressing a particular preference, without
pronouncing any judgment on the pertinence or the moral
value of the choice, or on the quality of the chosen objects.
They are meant to register the presence of such preferences
only, without seeking to know whether they are profitable

or good. In this sense, pure economics remain value-neutral. The preferences are treated as objective facts because they can be observed despite the subjective nature of the decision itself, given its dependence on the will of the agent who sees a utility in it. This is all that pure economics need in order to reconstitute the conduct of the human being that resorts to the available means and resources in order to obtain maximum satisfaction. It is a logical action, the end and means of which can be determined with precision, on the obvious condition of the adequacy of the selected means to the end. It is exclusively oriented to the quest for maximum satisfaction: 'Our study,' Pareto wrote, 'has for object the phenomena that are the consequence of human actions meant to enable people to obtain those things which satisfy their needs or their desires.'[8] If the structure of such actions presents no difficulty to analysis, not the same may be said about the generally used vocabulary which is a source of equivocal meanings. A case in question is that of the notion of utility.

In economics the term utility may mean two things: on the one hand, that which is profitable, beneficial or precious, in opposition to what is noxious, and on the other hand, that which is adequate to satisfy a need, no matter whether the thing is good or evil, harmful or not. However, this double meaning is a source of equivocalities, because quite often it happens that the economists shift from one meaning to the other, while making their audience believe all the time that they talk consistently of one and the same thing. In this way they arouse confusions which in turn disrupt the logic of their thinking and place the validity of their demonstrations under a question mark. In order to avoid such misunderstandings, Pareto suggested the use of two different terms corresponding to the two different concepts, respectively: that of utility to designate that which is profitable or beneficial, and the term 'ophelimity,' to refer to 'the ratio of convenience which makes a thing satisfy a need or a desire, whether legitimate or not.'[9]The wine, for instance, is ophelimic to the extent it quenches the craving of the alcoholic, although it may not be good for his health. Thus utility implies appreciation of worth whereas ophelimity points to the raw, objective fact of the adequacy of a thing to satisfy a definite need. One may talk of the utility of a thing in relation to a particular moral, political, or religious point of view, such as for instance, whether it would be better for a nation to increase its prosperity through economic activity or by military conquests. But one cannot talk in the same way of ophelimity which, though subjective in the sense that it is linked to a need or a desire peculiar to a human being, expresses an objective reality in the relation of adequacy between means and end. Ophelimity is subjective in the sense illustrated by the case of a stamp which is of interest to a stamp-collector but not at all to a non-collector. On the other hand, it is objective to the extent it is the stamp that meets the collector's desire. Consequently, it is a matter of ophelimity and not of utility whether pure economics consider the conduct of *homo oeconomicus* as that of an agent who seeks to obtain maximum satisfaction. It is under this aspect that it differs from other approaches in the field of economics, that want to make themselves useful either by offering solutions to given situations (should the output of an enterprise be increased or not), or by intending to bring about happiness to the human being (through socialism, for instance, and not through capitalism). Thus, *homo oeconomicus* may be defined as the individual who aspires to the highest ophelimity, provided this satisfaction is not mistaken for the greatest pleasure or the greatest enjoyment. After all in the case of the ascetic, for instance, it is the maximum of privations that is aimed at. The individual remains judge of his own preferences, but as soon as the latter are made public, it is ophelimity that expresses the most convenient or the most adequate manner of satisfying them.

Regrettably, the economists did not retain the distinction between ophelimity and utility, and the term 'ophelimity' was not given the opportunity which Pareto had hoped for it. He was willing to give up the term for any other, if found shocking by the linguistic purists. The language of economics would have gained in precision and many errors and paralogisms might have been avoided. Here is an example of the latter given by Pareto himself. Ricardo had written that water and air, the utility of which are so great and which are indispensable to human life, cannot despite all that be exchanged for other objects, in ordinary cases, while, on the other hand, gold, the utility of which is so small compared to that of air and water may be exchanged for a great amount of goods. About that Pareto correctly remarked that the comparison did not hold, because the term utility had been employed by Ricardo in two different senses, once as ophelimity and then, a second time, as utility in the current meaning given to the term.[10]

Originally Pareto showed great confidence in the possibilities of pure economics which he thought capable of resolving all the problems, so to speak. His confidence was founded on the idea, which he cherished at the time, namely that economics in general were a natural science in the same way as chemistry or physiology: in his opinion, pure economics would serve as its mechanical groundwork.[11] In 1898, he used to write, for instance, that pure economics were not only similar to mechanics, but rather more, a branch of mechanics. And he was adding: 'By posing the problem of economics, one arrives at equations that are identical to those of mechanics in a space of n dimensions. The equations being identical in both instances, the solutions, too, are the same.'[12] With time, Pareto became more cautious. Sociology allowed him gradually to realize that the solutions worked out theoretically were not automatically adopted in practical life, because of the impact exerted by the non-economic factors and by the social and political life in general. He became aware of the fact that life did not conform to the rigid tools of theoretical analysis. This is what he was writing in 1913: 'Whoever wants to derive the solution to a practical problem exclusively from the theories of pure economics, or even from those of applied economics is by and large mistaken; one must add a great number of propositions made available by other social sciences. Likewise, whoever wants to cultivate a field under the exclusive guidance of agricultural chemistry would be in the wrong. Is one then to draw out of these undeniable facts the conclusion that the economic theories are false, that they are useless to the understanding of social phenomena, or that the chemical theories are also false, that they are useless to the understanding of agricultural phenomena? Obviously not. The sole legitimate conclusion is that these theories take into consideration one aspect only of the phenomena, and that it is necessary to bring others in, which would account for the other parts.'[13] I shall not insist too long on Pareto's intellectual evolution in this field where he ended by acquescing in the good parts of economic protection, after he had fought it unrelentingly in the name of his intrasigent faith in the principle of free trade. Nevertheless, it seems to me relevant to linger a while on the limited and precise task which he assigned to pure economics.

a) According to Pareto, it was to define basic concepts rigorously, such as those of value, exchange, capital, monopoly and so on, without which economic life would not be possible. The scope assigned by Pareto to pure economics is considerable. By their means he expected to arrive at a general economic system valid under any political régime, be it capitalist or socialist. 'Pure economics,' he wrote, 'must equally serve to establish the laws of phenomena in a society ruled by private property, as well as in a society where collective property is generally prevalent. Given a certain organization, pure economics must enable us to forecast the economic consequences.'[14] He insisted on the presence of certain fundamental laws which no régime could overlook in practice, even if it were to deny them theoretically or ideologically, unless it wanted to block economic development, and as a result, the normal flow of social life.

b) In Pareto's opinion, it had to define the permanent conceptual implications of economic notions in order to separate what was strictly relevant to the economic process from what belonged to moral judgments or to historical contingencies. In the lecture he gave on the occasion of his appointment as full professor, Pareto said the following words: 'Does it not occur to you that in order to give an enlightened opinion on the question whether the appropriation of capitals is useful or harmful to society, one must first of all know what is meant by capital and its economic functions? Would it not be as appropriate to ask historiography and statistics to inform us on the ways economic goods are transformed one into another? Do you think it superfluous to try and bring a little order to this huge number of facts, to classify them and to try to derive general laws from them? Well! This is the only aim of economics.'[15] He was convinced of the existence of conceptual characterstics that made the rent be the rent, irespective of the varying historical conditions that added a specific, secondary trait to them and did away with another which appeared more important to a previous age. He noted that many economic theories were concerned with these varying and secondary aspects, mistakenly raising them to the level of essential characteristics. Whence the confusions so pernicious to the rational understanding of the economic phenomenon. Pareto did not doubt that the concepts worked out by theoretical abstraction were unavailable as such in concrete, empirical life; yet their unreality was just what helped to know reality better. If the implicit naturalism of his reference to rational mechanics is left out, Pareto's method approximates Weber's ideal type in more than one way, although it is less developed theoretically; 'Thus pure economics come to resemble the the so-called rational mechanics which also deal with the properties of ideal bodies. The solid bodies of rational mechanics are no more to be found in nature than is the *homo oeconomicus*.'[16]

c) Finally, he regarded them as having the task to rationalize the economic process on the basis of a logical analysis of action: 'It is an undeniable fact that for some time now there has been a tendency to give a new form to economic doctrines. One tries to make them rational, and in order to do so one resorts to mathematical reasoning.'[17] He thought that thanks to this rationalization it would be possible to discover the uniformities, the constants or the laws of economic life, granted that such research would not be held to account exhaustively for all the economic phenomena: 'Meanwhile we see that pure economics, and political economy in general, do not have any direct, practical utility of any considerable size. For the time being, their utility is only theoretical, namely of enabling us to know the experimental uniformities of certain phenomena which are usually given the name of laws.'[18]

In order to lend more precision to reasoning in economics, Pareto waged on a sustained battle for the introduction of mathematics, and in the process kept casting shafts on the literary economists, as he called them. Eventually, he was to abandon that position, too. If in his younger years he had been convinced that everything could be solved by means of equations, in the long run he came to criticize even Walras, his former teacher, for having been too rigid with regard to this aspect of economics. As a matter of fact, in his preface to A. Osorio's book on the mathematical theory of exchange, Pareto was writing the following in 1913: 'One used to imagine that by applying mathematics to political economy, one was lending precision and pregnancy to the demonstrations of the latter science, so short of them, and that as a result everybody would feel compelled to accept them. Walras plunged head over heels into this error, not only as far as pure economics were concerned, but also with regard to practical problems about which he believed that he could impose his solutions in the name of mathematical precision. It is useless to add that he failed entirely.'[19]

Nonetheless, Pareto remains a forerunner of econometrics. He saw a twofold advantage in the use of mathematics. On the one hand, it would contribute to the creation of a technical language indispensable to any branch of science that is intent on making up for the vagueness inherent in the terms of ordinary language. In that way, he thought, it would be possible to eliminate certain errors like those made by the literary economists who were ignoring the notion of continuous growth, or in mathematical terms, mistaking the tangent for the curve. On the other hand, Pareto held it to compensate for the shortcomings of ordinary logic: 'The latter might conveniently deal with problems concerning causes and effects; however, it showed its inadequacy as soon as it was made to tackle questions about mutual dependence. To make up for it, one was forced to turn to a particular logic, namely mathematical logic.'[20] That said, there was enough room left for everybody: literary economists, as well as mathematical economists. Returning to the model of the natural sciences time and again, Pareto came to the conclusion that: 'Each and everyone may choose the method which he likes best. Even among astronomers, some develop the mathematical theory, while others make observations without concerning themselves with theory. All have contributed equally to the advancement of that branch of science. ...Those economists who do not wish to busy themselves with mathematics still have a vast field open to them in their activity, and they need not covet that which some of their colleagues try hard to make bear fruit.' [21]

Despite his exigencies about precision, Pareto rejected any indiscriminate methodological rigidity: 'There is no infallible scientific method: there are only some which are better than the others. Going to the other extreme, some innovators have concluded that one can no longer deal with political economy unless one resorts to the mathematical method. As their own contribution to science had been denied earlier, so nowadays they in turn are denying any merit in its development to their predecessors.'[22] With time and experience, Pareto became more refined in his conceptualizations, though no less sarcastic in his style of writing. Likewise, he became increasingly critical of his own opinions and so eventually he was able to appreciate correctly John Stuart Mill's idea that no principle could be considered true which successfully rejects all the attacks directed against it.[23]

2. THE ECONOMIC EQUILIBRIUM

The reason for alloting a special section of this chapter to Pareto's theory of economic equilibrium lies in its key importance to the understanding of his sociological theory, and particularly his basic concepts of social heterogeneity and of mutual dependence of phenomena, respectively. It was also from Walras that Pareto inherited the notion of equilibrium. What he himself did to it was to extend it in such a way as to accommodate the parallel tackling of the economic and the social equilibria. The idea of balance represents the warp, so to speak, of Pareto's thinking in general, and that from an early time. His BSc thesis in physics had been about the equilibrium in solid bodies. Later on, his economic thinking became centred on the notion of equilibrium. As soon as he found the elements which he needed for his theory of society, Pareto concluded his TREATISE with a chapter on social equilibrium. Thus, throughout, one seems to find oneself in the presence of a fundamental concept which informs his entire outlook and philosophy.

With the help of this notion of equilibrium, Pareto wanted

to make available a quantitative representation of the forces,
or the conditions, which act concurrently upon a particular
system, be it the system of production, consumption, or that
of the population. It is linked to the law of the mutual
dependence of the phenomena, as he called it. According to
this law, every state is each time conditioned by a plurality
of causes or phenomena which act and react each upon the
other without interruption. In other words, a state is not
the result of one cause only, but always of a multitude of
causes. Under this aspect, Pareto among others has undeniably
exerted a decisive influence on the evolution of modern epistemology in the field of the social sciences. He was one of
those who strongly attacked the long prevalent idea of the
unique causality, in virtue of which it had been enough to
know the causes of a phenomenon in order to be able to foresee
its consistent effects. Implicitly he attacked all the theories which had been looking for **the** cause of value, or **the**
cause of the population movement. In his opinion, there are
always causes that act correlatedly in covariance. In consequence, causality in the singular should be replaced by it
in the plural. Pareto considered the misunderstanding of
the mutual dependence of phenomena as the source of a great
many errors, such as the tendency to explain a social situation exclusively in economic terms, or solely in political
terms, or still, exclusively by the physical conditions of
climate and geography, or solely in terms of race, and so on.
'Formerly and still nowadays the idea that the moral and the
economic well-being of a people depend exclusively, or at
least mainly, on the form of its government was and still is
quite widespread. Intent on reacting against this error,
some economists have fallen into the opposite error by denying
to the form of government any influence on the welfare of the
people. The same mistakes become manifest with reference
to the action of legislation. It is equally mistaken to think
either that laws are all powerful in the alteration of the
social state of a people or that they are utterly impotent.'[24]

Pareto admitted that in certain well-defined conditions,
a series of causes might indeed exert a prevalent impact,
but he was reluctant to concede that it was always so, whatever
the circumstances. He pointed to the fact that it was the
belief in uni-causality with its implicit one-sidedness that

lay at the basis of erroneous solutions propunded by certain economic and social doctrines. They held the distribution of wealth to be the main cause of the configuration of a social system. Whence the inference that in order to change the effects of the social system as a whole it was enough to alter one cause only; in that particular case meaning to do away with private property. Pareto argued that to say with Marx that the economic sector was in the last instance the determining factor, simply meant to express the primacy or the preponderance of a single cause by using different words. The infrastructure-superstructure dialectic did not alter, in his opinion, the absolute causality that lay at the foundation of that doctrine. Rather, he was inclined to think that if the social and the economic conditions determined the evolution of the intellectual aspect of society, this latter aspect is equally determinant of the economic. To give preponderance to any one of these causal categories meant in Pareto's eyes to risk the scientific framework for the sake of metaphysical divagation. Actually: 'A given distribution of wealth is the "effect" of these conditions. It is easy to supply the evidence. It suffices to notice what is going on within different social classes. Individuals, either lazy or lacking in foresight, are born both among the poor and among the rich.'[25]

Given the plurality of causes and variables which act in correlation and mutual dependence (for Pareto correlation and mutual dependence were synonimous), the idea of equilibrium appeared to him as the most appropriate concept for the definition of a social and economic situation. In pure economics, the problem is easier to solve than it is in sociology because in economics one deals with uniform conditions and the recurrent actions of individuals aiming to satisfy their desires. Pareto's definition of the economic equilibrium reads as follows: 'It may be said that the economic equilibrium is that state which would reproduce itself indefinitely were there no change in the conditions in which it is observed. If for the time being we take into consideration the stable equilibrium only, we may say that it is determined in a way that, once slightly altered through the smallest interference, tends to re-establish itself immediately and return to its original state. The two definitions are indeed equivalent.'[26]

This definition may be illustrated by quoting one of Pareto's own examples: 'From one meal to the other, the individual receives a certain stimulus which is made manifest through a need of food. As soon as the individual has had his meal, the stimulus ceases and the need is appeased. In economics this is the state to consider if one wishes to avoid losing oneself in idle and useless details. It may be given a name, or be designated by a simple letter of the alphabet and so be called the X state, for instance. Nevertheless, by analogy with mechanical phenomena, it may simply be called the **state of equilibrium.**'[27]

It was Pareto's opinion that as soon as an equilibrium was defined, it was possible, at least relatively, to determine the causal impact it exerts, provided the alteration of one of the implicit conditions changes the state itself. Thus he became convinced that thanks to this concept one could scientifically establish the variations and modifications likely to affect any given economic or social system.

Indeed Pareto was dealing with a highly abstract notion, because the conditions to be considered define an 'ideal phenomenon' without validity outside the limits imposed by the determining conditions. Notwithstanding, Pareto regarded it merely as a first approximation in a series that would allow to seize the empirical phenomenon better. Epistemologically speaking, the principle of mutual dependence has as its complement the principle of successive approximations. By these latter terms one should understand the multiplication of ways of approach or points of vantage in order to obtain an ever clearer idea of the phenomenon which otherwise, even with the best of intentions, could not be explained exhaustively. 'The study of economic phenomena,' Pareto wrote, 'may be compared to that of the surface of the Earth. It is already a very important notion, namely that of the more or less spheroid shape of our planet, but this is only a first approximation which disregards the highest mountains and the deepest crevices of the oceans. Geography yields a second, and topography, a third, but never would we get a description of the Earth which would take into account the smallest molehill and the tiniest pebble. Likewise, the economic phenomenon would never be known to us in the minutest

detail, yet we may obtain ever closer representations of
it. The concept of economic equilibrium, which is basic to
science, leads to the first approximation of the economic
phenomenon.'[28]The same goes for any scientific theory, because
none accounts fully for the phenomena it covers. It is only
an approximation which needs incessantly to be revised, and
sometimes even given up in favour of another, more adequate.
It is in this epistemological context that Pareto's concept
of equilibrium should be grasped. Otherwise, one risks making
the same mistake as Guy Perrin in his own book on Pareto's
sociology. Perrin discarded this very context from his critical analysis of the latter's work.

For reasons related to the possibilities offered by mathematical explanation, Pareto confined his positive analysis
to statics, that is to say, the study of isolated phenomena,
such as the production or the consumption of a determined
quantity of goods, as also the study of continuous phenomena.
such as the very production or consumption within a definite
time-unit. Contrary to what some of his interpreters criticized
him for, Pareto never neglected nor underestimated the dynamic
aspect of phenomena. His own observation on the matter was
that usually the economists had too few elements at their
disposal and no adequate mathematical theory to tackle the
dynamics of phenomena in a satisfactory manner.[30] In fact,
dynamics implied successive equilibria, granted that the
correlation between them would result into a theory of growth,
as for example, an increase in production. Pareto paid particular attention to the phenomenon of economic crisis, as one
of the aspects of economic dynamics. It covers a whole chapter
in Pareto's COURS. There, he showed that it would be incorrect
to interpret economic crises simply as depression-related
phenomena. They become manifest in periods of 'ascendancy'
as well as of 'decline.' He also pointed out that they are
not necessarily abnormal phenomena or accidents. On the other
hand, he noted that the necessary mathematical tool for the
explanation of these normal oscillations was still missing,
as was a much needed theory of undulatory mechanics. He conceded however that crisis could be interpreted simply by
means of statics. Regarding crisis as an unavoidable aspect
of growth, given its undulatory character, Pareto raised
the question whether it would be useful to prevent crises

from occurring altogether, provided it could be done. 'One
tends to answer in the affirmative, but a closer examination
of the question gives rise to a lot of doubts. It is not
at all sure that the rhythmical movement is not one of the
conditions of economic progress. On the contrary, it seems
highly probable that this motion is a manifestation of the
vitality of the economic organism. The alternatives of rest
and excitation seem necessary to all superior living organ-
isms.'[31] It is from this point of view that one should consider Perroux's criticism of Pareto's theory of equilibrium.
Perroux remarks that in itself equilibrium is neither a correct
representation of the life of market economies, nor a satisfactory representation of the optimum conditions. He does
not find it a sure means of classifying and understanding
the implicit changes, either. 'Each time the relations between the agents, that is to say, between competitors are
represented as relations between objects, in other words,
as physical contiguities, the fertility of the schema is
compromised.'[32] Furthermore, Perroux writes: 'The logical
expression of Pareto's universe may be perfected and refined
as much as one wishes; nonetheless, the notion of macro-
decision cannot be rendered intelligible unless one changes
the central attitude of the reasoning suggested to us by
Pareto and his idea of equilibrium, too.' This is so because
as Perroux goes on to explain: 'Pareto's equilibrium is a
device for the elimination of the global intention and decision.'[33] These remarks are perfectly correct to the extent
one focusses upon the theory which Pareto effectively worked
out in terms of statics. Nonetheless, his writings show that
he did not exclude the necessity of building up another schema
as soon as one was turning to economic dynamics to which
macro-decisions belong. In consequence, Pareto did not deny
the need of starting from other data than those relevant
at the level of statics. Perroux's criticism is highly perti-
nent from that point of view: the political will which is
determinant in the sphere of macro-economics represents a
variable hardly amenable to quantification, at least not
in the present circumstances. For this reason a dynamic theory
of equilibrium would not only register difficulties in the
translation of growth into mathematical terms, but also face
the challenge of the irreducibility of the political will.

Considered from its static aspect, the economic equilibrium raises a question about the opposition between needs and scarcity, or to use Pareto's own terms, 'the opposition that exists between the tastes of people and the obstacles encountered on the way leading to their satisfaction.'[34] As he figured it, the problem was not that of knowing whether a certain person prefers to buy sausage rather than wine, and another a motor-car rather than a piece of jewelry, but to trace the process characteristic of various actions. Whence the need to consider it an ideal, abstract manner, independently of the contingency of particular desires. In practice, the abstraction meant that only the economic aspects of the phenomena in question would be taken into consideration. They were so numerous in virtue of their mutual dependence that ordinary logic was no longer good enough, and so it became necessary to resort to mathematical logic which, as Pareto was quick to stress, was not a method 'opposed to other methods. Rather it was an additional research and demonstration procedure.'[35] As a mode, it does not represent any difficulty, although one may challenge the latent naturalism in Pareto's reference to rational mechanics. 'The equilibrium of an economic system reveals striking analogies with the equilibrium of a mechanical system. As soon as one becomes familiar with the latter equilibrium,' Pareto wrote, 'one also gains some clear notions of the former.'[36] Even in his COURS, one finds Pareto sketching a whole series of correspondences between mechanics and pure economics.[37] As in mechanics one was studying the relations of equilibrium and motion among given material bodies, controlling for all the other properties, so in pure economics, Pareto would argue, one was dealing with the relations between production and exchange of wealth for the inhabitants of a given society, irrespective of the other circumstances. Obviously, as a material body could not be reduced to its mechanical properties, nor could a social phenomenon be reduced to its economic properties. This is also another way of saying that pure economics are only a part of general economics and that economics are in turn only a part of the social phenomena. Nonetheless, in spite of Pareto's insistence on the fact that there was only a matter of analogy of no demonstrative value between those two orders of phenomena, he happened to talk of them in identical terms more than once. Without going to the extreme taken by those critics that make most of such confusions in order to reject Pareto's analysis entirely, one cannot help remarking that his naturalistic attitude weakened his argumentation time and again.

Pareto expected to extend his notion of equilibrium to society, and eventually to build up a theory of social equilibrium. He was fully aware of the difficulties involved in such a project. All the more so because he was reluctant to give up the solid ground of experience, and besides, wanted to resist the lure of certain hypotheses. The obstacles were even greater than those related to the dynamic theory of economic equilibrium, because the nature of the mutual dependence of the physical, economic, political, moral, religious and intellectual conditions was still unknown despite the researchwork carried out in the social sciences. Above all it was not easy to find a uniformity among those conditions so necessary in the elaboration of a mathematical theory. 'The observation of facts induces us to acknowledge that the distribution of wealth and the other economic conditions, alongside religious, moral and philosophical beliefs, the character, the qualities and the shortcomings of nations, and so on, are all phenomena connected among them by certain conditions. However our knowledge does not go farther than that, and we are in no position to determine the nature of these conditions, whereas in the case of economic phenomena we could define them with accuracy.'[38] Thus, in order to make up for the defficiency, Pareto thought it useful to complete the mechanical model, which had served him as a frame of reference for the theory of economic equilibrium, by an organic model. His reason: 'The comparison with a living organism is the best, as soon as one intends to acquire an idea about the evolution of societies.'[39] Nonetheless, scientific caution of which Pareto was not short entitles nobody to attribute to the analogy between an organism and the social body more meaning than it contains. Besides, it was not worth repeating the errors of certain theories which applied Darwinism too rigidly to matters concerning the evolution of societies. That was the tricky rock to be avoided in order not to give too doctrinaire an interpretation to the processes of social adaptation and selection. Pareto was aware that social heterogeneity, which was the result of a differentiation process characteristic of societal development, did not offer any argument in favour of the socialist theories which expressed the belief in the possibility of a re-established social homogeneity at an indefinite moment in time by artificially building up a radically new society. Actually there was every probability that the social differentiation would persist, 'even in the aftermath of the instauration of a socialist régime, unless society lapses into savagery.'[40]

This project of applying the notion of equilibrium to society with the intention of working out a more synthetic concept turned Pareto into the subject of many a criticism, sometimes very harsh. Among his critics, Sorokin, for instance, denied Pareto any merit because of his inability to offer a coherent theory of social equilibrium, and that despite his reasoning by analogy and his transcriptions in mechanical or mathematical language by means of symbols and geometrical signs. Because of that, Sorokin conluded that Pareto's work was a fiasco, and his concept of equilibrium had no heuristical value, being purely parasitic, in Sorokin's opinion.[41] Such animosity is hard to understand because it pronounces peremptory judgments when it is enough to read Pareto's texts in order to realize his hesitation and circumspection in the attempts he made to extend the concept of equilibrium to society. Indeed, he was less dogmatic than his critics who have seen no merit in his efforts. As a matter of fact it is precisely anti-scientific to deny a priori any legitimacy to his project which was at least worth undertaking as an experiment. Nor can it be said that Pareto failed, because he himself had acknowledged the difficulties inherent in the enterprise and as a result remained content to sketch out some preliminary points only. Besides, he never thought himself capable of providing an exhaustive explanation of the social phenomenon by embarking upon that path, for the simple reason that he was referring to an approximation which alongside others could facilitate the understanding of the global social phenomenon and nothing else. It is still a path to be explored and not to be discarded just because a first attempt did not yield the results hoped for.

Rather than review all the criticism directed against Pareto (and part of it is utterly uninteresting), it seems wiser to insist on the significance of Pareto's research efforts at the time when he was writing his COURS and the MANUAL. Little as one may be acquainted with the texts he wrote during that period, one is quickly made aware of the fact that Pareto wanted to generalize the theory of pure economics, as any other scientist using the mathematical apparatus. On that basis, he intended to work out a general theory of society. Starting from the premise that the economic fact was one of the social facts to which it was correlated, he hoped eventually to be able to account mathematically for the whole of society. Examining the notion of social equilibrium in the TREATISE, one comes across the following: 'Let us look for analogies in a field closer to ours. The states X_1, X_2, X_3 ... are analogous to those which pure economics take into consideration in the case of an economic system. The analogy is so inclusive that the states of the economic system may be regarded as particular cases of the general states of the sociological system.'[42] That was his project. Nevertheless it should be noticed that Pareto remained at that analogical level peculiar to the research stage, and that he did not affirm that he had arrived at any positive result. In reality he was seeking a system more synthetic and at the same time more comprehensive, and in which pure economics would be a first, tentative approach or approximation. However, given the lag in the social science research, it was impossible to work out such a theory on the spot. Pareto was forced to resign himself and turn instead to a less ambitious project though no less scientific, namely to trace the variables implicit in a theory of social equilibrium by logical-experimental means. I shall return to this project later on.

3. PARETO'S LAW

By and large this law of the distribution of wealth consolidated Pareto's notoriety among economists. To us nowadays its significance is twofold. On the one hand, Pareto used it as an allegedly scientific piece of evidence in his opposition to the claims of the socialist systems, and on the other, he regarded it as a confirmation of what may be called the philosophical presupposition of his sociological theory. The latter refers to the identity of human nature through time. Originally, however, Pareto had seen in what eventually became known as his law the justification of the use of mathematics in political economy. In other words, the elaboration of his law was proof of its own legitimacy and fruitfulness.

The classical liberal school in economics had been concerned mostly with the question of production and had regarded the distribution of wealth as subordinate, and that from a point of view esssentially optative. Said differently, the classical liberal economists had been hoping that growth would end in harmonizing capital, labour and property by the play of offer and demand. It was the socialists who laid stress on the problems of distribution and turned the latter into their whipping post. On the other hand, the academic economists of the German historical school turned the distribution of wealth into the subject-matter of their debates with the consequence that the partisans of liberalism could no longer ignore it. Aware of the trend, Pareto began researching the problem as early as 1893, when he was appointed to a professorship at the University of Lausanne. With the assistance of the Vaud Canton, he was able to obtain the statistics of France, Britain, Germany, Belgium, United States, Switzerland and Austria. He had no intention to join in the quarrel of claims and objections picked up by the literary economists. Rather he wanted to examine the problem scientifically, on the basis of documents. Employing Cauchy's method of interpolation,[43] in order to standardize the various data, and also by making the most of the statistical works of the French Foville and the Briton Giffen, Pareto succeeded in seizing a certain uniformity as concerns the phenomena of distribution of revenues, empirically. He managed that, as early as 1895. The following year, he published the results of his research in the RECUEIL of the Lausanne Law School. In order to spare the readers of the present book the intricacies of Pareto's graphs and equations, only the conclusions of his findings will be summarized here.[44] The curve of the distribution of wealth varies very little from one period to another in the countries under consideration, despite the great difference among them with regard to their economic and social systems.

Graphically the curve assumes the shape of a curl with the peak, representing the higher revenues, pointing upwards, while the lower base represents the lower incomes. That is to say that the increase in the number of higher incomes does not mean a general growth of wealth at all, nor does an increase in the number of poor people mean general impoverishment. Furthermore it shows that the inequality of revenues, on the one hand, and impoverishment, on the other, are not inversely related. Rather, they are two, altogether different things.

Without wasting any time, Pareto conferred on this uniformity the validity of a law. Nonetheless, as soon as it was made public, it was contested by the economist Edgeworth (a fact which ulcerated Pareto deeply), despite the enthusiasm which it aroused in a statistician like Foville. Georges Sorel found fault with it, too, and stated that its validity was limited to the capitalist nations. Since then, Pareto's law has remained an object of polemical debate. Some authors tend to confirm Pareto's point of view and sometimes even try to improve upon his formula, while others question its pertinence on the pretext that his statistical sources were unreliable, or that they lacked precision. It is worth recalling however that its validity has been reasserted in the cases of the Ancient Peru and the Rome of the Caesars,[45] and more recently, in the case of the rural communities of the Japanese island of Hokkaido.[46] It has been successfully applied to other phenomena besides the economic, such as for instance, in biology. Moreover, it has been the object of further refinements thanks to the efforts of Amoroso, McGregor, Gibrat and Gini. Instead of getting into the details of the controversial debates, it seems to me more appropriate to stick to the conclusions drawn by Pareto himself, because they cast light upon his other works as a whole.

a) This law served him, as already said, in his struggle against the socialist theories, and one may wonder whether it was not under its influence that he wrote his SYSTÈMES SOCIALISTES. In Pareto's opinion, the socialists were wrong to believe that the solution of the social question lay in the redistribution of wealth by assigning the fortunes of the rich to the poor in one form or another, so that: 'By

equalizing the expenses for palaces and for hovels, the mean
would yield the equivalent of the expenses for "ellegant and
comfortable" houses. The available statistical data are absolutely contradicting this hypothesis. Perhaps they are inexact
or wrongly interpreted. All that is possible, and that is why
more evidence is needed.'[47] Ultimately, as Pareto saw it, the
socialists' error consisted in their upholding the idea that
the distribution of wealth was the cause of social inequalities
and that as a result, it would have been enough to modify the
cause in order to alter its effects, and so create a different
social situation. On the contrary, Pareto would argue, the
actual solution was not the fragmentation of wealth, but an
ever increasing production, as the classical economists had
seen it:'In order to raise the level of the minimal income, or
in order to reduce the inequality of revenues, the wealth must
increase faster than the population. Accordingly, the question
of the improvement of the economic condition of the poorer
classes is above all a question of wealth production.'[48]

   b) Pareto's main philosophical premise was that the human
nature remains identical to itself in its depths, despite the
alterations operated on it by history and evolution. The distribution of wealth might, in his opinion, depend either on the
nature of the people involved, or on the type of societal
organization. It would differ with the time sequence and the
geographical region, for causes that are still unknown. On the
other hand, the uniformity of the law and the regularities to
which it bears witness show that the distribution is not a
matter of chance. If it were, the curve would have assumed the
slope characteristic of probability curves, which it does not.
Because it varies little in relation to geographical region,
time sequence, and societal organization,[49] the distribution
of wealth is not dependent on social systems, either. Thus
only one way is left: 'Without deliberately overlooking the
other causes, one must search for the main, determining cause
in the human nature.'[50] In Pareto's case that meant not only
the action of natural laws,[51] but also the interplay of permanent human inclinations which Pareto termed 'residues' in the
TREATISE. Social inequality was not an institutional problem,
but rather a natural phenomenon. No better society capable of
doing away with it was ever possible.

4. FROM ECONOMICS TO SOCIOLOGY

From what has been said so far it may be easily inferred that Pareto took an interest in sociology quite early in his research, almost conconmitantly with his beginnings in pure economics. That happened after his appointment at the University of Lausanne. Logically this interest of his was motivated by the reason that he had to acquire a global idea of economy and of its role in society before he could increase the generalizing power of his theory of pure economics as was his intention. He was not slow in realizing that despite his scientific interest, pure economics made no sense unless they could be informed by applied economics. The latter in turn were on each and every occasion linked to a given social context that was likely to offer resistance for political reasons, as in the case of protectionism, for instance, or for moral or religious causes. Whence the need of sociological research which would have enabled him to size up the place and the impact of economy in society. Pure economics were dealing with the economic phenomenon in its ideal state, independent of any other determining influence, in order to concentrate upon the process facilitating the maximum satisfaction of a need. Likewise, the economic equilibrium took into account the economic conditions only. In empirical reality, however, the economic action, not unlike the economic equilibrium, met with obstacles that doomed to failure the application of theoretical solutions derived from pure reasoning. Here is what Pareto was writing in his SYSTÈMES SOCIALISTES: 'The economists had been wrong to have attached too much importance to reason as determinant of human action. They had believed that by revealing the falsities and the nonesense in the theories of their opponents they would render the latter impotent. The success of Cobden's League was regarded as an expression of the victory of reason over prejudice, whereas in fact it was simply the victory of certain interests over others.'[52]

While acknowledging the influence of economics on his sociological research, various interpreters of Pareto's works accuse him of incoherence and criticize him for having set side by side two ways of thinking that make odd bed-fellows. Thus Perrin writes that Pareto's sociological theories reveal a genuine incompatibility of essences and as a result, any conciliation between the two types of analysis is impossible.[53] In this manner, he also rejects Pareto's own statements about the continuity of his own thinking, qualifying them as retrospective justifications. Perrin refers in particular to the speech delivered by Pareto on the occasion of his 1917 Jubilee at the University of Lausanne. At that time, Pareto reviewed his work and went on to say: 'As soon as I reached a certain point in my research in the field of political economy, I found myself in a deadlock. I could see the empirical reality, without however being able to reach it ... Pressed by the urge to bring an indispensable complement to the study of political economy and moreover, drawing inspiration from the example set by the natural sciences, I was induced to put together my treatise of sociology, the sole purpose of which - I say sole and insist on it - was to investigate the empirical reality by applying to the social sciences methods of research tested in the fields of physics, chemistry, astronomy, biology and other similar sciences.'[54]

Undoubtedly Pareto became interested in sociological problems while seeking to complete his reflections on economics. The SOMMAIRE, published in 1905, reproduces the mimeographed text of the series of sociological lectures delivered at the University of Lausanne for some time.[55] Besides, his writings on economics, such as the COURS and the MANUAL, deal conjointly with the two subject-matters. The first sentence of the MANUAL points out that it is both an economic and a sociological book.[56] Various explanations offered in these two writings announce some of the topics which would be dwelt upon and expanded in the TREATISE later on. In them, one even comes across the idea of residues and derivations, though not in those terms. As early as that Pareto was associating the notions of sentiment and interest in his intention of turning them into the general motives of human action. Thus in the MANUAL, for instance, he wrote the following:'It is mainly to sentiments and interests that one is to turn in order to make people act and follow the path one wants them to. Theoretically little is known about these phenomena, and here we cannot go any farther.'[57] True, his conception of economics had taken shape before that of sociology. At the beginning he had thought that he could deal with sociology by employing the same criteria that were used in economics; his early ideas of social and economic equilibria testify to that. It was only later, and more specifically as soon as he wanted to master sociology as much as economics, that he devoted his research efforts mainly to sociology. Incidentally, he found out that the parallelism he had previously upheld between the two fields was untenable. In other words, it was as a result of deep reflection on the social phenomenon that Pareto became aware of the need to alter his approach to the two categories of phenomena. The apparent watershed between his economic writings previous to 1900, on the one side, and his sociological works after 1900, on the other, is due to his change of method and perspective when he embarked upon the analysis of social phenomena. However, while building up his sociological system, he also managed to grasp the limitations of his idea of economics. This transition needs to be explained because on it depends the understanding of the TREATISE.

a) The disappointments experienced by Pareto during the interval of time which he spent in the service of free trade made him realize that economy was not the only factor affecting society. The practical application of any economic theory was handicapped by political, religious and other social resistances. As a result and in order to acquire a broader idea of the economic reality, it appeared to him indispensable to consider the economic fact as social and in correlation with other facts, according to the principle of mutual dependence. At the same time, it occurred to him that pure economics and the mathematical approach were but a first approximation of the whole economic reality, and that sociology was just another approximation. Whence the need to penetrate deeper into the territory of sociology as he had done in the field of mathematics. Increasingly concentrating on this new approach, of which he grew keener by the way, Pareto gave up part of his economic research in its favour. The conclusion to which he arrived in the process may be read in the TREATISE: 'Let us consider certain people who have appetites or tastes and who meet with certain obstacles on their way to satisfy them. What would then happen? Pure economics provide the answer to that question. It is a very comprehensive science because of the great variety of tastes and the extraordinary diversity of obstacles. The results which pure economics yield are an important and integrant part of sociology; yet it is only a part which in certain situations may be very small, almost negligible, and which at any rate needs to be combined with the other parts in order to reconstitute the image of concrete phenomena.' [58]

b) As his reflections on society advanced, Pareto also became increasingly aware of the hypothetical-deductive nature of pure economics: the latter deal with ideal situations and so are valid within those circumstances alone. 'In the same way as pure jurisprudence draws the consequences of certain principles, pure economics draw the consequences of certain hypotheses. Both sciences are applied to concrete phenomena as long as the given hypotheses play a prevailing role within those phenomena.'[59] Somehow Pareto became convinced of the sterility of that sort of abstract research with no reference to real life. With time he arrived at the conclusion that the kind of action tackled by pure economics was logical only to the extent it was based on the premise that tastes were data and no attention was paid to the valuations to which they were subjected in real life. He realized that the concrete action which was analysed by sociology depended on a great number of variables. 'Practice,' Pareto would say, 'is essentially synthetic.'[60] The study of sociology enabled him to appreciate the difficulties linked to the incoherence of determining factors at play in practical life. Accordingly, he ceased to conceive sociology in the image of pure economics, and instead looked at it for what it was, namely an autonomous field of research which had only an accessory interest in the expressions of rational conduct made available by pure economics. Notwithstanding, he never discarded the possibility of working out a pure theory of social equilibrium. With pure economics in mind, Pareto kept wondering whether the same approach could not be used in the social sciences: 'Thus one would have a science resembling pure economics or even applied economics. Unfortunately the similarity ceases as soon as the correspondence with reality is taken into account.'[61] The level at which sociology operated was not the same as that of pure economics, because the questions addressed to each of them were different.

Whence the unavoidable break in the approach to each of the two subject-matters.[62]

c) Given the fact that the questions posed to them were different, Pareto concluded that their research methods were equally different. He realized that in sociology it was not possible to go by the methods peculiar to geometry, which did not mean that the application of mathematics to the social sciences was irrelevant. Rather it meant that their usefulness was not the same, given the nature of the object of investigation. As a result, he argued, one had to resort to another method, equally scientific, namely induction, characteristic of the empirical sciences. Pareto called this method logical-experimental. In his opinion, sociology had for its object of study precisely what pure economics hypothetically considered a given, namely the variations of taste under the impact of sentiment and other empirical determinants.'The field in which we work is exclusively that of experience and observation. We are using these terms in the sense lent to them by the natural sciences, such as astronomy, chemistry, physiology and so on.'[63] Thus the difference was the same as that between a purely deductive, mathematical method, on the one side, and the experimental method, on the other.

As already said, Pareto changed some of his ideas gradually as he advanced in his research, learning to use scientific doubt and avoid dogmatism of any kind, even at the risk of putting his early, original ideas under a question mark. Pure economics were valid within the limits of and in the conditions defined by their hypotheses. The logical-experimental method was valid in other conditions, namely of the direct observation of phenomena.'The aim of science,' he went on, 'is to know the uniformities of phenomena; as a result one should use all the methods that enable us to reach this aim. The good and the bad methods are recognizable as such by testing. The method which leads to the objective aimed at is good as long as one has not yet come across a better method. History is useful to us in the sense that it extends past experience to the present and offers substitutes for those experiences which we cannot undergo ourselves. In consequence, the historical method is good. On the other hand, the deductive or the inductive methods that are applied to facts of the past are as good. One is content with ordinary logic whenever it suffices for various deductions. There where it does not, one replaces it by the mathematical method, and that without any hesitation.'[64] All that said, it is obvious that like any other scientist, Pareto was influenced by the ideas of his time. Like most of the specialists in the human sciences at the end of the nineteenth century, he believed that psychology was the basis of political economy and, in general, of all the social sciences.[65] Nowadays he may be criticized on that point because psychologism has in the mean time been discarded, although Pareto himself was not too keen on that trend either. Whatever the case, the break which occurred between economics and sociology in his own theorizing should disconcert only those who think that one and the same method may be used one-sidedly, be it the Marxist, the historical or any other, in order to analyse any category of phenomena. It is that one-sidedness which is unscientific. That is why one finds it hard to subscribe to Guy Perrin's thesis which claims that Pareto's sociology excludes economics.[66]

On the contrary, Pareto should be appreciated for having revamped and corrected his own ideas, as made evident by a paragraph in the TREATISE and which is essential to the interpretation of his thinking. Unfortunately his critics overlook it. In opposition to what he had thought earlier in his life, Pareto admitted in this paragraph that economy could not be explained solely by means of economics: 'One could not learn about those various effects by means of political economy alone, although they were economic in nature. It was necessary to adduce the means of another science, more general, which taught us to pay less attention to those derivations on the basis of which erroneous theories had been worked out. That science showed us how many were the forces acting upon phenomena in real life, and revealed to us their nature. These phenomena, though strictly economic in appearance, were actually dependent on other social phenomena.'[67] One cannot sustain a meaningful discussion of Pareto's transition to sociology without considering this text.

III

THE SOCIOLOGIST

The TREATISE is a dense, unbalanced work, hard to stomach in places, prolix in others. Briefly, it is a monster. Without harm, Pareto might have easily shortened it at least by half. Neither the force of his argument, nor the validity of his analyses would have suffered in any way. One cannot help subscribing to the unflattering remarks made by its reviewers. Firstly about the form: 'A case of scientific teratology' (B. Croce); 'He abused the right to be long, as if the multiplication of anecdotes could have made up for the doubtfulness of the evidence' (R. Aron); his inductive method 'consists above all in the absence of any indication of the aim it was supposed to lead to; the same questions are dealt with in ten different parts, time and again' (Bousquet). About the content of the TREATISE and the method employed in it, Halbwachs reproached Pareto the confusion between experimentation and exemplification, that is to say, between verification by means of proof, on the one hand, and the illustration of a statement, sometimes little grounded, by means of examples, on the other. Pareto had made random and extensive use of newspaper articles whenever they were confirming his assertions:'With equal confidence Pareto accepts the most diverse and questionable evidence, provided his conceptions are confirmed once more through the satisfaction of his hatreds. Press reports, gossip, anything goes as long as it can vex democrats and humanitarians alike' (R. Aron). Actually he took reckless pleasure in choosing as the target of his sarcasm and invectives the idea of progress, equality, peace, good-will, and so on, often at the expense of scientific rigour. Likewise, in certain sections of the TREATISE he resorted to libel rather than to a reasoned analysis of the facts.[1]

All these shortcomings however do not diminish the originality of his thinking, because it must be admitted that Pareto approached the social phenomenon in a way quite different from that assumed by the other sociologists, accustomed to the academic style. His work is not only rich in suggestive observations and unexpected points of view, but also permeated by a sharp sense of in-depth analysis, although quite unlike that characteristic of psychoanalysis. Contrary to what some of his critics said about it, the TREATISE shows a high internal consistency of thinking that impresses by its refusal to pay tribute to contemporary ideologies, to the reassuring beliefs, or even to the habitual categories employed by sociologists. His thinking has often had the effect of a corroding agent, not only by its biting style of expression, but also by the way it disturbs our intellectual tranquillity, undermines allegedly well-grounded convictions and hurts our humanitarian feelings and generosity. Pareto's thinking was intent on unmasking unconscious dissimulations which most often are adopted in good faith and with impartiality.

One must trace and point out the main directions assumed by Pareto's sociology in this voluminous work, full of digressions and the reading of which often turns into an unnerving and demanding pursuit for whomever dares to embark on it. As a matter of fact, the topics referred to in the TREATISE are not many. That does not also mean that I intend to turn them over and upside down in the Paretian manner with the result of effacing his alleged cynicism by my restraint.

1. THE LOGICAL-EXPERIMENTAL METHOD

Sociology is a science and as such it must submit to the servitudes of scientific research and analysis. Pareto took the concept of science in its strictest meaning which to some may seem too narrow. He saw it as an intellectual activity concerned to determine the relations between objects and between phenomena, and to bring to light the uniformities implicit in these relations.[2] This definition is to be looked into for what it contains and also for what it excludes.

Pareto's idea of science is very close to that put forth by Claude Bernard in his INTRODUCTION À LA MÉDICINE EXPÉRIMEN-TALE.[3] However, I shall not go into any detailed discussion of this comparison. Essential from Pareto's point of view was that the natural sciences provided the model for any scientific approach. In the already mentioned Jubilee speech delivered at Lausanne, Pareto stated that: 'The main purpose of my studies has always been to apply to the social sciences the experimental method which has yielded such brilliant results in the natural sciences.'[4] Factual reality is the only basis for research and sole criterion of verification. As he explained it in § 144 of the TREATISE, the task was to classify the facts with a view to discovering relations and possibly uniformities or laws. From that inductive stage one was to proceed to that of deductive verification of the validity of those uniformities with the facts of life. Furthermore, there were conclusions to be drawn from them as soon as the verification was completed. Pareto always returned to facts wherever he talked about methodology in any of his books. This limitation imposed on analysis was, in his opinion, the only guarantee of objectivity. By the latter he meant a total indifference to values and beliefs. That was not however to say that sociology was to ignore those values or beliefs. Rather, it meant that sociology took them for facts without worrying whether they were just, worthy or legitimate. 'We accept all the facts, whatever they are, provided they can directly or indirectly lead us to the discovery of a uniformity. Even an absurd or silly argument is a fact; and if it is accepted by a great many people, it becomes an important fact for sociology. Beliefs, whatever they are, are facts, too, and their importance is not linked to their intrinsic merit, but rather to the larger or smaller number of people that profess them.'[5] Pareto was interested in the objective and verifiable relations among facts only, and not in the knowledge of facts in themselves, in their nature or essence. Whenever causality was not regarded as a relation, but rather as an alleged descent to the ultimate source of things, he rejected it, because such attempts surpassed the limits of experience. As a consequence, they were for him mere speculations outside the field of science. Moreover, scientific laws were relative to the conditions of a particular time and space. Whence Pareto's conclusion that all scientific knowledge is relative.

Pareto's idea of facts excluded any reference to any particular creed, religious or otherwise, to metaphysics, because the latter wanted to know the nature of things, or to any encompassing theory capable of explaining everything on the strength of a previously drawn-out schema, such as Marxism, for instance. Likewise it left out the knowledge of the utility of the phenomenon under examination and of the profitability of the scientifically established relation: 'An important consequence is that I do not think it useful to have all sociologies modelled upon mine. On the contrary. Generally speaking, any author wants to persuade and is convinced that in this way he does a useful thing, because he believes that he knows the truth and the truth is always good, useful, and so on. As far as I am concerned, I do not wish to persuade anybody, and I strongly doubt that it would do any good, at least most of the times. I do not believe at all that I am in the possession of an absolute and ultimate truth. I do not believe either that experimental truth is always useful. I do not know whether it is good, because I do not have the slightest idea of the meaning of that word.'[6] Thus when tackling Pareto's methodology, it is important to make a clear distinction between, on the one hand, a theoretical truth confirmed by experience and, on the other hand, a useful theory, because the utility of a theory is not a matter that falls within the jurisdiction of science. Rather it is a matter of subjective beliefs and valuations. In short, it is a matter of interests. What is true is not automatically useful and what is useful is not necessarily true. Whence his much criticized remark: 'Thus I ask the reader always to remember that wherever I show the absurdity of a doctrine I do not mean in the least to maintain that it is harmful to society; on the contrary, it may be quite profitable to it. Likewise, wherever I speak of the utility of a theory to society, I do not intend to imply that it is experimentally true at all. To sum up, one and the same theory may be rejected experimentally, but accepted for its social utility, or the other way round.'[7] He had stated that idea already when he had noted that a proposition in political economy was true if it was confirmed by the facts and not in the least because it conformed to the liberal, christian, catholic, socialist or any other doctrine. Scientifically, a doctrine of the latter sort was meaningless.[8] According to Pareto, faith in socialism was in no way different from the faith in one's fatherland, or in the nation, or else in the army, in terms of science. It expressed a simple conviction which was not amenable to demonstration. Thus one would obviously reject as absurd a demonstration of Pythagora's theorem by means of an appeal to the 'immortal principles of 1789.' Nonetheless, Pareto would say, one seldom realizes that one does just that whenever one claims that an economic determination is just, simply because its character is socialistic.[9]

Pareto's epistemology seems to have been strictly positivistic. More than once did he restrict his propositions to facts alone in a way that led him to a kind of fetishism. Thus, for instance, in a letter addressed to Pantaleoni, he wrote that were he to re-edit his COURS, then he would add still more facts.[10] That was exactly what he did in the TREATISE. Unfortunately there he happened sometimes to offer for facts the unchecked and subjective interpretations given by journalists. His only reason was that they seemed to corroborate one or the other of his analyses. On the other hand, it would be a mistake to attribute to him the idea that science was but a copy of reality, or the belief that the sign of equality could be drawn between ideas and reality. By the way it deals with ideal phenomena, his theory of pure economics would have sufficed to put him on his guard against such errors. Not only did he admit that the scientific fact was a conceptually reconstructed fact, but time and again he also stated that it was impossible to grasp any phenomenon in its entirety. 'No concrete phenomenon can be known in all its details; there is always a residue left, which at times may be materially apparent. We can have only approximate ideas of concrete phenomena; so divergencies are unavoidable and all we can do is to reduce them to a minimum.[11] It was for this very reason that he rejected the theories which were claiming to explain everything by means of a single factor, as socialism was doing when it claimed that everything was ultimately reducible to the economic sector. That implied a priori knowledge of the nature of things as well as the ability to explain everything. All theory, Pareto argued, was provisional, and nobody could uphold the absolute superiority of any of them: 'From the scientific viewpoint, no theory should be rejected off hand. One must always compare it to the facts in the first place; if it agrees with them, then one may accept it. If not, then one rejects it.'[12]

Despite all that, Pareto's positivism was never rigid or narrow. I have already drawn attention to his statements about the need of resilience in the choice of methods, and to the fact that Pareto had no explicit reason for imposing any particular research method a priori. Furthermore, it was his opinion that the decision how far to carry on one's investigation was a matter of opportuneness lying entirely with the scientist: 'The economist, like all those who study very complex phenomena, has at each step to solve the question how far it is feasable to go into the examination of details. One cannot in an absolute manner determine the point where it is advantageous to stop: this point depends on the proposed objective.'[13] Pareto was the first to become aware of his own mistakes and to alter his approach as a result. Nothing is more enlightening in this respect than his own confession, inserted in a note to the TREATISE: 'A learned personality asked one of my students whether my science was democratic! It had been said and written of it that it was socialistic; another claimed that it was reactionary. The science which seeks factual uniformities (laws) exclusively is none of the above: it bears no epithet. It is content to look for these uniformities and nothing else. Personally I had been a supporter of free trade in the COURS, but in the MANUAL I had already given up that position and ever since I have avoided taking any stand while I am concerned with science alone.'[14] On the other hand, it would be wrong to consider him a partisan of scientism. What he meant in his confession is the following: when I am doing science I submit myself to the conditions and the presuppositions peculiar to the scientific activity and during that time I am not concerned with morality or with metaphysics; I do not seek to give advice or persuade. 'One wants to know,' he was saying, 'to know, and nothing else.'[15] Also, Pareto never favoured the idea that science was a privileged activity, or a profession superior to others such as politics, or the arts, for instance. Nor did he profess that the value of an object was enhanced by its scientific explanation. 'Let us be wary of endowing logic or experimentation with any superior force or dignity in the ways of the dogmas accepted by sentiment, and which are also shared by a certain materalistic metaphysics. Our aim is to make distinctions, and not to compare, and above all, not to judge the merits and the virtues of this or that.'[16]

Nevertheless, no researchwork could be carried on blindly, and while admitting that it has to follow certain guiding principles, Pareto warned that no metaphysical significance needs to be attached to them. They are mere research or rather, working hypotheses. In my opinion, four such basic principles might be singled out in Pareto's work. The first two have already been dwelt on; they are the mutual dependence of phenomena, and the principle of successive approximations. In the MANUAL, a third principle comes to the fore: 'There is no proposition that cannot be proven true under certain conditions that need to be determined. The conditions that affect a phenomenon are an internal part of that phenomenon and cannot be separated from it.'[17] In other words, a proposition is valid only in the conditions which made its formulation possible. This principle will facilitate the understanding of non-logical actions because these actions are characterized by a claim to a validity that exceeds the defining conditions. The fourth principle is that of causal pluralism. A phenomenon is never explained by one cause only; rather it is the result of a great number of interfering causes that are in continuous interaction. Causal one-sidedness is metaphysical. It is not in the least scientific. Even if there were a preponderant cause in a given situation, it could not be an absolute determinant. In a different situation that cause might cease altogether to be preponderant.

It is in this epistemological context that one must consider Pareto's logical-experimental method. As its name shows, it implies two procedures which more often than not are used in combination, though if need be, they may be used separately. On the one side, there is the classical experimental method which acknowledges as scientifically valid those propositions and theories alone that are verified empirically. On the other side, there is logic which deducts the consequences on the basis of observable and verifiable relations by means of reasoning. Meanwhile it is understood that the scientist is free to rely either on classical or on mathematical logic. According to Pareto, all the propositions that are worked out with no regard to these two methods are unscientific. Said differently, the only judge of the validity of a scientific proposition is experience. If the observations, on which the inference is based, elude the control of experience, the conclusions drawn from them have no scientific value. Whence: 'Whoever states a logical-experimental proposition may present his contradictor with the alternative either of accepting it as true or of denying any reliability to experience and logic.'[18]

Thus understood, the logical-experimental method sets a pathway to follow, which Pareto underlined in § 69 of the first chapter of the TREATISE for everybody to see. I shall return to it.

Briefly, Pareto's methodological position may be described as follows: there is no ground to conclude that this method is better than the others, because the very term 'better' is meaningless in this context. What is called in question is merely the opposition between the scientific investigation, on the one hand, and the speculations on the absolute or the essence, on the other. They are two heterogeneous orders that need not be mistaken one for the other. That does not mean that in the name of science one should accordingly discredit the attitude of those who explain events by referring them to theology, morality, ethics, or politics, provided they do not try to present their interpretations as scientific. What matters is to know which judge has been chosen: experience; authority; utility, or the revelation. All of them are legitimate and authoritative within their particular areas, but incompetent in any situation the conditions of which exceed their respective jurisdictions.

There is still another aspect of Pareto's methodology worth considering, because Pareto returned to it time and again with singular emphasis. That did not prevent him from betraying it more than once. It is what Bousquet called 'the illusions of the vocabulary.'[19] In short: it would be preferable to be able to work with simple signs as in algebra, but such a procedure risks to introduce more confusion than it can forestall. Thus Pareto conceded eventually that one must resort to concepts expressed in words. Unfortunately too often, he used to remark, sociologists cling to these words instead of the real facts which they describe. He saw a partial solution to that inconvenience in the definition of the terms likely to be employed, and in their consistent use afterwards. Another alternative was to work out a technical vocabulary made up of terms sufficiently univocal. Pareto remarked that both the 'literary' economists and the sociologists, in general, did not pay much attention to such precautionary measures, but grounded their reasoning in the affective charge built in the very words. Thus, while discussing such concepts as capital, justice, peace, equality, progress or democracy, they would start by blending their arguments with feelings of sympathy or aversion which would mar their analyses. In such cases, he noted, verbalism often displaces science. Language, he insisted, lays many a trap for the specialists in the social sciences. They either mean something else than what is ordinarily understood by the term, without making that clear, or employ one and the same word giving it different meanings and playing on them. Sometimes they attach feelings to those words, or introduce a priori decisions without any open warning. They hold for precise what is not, and happen to mistake wishful thinking for demonstration. Pareto drove his point home by showing, for instance, that speeches that exalt freedom approve, implicitly and in good faith, of an oppressive system at one and the same time. One uses the term 'socialism,' Pareto would remark, as if everybody was understanding the word in the same way, as if Marx agreed with Proudhon, Guesde with Sorel and Jaurès, Sombart with Bernstein, and so on. Under such conditions, he noted, the evidence put forth is often exclusively verbal. Pareto himself provided a wealth of analogous examples, but I am not going to insist on them. What I want to stress, though, is Pareto's necessary contribution to a theory of argumentation by his discussion and his insistence on the need of clarification. As Bobbio also observed: 'The main contributions which Pareto brought to the theory of argumentation are two: 1.the importance which he attached to the difference between the scientific and the rhetorical discourse in the study of the human society, and the delimitation of the two areas through criteria of identification of the two different types of discourse (the first, truth-falsity; the second, efficiency-inefficiency); 2.the finding that in rhetorical discourse one has in turn to differentiate between the sentiments which it conveys or wants to arouse, on the one side, and the arguments adduced to obtain the so-called accord of the sentiments, on the other. Pareto also found that this latter aspect is sociologically less consistent and less important than the former.'[20] Seen from this angle, Pareto's work yields the first elements for a sociology of ideologies.

2. THE LOGICAL AND THE NON-LOGICAL ACTIONS

The distinction between the logical and the non-logical actions became manifest in Pareto's sociological thinking quite early, and well before that between residues and derivations. It might even be said that this distinction began to inform his thinking directly as soon as he realized that he could no longer uphold the parallelism between economics and sociology. Notwithstanding, one finds it mentioned already in an article published in the RIVISTA ITALIANA DI SOCIOLOGIA in 1900, under the title 'Une application des théories sociologiques.' There one may read, for instance, that : 'Although pressed by non-logical motives to act, the human being likes to link his actions to certain principles in a logical manner, and for that purpose he thinks of the latter after the act, in order to justify his conduct. The human being who in this way deceives the other by his own statements started by deceiving himself into firmly believing in his own words.'[21] This distinction became a subject-matter of his lectures delivered at the University of Lausanne, as made evident by the SOMMAIRE of his course of sociological lectures printed for the benefit of his students. The logical-experimental method enabled Pareto to lend a solid groundwork to the distinction which had been his concern for several years already. As a matter of fact, by defining the necessary conditions for logical reasoning, the method made it possible to determine whether an action was logical in regard to the reasoning that supported it. Said differently, it is in relation to logic that actions are pronounced to be logical or non-logical by Pareto. His procedure has been held by Schumpeter, among others, to have fallen short of distinguishing between the rationality of thinking, on the one side, and the rationality of action, on the other.[22] An action may be rational without necessarily conforming to the categories of logic. This argument, set forth by Guy Perrin who questions Pareto's distinction, is actually irrelevant to the latter's preoccupations because, as Raymond Aron stresses: 'Pareto reminds us that objectives are not logically determined by science. There is no scientific solution to the problem of action. Science cannot go any farther than to suggest the means by which goals may be reached efficiently. The determination of ends is not a part of science. Ultimately there is no scientific solution to the problem of individual conduct. Nor is there any scientific answer to the question of social organization either.'[23] The rational action is that kind of action the ends of which have been well chosen. On the other hand, for Pareto the determination of ends is a question of valuation in keeping with the norms of utility, morality, and so on. His interest is more circumscribed, namely to understand the relation between the chosen end, considered as a given, on the one side, and the means put to work in order to attain the given end, on the other. It is from this point of view alone that Pareto posed the problem of the logic of action.

One thing should be made clear from the beginning if we want to get a correct idea of Pareto's sociological research project. He had never intended to work out a scientific or more specifically a sociological theory of action in the way Parsons tried to do. As Busino remarks to the point: 'Pareto remained aware of the impossibility of working out an analytical schema of action solely on the basis of action itself.'[24] He always stated that action is synthetic by its very nature. 'The concrete actions are synthetical; they originate in combinations of elements that need to be classified.'[25] Or in another place: 'I declare that I do not wish to resolve any practical question. Nonetheless, whenever one steps out of theory, wishing to put together rules for real life, then one has to resort to synthesis.'[26] By those words he wished to say that the concrete action is always affected by a coefficient of indetermination and of the unpredictable, because it combines the agent's insight and sense of opportuneness, as need arise, with extremely different factors. Furthermore, during its actual unfolding the action elicits the intervention of other elements, originally unforeseen. Volition plays havoc with the predictions and in consequence with any scientific theory of action. In other words, the indefinite number of factors which are likely to intervene in an action defies the capacities of any analytical study. Each individual is prone to choose a different set of factors even whenever they all want one and the same thing. What Pareto called logical action is sheer abstraction of an ideal type which approximates reality to a lesser or greater degree. Besides, he insisted on the fact that one and the same action may imply both logical and non-logical phases. [27]

Pareto's definition of logical actions is more precise than that of non-logical actions. On one occasion he came to describe the latter almost exclusively by contrast to the former: 'Once and for all we shall call logical actions those operations which are logically connected to their objective not only from the point of view of the agent, but also of those who have a broader knowledge; in other words, the actions which have objectively and subjectively the above meaning. The other actions would be called "non-logical," which does not mean illogical.'[28] Before going on to discuss these definitions, a look at some of the examples given by Pareto himself might be helpful. The engineer who builds a bridge acts logically when in the process of execution he takes into account the nature of the soil, the most adequate span system, the resistance of the materials, and so on. He accords the means with the anticipated end accurately. The Stock Exchange speculator acts in the same way when he achieves the expected result. These are logical actions. Among the non-logical actions Pareto would quote the attitude of the Roman consul who before engaging in battle consults the oracles in order to find out whether the gods favour a successful outcome of the campaign. Other examples are the anthropomorphisation or the animation of material objects. A closer look at these examples makes evident that objectively, the relation means-end in the case of the engineer of public works corresponds fully to the subjective calculation implicit in the elaboration of the project. In the case of the investor, on the other hand, the objective outcome may happen not to correspond to his subjective estimations; he might have been mistaken in his forecasts. Furthermore, in the case of the Roman consul, the subjective means employed have no logical relation to the envisaged end, in this particular instance, military victory. Thus, non-logical behaviour may be of different kinds, in keeping with the different ways of estimating the relation between end and means, objectively and subjectively. Said differently, the logical action is that in which the means-end relation, which is achieved objectively in concrete circumstances, corresponds entirely to the agent's subjective awareness of this relation. All others, that is to say, all the actions that imply an inadequacy between the objectively aimed-at end and the agent's subjective estimation of means, are non-logical. The logical action is characterized by two specific traits: a) correspondence between the employed means and the envisaged end, and b) adequacy between the objective reality and the subjective awareness of the agent. There, where either a) or b) are absent, one finds oneself in the presence of non-logical actions which in turn may be of different kinds. By using these two characteristic features, one may together with Pareto draw up the table below.

By an objective end one should understand a direct, real end which may be empirically observed and experienced, as distinct from the imaginary end that eludes observation.

GENUS AND SPECIES	DO THE ACTIONS HAVE A LOGICAL END?	
	Objectively	Subjectively
Logical Actions The objective end is identical to the subjective end		
	Yes	Yes
Non-Logical Actions The objective end differs from the subjective end		
1st genus	No	No
2nd genus	No	Yes
3rd genus	Yes	No
4th genus	Yes	Yes
Species of the 3rd and the 4th Genera		
3a and 4a	The agent would accept the objective end, were he to know it.	
3b and 4b	The agent would not accept the objective end, were he to know it.	

A. The Logical Actions

Most of the times they are grounded in reason (§ 161): to the extent they use the means logically appropriate for a definite end through calculus or other logical method. Pareto thought that such actions were more frequent among the so-called civilised peoples. He associated them with the development of science and technology, and also of a more rigorous logic, which in turn tends to expand the scope of knowledge and favours the verification of information for accuracy by means of the logical-experimental method. From all this it may be inferred that at least implicitly Pareto accepted the idea of the advancement of knowledge. It accounts for the increase in the number of the manifestations of the logical conduct as the rational civilization develops. Logical conduct is most often encountered in the scientific, technical and artistic activities, as well as in economy, and in military, political and juridical actions. There is no doubt that Pareto had become aware of this genus of action through his analyses of economic activity, though he never limited the former to the latter. Besides, there is no ground to affirm that he had in mind contemporary and past societies alone. On the contrary, by taking one of his examples from military strategy, Pareto let it to be understood that given the uncertainties of the future, there is the tendency of working out a great many combinations in order to direct one's conduct logically henceforward. Neither did he exclude the possibility of such actions from the animal world. Nonetheless, for obvious reasons, he thought their number to be the greatest among humans (§ 157).

As already shown, a concrete action may display both logical and non-logical elements simultaneously. In particular circumstances, a logical action may become non-logical, and the other way round. Thus the non-logical behaviour of the Roman consul who made the decision to go to war dependent on the responses of the oracles, became logical as soon as he turned the forecasting technique, in which he personally did not believe, into a means of augmenting his chances of victory. That is, to the extent the examination of bird entrails could have helped to lift the morale of the troops who for their part believed in such prodigies. Pareto pointed to the fact that many a non-logical action are amenable to some logical interpretation. On the other hand, the investor's operation becomes non-logical as soon as he does not obtain the expected result, owing to some error in his calculations. Thus one cannot determine the area of logical actions with any precision, because no activity enjoys the privilege of its undivided use, not even economy. This type of action may raise a good many questions. Personally I shall raise only one, about the affinity between the operations inherent in the logical action, on the one side, and the logical-experimental method, on the other. An action is not logical because its end is rational; rather solely in relation to its envisaged end. Said differently, it takes this end as given, and concentrates only on the performance of the means and its consequences. From this point of view, the application of the logical-experimental method appears as a logical action. On reading Pareto's works one may wonder whether the relation means-end is the only characteristic feature of a logical action. Although he never said it in so many words, his writings would suggest that an action is logical as long as it is limited to its initial conditions, that is, as long as it does not exceed its original objective. Thus it is not only a matter of employing the means that are appropriate to an anticipated end, but also of sticking to that end, in the same way in which the logical-experimental method refuses to overstep the limits of experience.[29]

B. The Non-Logical Actions

'The non-logical actions emerge mainly from a certain psychical state: sentiment, the subconscious, and so on. It is the task of psychology to deal with such psychical states. In our study we shall tackle it as a matter of fact without going any deeper into it.'[30] These lines are significant not only because they point to the method used by Pareto, and which was always the same, namely to start from facts regarded as data, without seeking to know their origins and history, but also because they define the backdrop of non-logical actions. Among other things, he insisted that the non-logical should not be confused with the illogical. Indeed, a non-logical action may be illogical and absurd, but it may also be partially logical, or just seemingly logical. It does not exclude reasoning, but the latter is either false or quite sophisticated, and so on. In order to avoid any error in the interpretation of Pareto's ideas, it is worth repeating that it is only in terms of the abstract notion of the logical action that it is possible to identify what he regarded as non-logical actions. That is also why he did not bother to define the type. He was content to state that all action that is not wholly logical is non-logical, no matter whether by its contents, it is paralogical, simililogical, pseudological or illogical. This was made clear in a passage in the MANUAL: 'We must note that non-logical does not mean illogical; a non-logical action may represent what one could find best in terms of empirical observation and logic to adapt the means to the end; but this adjustment has been carried out by another procedure than that of logical reasoning.'[31] Thus Pareto examined the non-logical actions from the point of view of logic alone, and in no other way.[32] That is also the reason why he refrained from examining the part played by sentiment in that kind of action, or the degree of its involvement. Likewise, that is why he abstained from regarding it either as error, deviation, or a pathological form, and why he was content simply to categorize it according to the two traits which he considered characteristic of logical actions and which he used as criteria of classification. Actually by doing that he replied in advance to all those who have eventually seen him as an author that exalts the irrational: 'By granting reason and sentiment their part in the composition of social phenomena, by attributing to each a definite domain, one does not at all mean to depreciate either. Because I stick to reasoning naturally and necessarily while writing a scientific book, that does not mean that I deny the existence of a field of the sentiment and of faith. The reader will see rather the opposite, namely that I assign to the latter a scope which many would find exaggerated, perhaps. What I wish to avoid are the dissertations in such wide circulation in the social sciences, and in which reason and sentiment are mixed together into a strange alloy.'[33]

In contrast with the logical action, the non-logical action is amenable to a classification into four genera:

- The genus no-no, characterized by the fact that the means

do not correspond to any end either objective or subjective, and as a result there is no obvious reason for that action. Pareto quoted as example Hesiod's precept 'Do not urinate at the mouth of a river that flows into the sea.' Actually one cannot see the reason why one has to refrain from such pollution. Under this category one may also range certain gestures imposed by custom or etiquette. Anyhow, in Pareto's opinion, they are seldom encountered among people, perhaps with the exception of savages and barbarians, because the human being always tends to justify his acts and to apply to them a coat of logic, thus making them amenable to classification in the second genus or even the fourth. [34]

- The actions of the genus no-yes, on the contrary, are current. People invent means that do not correspond to the objective end. In other words, the relation means-end which is subjectively envisaged has no effect upon the objectively anticipated end. This is the case of those who think themselves capable of making rain or arousing a storm by prayer or offerings. To this genus belong most of the acts grounded in magic, and the majority of gestures linked to the religious cultus and ceremonial.

- The third genus, that of non-logical actions yes-no, is characterized by the fact that the agent attains the end objectively, but without being aware of it. Said differently, he uses the correct means and applies them accordingly to that purpose, but without being aware of all that. For Pareto this is the pure type of non-logical action.[35] The actions of this genus also occur frequently in real life. For illustrations of this genus of action Pareto searched the works of the French entomologist Jean Henri Fabre. Thus he chose as examples instances of animal behaviour that is adequate objectively yet only adopted by instinct and without awareness. On a human plane, one may subsume to this genus some of the ancient medical treatments which were correctly applied, though without any scientific knowledge of their action on the body. The same applies in the case of Hesiod's piece of advice, namely not to urinate in a well. Objectively it was correct, although Hesiod was no aware of the fact that by following that advice the spread of certain diseases could be prevented.

- Finally, the fourth genus, that of non-logical actions yes-yes, stresses the relation between the objective and the subjective ends. It points to those actions the means of which lead objectively to a result different from the subjectively desired end. Thus in the sphere of the economy, the entrepreneur who wants to reduce the cost price ends, against his will, by reducing the retail price, as well, in virtue of the fact that in the market system competition tends to bring the two prices to the same level. Something akin happens with the revolutionaries who want to set people free. Eventually they are forced to set up an oppressive régime because, Pareto argued, they have resorted to violence as a means of attaining their end. In other words, this genus includes actions in which the employed means lead to the disruption of the correspondence between the subjective and the objective ends, and ultimately to a result which objectively does no longer coincide with the subjective end. That is also what happened to Bismarck who, in his desire to weaken the socialist and the catholic parties, abolished the former and waged the *Kulturkampf* against the latter. By an inadequate appraisal of the circumstances, and in spite of his original intention, he ended by strengthening both organizations.

As for the two species 3a and 4a, and 3b and 4b, respectively, they do not need a long explanation, they can be easily understood. Would Bismarck or would he not have embarked upon the *Kulturkampf*, had he known that the catholic party would emerge stronger out of it? Or, was his hostility to that organization so strong that he would have waged the campaign no matter what?

On a closer examination of these four genera of non-logical action, one finds that experience is ultimately the determining criterion in all of them. Even when an action is carried out in keeping with the norms of logic but the result does not correspond to the original intention, Pareto would not have hesitated to classify it among the non-logical actions. That is made evident in his article on pure economics, already quoted. There he also drew up a typology of actions on two exclusive criteria, the logical and the experimental, respectively. Thus he grouped actions into the logical and experimental; the experimental and non-logical; the logical and non-experimental, and finally, the non-logical and non-experimental actions. One may question the pertinence of such a criterion as experience to determine the logicality of conduct in a particular situation. All the more so, as the distinction drawn by Pareto between the experimental and the logical actions does not preclude the inference that other criteria than those mentioned in the TREATISE could have been chosen as well. Consequently, some interpreters of his work, and in particular Raymond Aron, have not missed the chance to raise several objections. Is an action logical when it achieves an objective end, validated by experience? Did Pareto deliberately ignore the fact that certain customs and myths have an occult logic of their own, as structuralism has demonstrated of late? Would the ethnologists not smile condescendingly when reading some of his analyses? Besides, Pareto's procedure is circle-like. After having posited at the start that the logical/non-logical opposition applied only to the means-end relation, he had no difficulty in showing that the actions which did not correspond rigorously to the criterion, were non-logical. On the other hand, is it true that the non-logical conforms to sentiments only? This is not self-evident, and moreover, Pareto did not offer any proof in its favour. One may wonder whether he was not pursuing some other goal besides the purely scientific.[36]

It seems that in effect Pareto wanted to show that most of the intellectuals either are mistaken or delude themselves about the value of their work because they are convinced that they are right. Whereas actually the conclusions they are drawing do not correspond logically to the original data. That is what emerges from the long chapters following that on non-logical actions in the TREATISE. In them Pareto examined extensively the theories that exceeded experience and for that reason he regarded them as pseudo-scientific. I shall spare the reader the great many examples quoted by Pareto to back his case. On the other hand, it is true to say that he endangered his position when he tried to prove that intellectuals make mistakes in good faith. He affirmed that they are not intent on being wicked; rather they themselves lack lucidity while attempting to enlighten the whole of mankind. In other words, Pareto did grant the intellectuals two alternatives

only, that of hypocrisy (whenever they are of bad faith), and
of naïveté (whenever they are of good faith), respectively.
To sum up, he tended to see the intellectuals as essentially
naive: by being forced to reason they become unreasonable. It
is difficult to forgive someone who so ruthlessly ridicules
convictions that pass for sound and well grounded.

His unsparing derision is shown at a greater advantage in
his SYSTÈMES. There he denied any demonstrative value to a
series of propositions which Marx had considered scientific.
Relatedly, Pareto upheld that the dissemination of a doctrine
had little if at all to do with the logical value of that particular doctrine.[37] There, too, he went on praising casuistry
because, as he put it, without it social life would have been
impossible.[38] In the same context he remarked that people are
inclined to give to their deeds motives that are more imaginary
than real. Accordingly, he maintained that theories merely
dress with the garb of logic choices made for other reasons,
such as prejudices, sentiments or specific beliefs. He argued:
'Many people are socialist not because they have been persuaded
by a particular kind of reasoning, but rather they acquiesce
in that particular kind of reasoning because they are socialists, which is another matter altogether. The sources of
the illusions which people nourish with respect to the motives
of their actions are multiple... These actions are purely
instinctive, but the agents experience a feeling of pleasure
when they attribute to them logical causes, though quite
arbitrarily. In general, the agents are not very demanding as
regards the quality of such logic. They are easily satisfied
with make-belief.'[39] Then Pareto went on: 'Whenever people feel
drawn either to a religious or a moralistic or still, a humanitarian movement, they believe, and almost all in good faith,
that their convictions have been formed through a series of
rigorous syllogisms based on real and undeniable facts.'[40] There
is no doubt that Pareto turned his theory of non-logical
actions into an inexhaustible source of sarcasm levelled at
the intellectuals, the philosophers, the pacifists, and the
progressives, as well as at the various Christian churches of
his time. Their reaction in turn proves that quite often he
did hit the mark.

3. RESIDUES AND DERIVATIONS

The discussion of these two concepts represents the kernel
of Pareto's sociological thinking. He had started by putting
together a theory of logical action from the point of view of
pure economics. In the process, he reached the conclusion that
in practical life such actions were rare and that, on the
contrary, most human actions revealed non-logical elements
as well as pseudological and simililogical aspects. Eventually
he felt the need to understand those non-logical aspects and
to round off his theory of pure economics by a sociological
theory. Indeed, he admitted that he was not the first to
lay stress on the non-logical actions, and even took a chapter
in the TREATISE to show that others before him had suspected
the existence of non-logical actions, but had not taken the
trouble to offer an explanation for them. In his own attempt,
Pareto started by using the inductive method to analyze empirical cases taken mainly from the field of law. In that way he
expected to obtain the elements for a theory which in turn
would facilitate a series of deductions. I shall not discuss
his procedure in any detail here. Instead, I shall concentrate
on the results of his investigation.

He reached the conclusion that the non-logical actions
contain two elements: one, a constant, which Pareto marked by
the letter (a), and the other, more variable, which he designated by the letter (b). The part (a) directly corresponds to
non-logical actions; it is the expression of certain sentiments.
The (b) part is the manifestation of the human need of logic.
It, too, partially corresponds to non-logical actions, but
couches them in logical or pseudological arguments. Part (a) is
the principle inherent in human awareness. Part (b) represents
the explications, the deductions from the principle.[41] To
illustrate the distinction I shall take two examples. In
almost every society certain numbers are worshipped or feared;
likewise, homicide is proscribed. This is the constant element
(a). Furthermore, one quotes reasons that explain why certain
numbers are occult and why homicide is forbidden. For some, it
is a matter of perfect numbers which consequently are beautiful, just and good. For others, they have a religious meaning.
Likewise, homicide is forbidden either because God willed it,

or out of respect for human dignity. It is the element (b) which varies in accordance with the civilizations. In real life, the two elements (a) and (b) are given indiscriminately, as if they were both part of the given phenomenon. Thus the ban on homicide is stated concomitantly with its justification. From a scientific point of view they have to be kept separate. This does not apply to actions alone, but also to theories, be they philosophical, moral or of other kinds. 'When one reads someone else's writings with the intention of making a scientific appraisal of the latter's theories, one must start by separating the parts (a) and (b), respectively, something which has almost never been done before. Generally speaking, in each and every theory it is necessary to separate the premises, that is the principles, the postulates, the sentiments and the deductions drawn from them.'[42] This is the way by which, in Pareto's opinion, one can find out whether a particular theory exceeds the limits of experience.

With this result in hand, Pareto set forth the following hypothesis: 'The element (a) may correspond to certain human instincts, because (a) has no objective existence of its own and besides, it differs from person to person; on the other hand, it is almost constant within phenomena and that probably because it corresponds to those instincts. The element (b) corresponds to the completed mental effort to account for element (a). That is why it is so much more variable. It reflects the labours of imagination... But if part (a) corresponds to certain instincts, that does not mean that it is all-inclusive. This can be seen from the way it has been discovered. We have analyzed the arguments and looked for the constant part. With this method we could have found only the instincts that generate arguments, and in the process we could have noticed those that are not concealed by arguments. Thus one has left out the simple appetites, tastes, dispositions and, in terms of social facts, that very important class of the so-called interests.'[43] If this hypothesis agrees with the facts, then it is retained to define a uniformity. Otherwise it should be rejected.

A. The Theory of Residues

Pareto never ceased to insist on the use of precise definitions in one's work. Nonetheless, with regard to the notion of
residue, he did not manage to get rid of all the imprecisions.
A thing, though, is certain: the residue represents a constant,
non-logical element of the human nature. He left the psychological element out, attaching to it only the value of a
heuristical concept or kernel, as he so often used to call it.
In order to discourage any psychological interpretation of his
concept, Pareto took pains to distinguish among the residue,
the sentiment, and the instinct, in turn, although more than
once he himself became guilty of mixing up the three notions.
Here is his definition: 'One must be on one's guard not to
mistake the residues (a) for the sentiments, or the instincts
to which they correspond. The residues (a) are the manifestation of those sentiments and those instincts as the rise of
the mercury in a thermometer tube is the manifestation of an
increase in temperature. To make a long story short we shall
say elliptically that the residues, alongside the appetites,
the interests, and so on, play an important part in the determination of the social equilibrium.'[44]This passage confirms
the one already quoted from § 851 of the TREATISE and in which
Pareto was stating that the residue corresponds only to those
instincts which give rise to reasonings, and so letting his
readers to infer that there are other instincts which do not.

Various analysts have been justified in questioning the
legitimacy of such a distinction between instincts, because in
the last instance any instinct could give rise to reasoning.
It seems to me that by his procedure Pareto only wanted to
avoid a purely psychological interpretation of the residue,
and save the sociological explanation. That is what emerges
from the paragraph on the sexual instinct. There the residue
appears as an instinct linked to reasoning, which is not
the case of the pure instinct as psychology views it. This
correlation with reasoning is essential to the point Pareto
was making, namely that reasoning might conceal pure instinct
and render it hard to grasp. Thus, to recall Pareto's example,
the purely sexual instinct is characterized by the simple
approach between sexes, whereas the sexual residue may go as

far as to assume the disguise of ascetism. 'There are people who preach chastity in order to have the opportunity of fixing their thoughts on sexual coupling.'[45] Thus the residue is no pure fact to be detected directly by means of psychological research methods. Rather it is a hypothetical concept accounting in part for the complexity of real life. This is what transpires from another paragraph in which Pareto wrote: 'The residues correspond to certain human instincts; that is why precision and rigorous delimitation are usually lacking in their case. This very characteristic feature may almost always help to distinguish them from facts, or from the scientific principles that they might resemble to a certain degree.'[46] The same holds for the distinction to be made between residue and sentiment.

In his usual manner, Pareto started by classifying the residues. The method which he used in the process helps us to grasp the very notion better. He likened his research to that of the linguists when they analyze the roots of words and their derivatives. The analogy is not far-fetched because, as Pareto himself noted, both areas are concerned with products of the human mind that share a common process.[47] One may recall that Pareto was a friend of Ferdinand de Saussure's, which may also explain his reference to linguistics. While leaving most of the analogies listed by Pareto aside, one should nonetheless have a closer look at one of them: 'Modern philology knows very well that language is an organism that has developed in accordance with its own laws, and has not been worked out artificially. Only a few technical terms, such as oxygen, meter, thermometer, and so on, are the product of the logical activity of the scientists. They correspond to logical actions in society, whereas the formation of most of the words in the common language belongs in the category of non-logical actions. Nevertheless, it is high time that sociology makes some progress and tries to rise to the level already attained by philology.'[48] Well before the advent of structuralism, though in a different sense, Pareto used certain aspects of linguistics to examine social phenomena. What he retained from that is the analogy that residues are like the 'roots' which in turn are rich in 'derivatives.' While talking about instinct and sentiment, this analogy helps to understand the notion of residue which at any rate is not an empirically observable fact.

Certain incoherences in the classification of residues may be puzzling, particularly in the case of an author who claimed to have applied the logical-experimental method in the strictest way. One the one hand, his vocabulary lacks uniformity and precision. To produce his six classes of residues, Pareto used the term 'need' for one of them, that of 'instinct' for another, the term 'residue' for the third, and so on. On the other hand, one cannot grasp the logic behind his classification, nor the criteria of categorization. Each of the six classes is divided into several genera which in turn are often subdivided into species. These subdivisions give the impression of the greatest disorder. Why, for instance, did Pareto include only the family and the social class under the category of groups while practically overlooking any other relationship? It seems as if he gave free rein to his intuition at the expense of systematic procedure. Anyhow, the residues quoted by him lack homogeneity to such an extent as to have induced Raymond Aron to refurbish Pareto's classification in order to make it more orderly. So deeply involved in the problem did Aron grow.[49]Nevertheless, in what follows I shall stick to the order established by Pareto himself.

The First Class:
The Instinct of Combinations

It is a human tendency to imagine all sorts of relations and connections between things and among ideas,and to draw certain conclusions from them. 'It is an instinct,' Pareto wrote, 'which is strong in man and which has probably been and is likely to remain an important cause of civilization.'[50]At the same time it is one of the determinants of the social equilibrium. It is by virtue of this spirit of combination that, in Pareto's opinion, man sets up rules, reasons, plays, and more generally still, innovates. Whence a subdivision into several genera according to the type of phenomena that are combined:

- The instinct of combination in general, without other precision or determination, which pushes man to innovate, to create the new;
- The instinct of combination of similar or opposite things,

in the sense that man has a tendency to associate what is similar or what is opposite. To this Pareto added: 'Often the non-logical arguments are formed by association of ideas.'[51] This genus includes various species, depending on the kind of things that are associated, that is, rare, exceptional, terrible, and also in keeping with the tendency of attributing to a happy state all the good things, and to a bad state all those that seem evil. Thus the person who is hostile to an institution or a régime holds them responsible for all the evils. By association, one opposes the devil, regarded as evil, to god considered good. In short, under this aspect, the instinct of combinations lies at the basis of all magical operations, divinations, oracles, legends, and so on.

- The occult power of certain things or of certain acts. This genus includes the gestures by which we mean to grant an occult power, propitious or nefarious, to objects such as amulets, relics, and so on. It lies at the basis of the beliefs in miracles, ordeals, and of various sorts of charms and spells. It compels people to attribute sacred virtues to numbers or particular days.

- The need of putting together residues as, for instance, logical knowledge and faith: 'Man loathes severing faith from experience; he wants a complete entity, free of any discordance.'[52] Here Pareto referred not only to religious beliefs, but also to revolutionary, political, and other creeds.

- The need of a logical sequence. It is a fundamental genus because it implies that the human being not only thinks but also reasons according to the strict rules of logic or pseudologic. As a consequence, even logical conduct is held by Pareto to rest on a residue as does the non-logical behaviour. Thinking may be both inductive and deductive and as such it gives birth to science. It may also be analogical, and then most often it results into fanciful logic.

- The faith in the efficiency of combinations that stands behind the spirit of invention, innovation, novelty and of foresight.

The Second Class:
The Persistence of Aggregates

Pareto described this residue as follows: 'Certain combinations form an aggregate out of parts that are united directly, and which as a result, acquires a personality of its own, similar to that of living beings. These combinations may often be recognized by the fact that they are given names of their own, distinct from the simple enumeration of the parts.'[53]More explicitly, it is the residue which imprints a lasting character on the particular combination, and in consequence endows it with an indepedent existence. As such, it is the opposite of the preceding residue. While the instinct of combinations points to intellectual and cultural development and change, the persistence of aggregates lends stability to the combinations formed by the former residue. Thus it lies at the basis of order, is inherent in the reinforcement of social achievements, and so is behind political, economic, religious and other institutions. Furthermore, Pareto compared it with mechanical inertia.[54] It rules over conservation and tradition. This class, too, is subdivided into genera, in accordance with the nature of the aggregate: abstract, objective, or human. Some of these genera are in turn divided into species. I shall pass them over and briefly review the genera only.

- Persistence of the relations among human beings, and with places. To this genus belong the sentiments which attach an individual to his family, homeland, mother-tongue or the soil. Whence the cult of the family gods *(penates)*,or the deities of the city, or the cult of the aponymous hero. It is to this residue that the division into castes and social classes may be attributed, with all the inherent consequences, such as certain life-styles, customs, beliefs or prejudices. The sectarian spirit belongs here, too.

- Persistence of the relations between a dead person and his life-time possessions. It refers particularly to the ancient customs of burying the dead with their weapons, in the case of warriors, and of placing foodstuffs and games for their entertainment, in their tombs.

- Persistence of an abstraction. The residues of this genus are at the basis of theology and metaphysics.[55]

- Persistence of uniformities. This genus of residues drives people to generalize on the basis of particular cases, to give the value of natural principles to specific circumstances and to make hypotheses pass for necessary relationships.

- Sentiments turned into objective realities. This residue lies behind the tendency to attribute the status of objective facts to purely subjective experiences.

- Personifications, that is to say the transformation of certain abstractions into objective individualities. Pareto wrote that language was an excellent means of making aggregates persist and assume a personality of their own.[56] The entities written with capital initials, such as Progress, Democracy, and so on, he went on, replace the anthropomorphism of former times as our contemporaries regard these powerful and beneficient entities with feelings akin to those nourished by their ancestors for the power of Rome, for instance.[57] Most of the new doctrines, such as socialism and pacifism, are presented as salvation doctrines on an equal footing with the abtract divinities of yore.

- Need of new abstractions. As soon as the old entities become obsolete, they are replaced by new ones. Folk mythologies are replaced by others more sophisticated, such as the mythology of Humanity, for instance. Science has become a mythology in the same way, since even the Church wants to be modern by becoming 'scientific.'

The Third Class:
The Need of Expressing One's Sentiments by
Objective Signs

Pareto dealt with this class quite briefly. 'Strong sentiments are generally accompanied by certain acts which may not have any direct relation with these sentiments, but which would satisfy the need to act.'[58] To summarize, it is the need to manifest our sentiments or our emotions by means of the most diverse gestures. This need of expression is almost tyrannical. Pareto worked out only two genera for this class of residues:

- The need to act which becomes manifest by combinations. Most often it is expressed in conjunction with the residue of the first class.

- Religious exaltation. The desire to manifest one's feelings often leads to enthusiasm and delirium, accompanied by songs, dances, contortions, albeit mutilations.

The Fourth Class:
Residues Connected to Sociability

They are residues which reinforce social life, essentially

on the basis of discipline, without which society cannot exist.
However, Pareto was very laconic when it came to the more
general explanations. Instead, he expanded the genera included
in this class:

- Private associations; people tend to get together within
religious communities, sports associations or literary clubs.

- The need of uniformity; it is the desire that makes the
human being demand that the others think or act like him
at the expense of persecuting or harming those who live and
think differently. The analysis of this genus gave Pareto the
opportunity to examine the phenomena of imitation and of fanat-
icism, respectively. The desire to preserve uniformity leads
to excommunications for heresy or heterodoxy, to condemnations
to the stake, and nowadays to sentences for offences committed
through the expression of opinions. On the one hand, there is
a genuine neophobia, or horror of everything that is new, and
on the other hand, there are people who admit that nothing is
good unless it is new.

- Pity and cruelty; although apparently opposite, these
sentiments are the contrary of indifference, and are often
associated, or alternate, in one and the same person. The
individual who pities the thief arrested by the police becomes
aggressive as soon as he himself becomes the victim of a
robbery. Pareto saw the extension of penal leniency, though
not without inherent contradictions. In his opinion, the laws
against offences increased in number, whereas the administra-
tion of justice tended to favour the offenders: 'It seems that
the pity for the offenders increases while the compassion for
their victims decreases.'[59] Pareto explained this contradiction
in part by resorting to the presence-absence dialectic: 'The
feelings of pity are particularly strong for those present and
are by far too weak for those who are absent. The jury see the
assassin and feel pity for him. The same holds good in the
case of the judge. One does not see the victim: the latter has
vanished. To think of the victim is a painful obligation. Note
that if the same jurymen, who today have acquitted an assassin,
happen to witness an assassination at a later time, they would
very likely join the rest of the crowd and would lynch the
criminal.'[60] Pareto went on to say: 'It is also this residue
that lies at the basis of the ease with which nowadays one
accuses society of all our misfortunes. Reaching the limit,

the leniency rebounds and turns into a reason to revolt and attempt the lives of others. People have a deep, instinctive aversion to suffering, in general, and also to unwarranted discomfort. Thus the citizens of a nation respect, hold in esteem, even cherish the mercy shown by powerful governments. They mock and despise the compassion expressed by weak governments. In their opinion, the latter is cowardice, whereas the former is generosity.'[61]

   - The tendency to impose an inconvenience upon oneself for the good of someone else. Every society demands a minimum of good-will from its members, that is a certain consensus, in order to survive. This may be more or less strong, given the degree of integration. There is no way of accounting for this good-will unless it is traced to a residue. Pareto saw it present among the animals that nourish and defend their offspring. 'One must have the sick mind of the fantasts of the "social contract," of the "social debt" and of "solidarity" in order to imagine that people defend their homeland in the same way as the partner of a commercial enterprise pays his share of taxes.'[62] Here Pareto was referring to the then fashionable theory of the quasi-contract aired by Léon Bourgeois. This good-will, Pareto admitted, might go as far as to become a sacrifice or the risk of one's life. To a lesser degree it makes people share their effects with the others. However, he warned, this tendency need not be given a humanitarian interpretation alone, because it is not free either of selfishness or of calculation. The logic of sentiments does not exclude their ambivalence. One does not become a socialist for the sake of an ideal only, out of concern for social justice, but also out of interest. In order to succeed in the pursuit of a career in France, during the Restauration, one had to attend mass. Later, during the reign of Louis-Philippe, it was preferable to read Voltaire, instead; under Napoleon III, to declare oneself apolitical, and more recently, it has become more convenient to pass for a socialist or a revolutionary. Pareto made haste to point out that it was the same with the heads of enterprises and the bourgeois that entered into alliance with the socialists. Whenever they demand welfare laws, '...one may think that it is out of sheer love for one's neighbour that one acts, and that enflamed by this love one burns to share one's assets. But pay close attention to what happens after the adoption of the "welfare laws" and you will see that their wealth does not decrease, on the contrary, it increases; that is, they did not give anything to the others; rather the opposite, they took even more.'[63] This mistake of the intellectuals as Pareto saw it was to allow themselves to be deluded by the declarations and the proclamations in favour of social justice, coming from both sides, from the right and from the left.

 - Sentiments of hierarchy; the relation of superior to inferior is essential to any society whatever the ideas on which it is based: 'The hierarchy changes, but does not disappear even in societies which proclaim the apparent equality of the individuals.'[64] This genus of residue is made manifest in several ways. First of all, by the obedience of the subordinates who may have various motives for it: fear, respect, affection. After all, one always accepts authority; it is only its sphere of action that shifts: 'There are plenty of anarchists who reveal a superstitious faith by the way they accept the authority of physicians and hygienists, even of those who are quacks, to a certain degree.'[65] On the strength of the persistence of abstractions, Pareto insisted that submission may be shown less to a person as to an attribute, such as prestige, for instance. There was a time when it was thought desirable to speak Latin; in a different age, it might be found suitable to be badly dressed, and so it always happens, Pareto argued, that a custom enjoys authority. A second manifestation of this residue is, according to him, the need of approval by the collectivity. 'The need which the individual experiences, namely of being well regarded by the collectivity and of winning its approval, is a very strong sentiment that lies at the foundation of the human society. It is a residue that acts tacitly, and often remains unexpressed. It may even happen that the person who seeks admiration and glory most of all feigns indifference to either.'[66]

 - Ascetism. Pareto considered it a very peculiar sentiment, characteristic of man alone, that is to say, without an equivalent in the behaviour of the other animals. It compels people to inflict suffering upon themselves and to abstain from pleasure. It was held by Pareto to be a tendency contrary to the instinct that makes people seek what is agreeable and shun what is unpleasant. He rejected the idea that ascetism was an oddity peculiar to Catholicism, since it was to be encountered in most societies. It was manifest in Ancient Sparta, and some of the Greek philosophers recommended its practice; the Budhists were not strangers to it either. Pareto did not refer to the Puritanism analyzed by Max Weber, but insisted on the case of the ascetics of the Christian Science. He wondered whether this residue should be placed in a class of its own, rather than be subsumed to a genus: '...the broad class which includes such acts as abstinence, the relinquishing of worldly pleasures, the injuries that the individual inflicts voluntarily upon himself. In this class, the genera are distinguished according to the purpose and the intensity of each of these sacrifices.'[67] Actually like Freud, Pareto realized that society cannot subsist without renunciations, constraints and discipline. Thus in this case one deals with a residue inherent in social life: 'The ascetic acts appear to us as acts dependent on the residues of sociability, in which the original intent diminishes, weakens, and may even disappear altogether, while on the other hand, the intensity of the act itself increases, expands out of proportion and becomes hyperbolic. In general, the abstinence practised by an individual, besides being useful to the individual himself, a case which would not concern us here, may be useful to the others, namely the collectivity. There where foodstuffs are in short supply, fasting is useful. There where riches are few, refraining from voluptuary consumption is useful to the collectivity. If all males would give way to the sexual instinct as soon as they see a woman, the human society would go to pieces.'[68] After all, the economic sector is grounded in the will to abstain from immediate consumption in expectation of future advantages. What Pareto condemned was the ascetism practised for its own sake, without any utility, that is to say, the ascetism that is not meant to control the senses but to mortify them. His opinion was that at the basis of this kind of life there lie such latent sentiments as envy, ambition or frustration. An example he gave was that of the great many feminists who hated men in general because they had failed to find one to their liking. This hypertrophy amounts in the last instance to a pathological phenomenon. Pareto threw his neutral stand over board and turned into a partial judge as he concluded: 'All these genera of ascetism, rendered more virulent in certain cases by casu-

istry, and which some people want to impose upon the others,
are the source of an enormous amount of suffering which has
been afflicting the human race. By tolerating and often by
accepting them willingly instead of rejecting them and destroy-
ing those who inflict them, the way venomous snakes are dealt
with, people clearly show how strong the corresponding sentiments are, although they represent but the perverted instinct
of sociability without which human society could not exist.'[69]

The Fifth Class:
Integrity of the Individual and His Belongings

According to Pareto, this class complements the precedent
because '...to defend one's belongings and to try to increase
their number are two operations that often get mixed up.'[70]
More explicitly, this residue is concerned with the defence and
the preservation of the person and his possessions. Nonetheless, the way in which Pareto used the term 'interest' raises
a question. Here is what he said: 'This group of sentiments
called "interests" is of the same nature as the sentiments to
which correspond the residues of the present genus. Thus for
better or for worse it should be added to it. However, it is
of so great an intrinsic importance to the social equilibrium
that it is useful to think of it apart.'[71] The question is
capital, because much of the criticism levelled at Pareto and
accusing him of incoherence springs from this apparent confusion of interest with sentiment.I shall return to it later on,
when I discuss the notion of interest. For the time being, let
me say simply that whereas the interest lies at the basis of
logical actions, the residue in question is the one that
affects the interests lying behind non-logical actions. The
different genera of this class are the following:
 - Sentiments which contrast with the changes in the social
equilibrium. They impel people to demand compensation for each
and every tampering with the social equilibrium whether that
in force, or merely an ideal representation. Among Pareto's
examples is that of the citizen without slaves in Ancient
Greece, who took as a personal offence the arrest of a slave
that had victimized his own master. Similarly, the partisans
of an anti-trinitarian doctrine were punished in the name of
an ideal justice in a society that upheld the belief in the
trinity. Pareto went on to point out that in a socialist

society one is likely to condemn in the same way those who profess a different doctrine. He also noted that the sentiment of justice is deeply anchored in the human being to the point that thieves expect from each other a fair share of the loot, in the same way as '...the soldiers who share the booty acquired from the enemy see an injustice in any change of the rules of distribution.'[72]

- Sentiments of equality among the inferior. This residue is opposed to the residue of hierarchy of the previous class. It points to the claim of equality made by the inferior at the expense of the superior. More often than not this sentiment of equality is but a disguised way of demanding to enjoy the same advantages and privileges as the others. In fact: '...the sentiment which very inappropriately bears the name of equality is vivid, active and strong, precisely because it is not effectively a sentiment of equality; it is not related to an abstraction as some naive intellectuals still believe. Rather, because it affects the direct interests of people who want to get away from the inequalities that are unfavourable to them, and replace them by others of benefit to them.'[73]

- Restoration of integrity by acts involving those whose integrity was impaired. This type of residue is at the basis of the so-called purification rites, very frequent in former times, rarer nowadays. The nature of change is of little importance in this case: it may be physical contact, defilement, or breach of an interdict or of a rule. What is important is the redress, the action of restoring the integrity. The methods are diverse: regeneration, ablution, lustration, aspersion or the Christian confession. According to Pareto, these residues have for their foundation the distinction between the pure and the impure, two categories of utmost importance to sociology. Obviously the phenomena regarding the taboo and the totemic rites belong in here, too. So does nationalism: the French Swiss, Pareto showed, demand that one speaks of 'Genève' and not about 'Genf,' and the Flemish in their turn speak of 'Brugge' and not of 'Bruges.'

- Restoration of integrity by acts involving the agents of change. 'There is a sentiment that urges animals or man to react against an offending agent, to render evil for evil. As long as this does not happen,' Pareto wrote, 'man experiences a feeling of unease, as if he misses something. His integrity is affected and is not set right again unless he performs certain acts aimed at his aggressor. Such kinds of sentiments are come across in people who seek vengeance or want to fight a duel.'[74] The object against which redress is sought may be an actual being or an abstract or imagined entity: an individual may give up his religious faith or stop praying because God has not granted his requests.

The Sixth Class:
The Sexual Residue

From the very beginning it should be noted that this residue is not divided into species as is the case with the third class. Nor is it divided into genera as all the other five classes. As already seen, Pareto was not interested in the sexual instinct which, in his opinion, was a subject-matter for psychology. His concern was only with the residue which finds expression in theories and arguments whether they are in favour or against sexual freedom. Actually, his book-size pamphlet, LE MYTHE VERTUISTE, shows a Pareto intolerant of those who were against sexual freedom. I shall leave his polemic aside, and instead list the various points he made with regard to the residue proper. Furthermore, I shall show how in his opinion this residue persists in innocent and chaste relations. Pareto maintained that this residue is behind most of the belletristic literature and the fine arts (sometimes obscene sculptures are to be found in cathedral churches). According to him, it permeates religion (the Romans, for instance, had specialized deities that presided over the allotment of dowries, the action by which brides were led to the houses of their bridegrooms, the brides' belts were taken away, as well as deities which presided over the consumation of the marriage, over child-birth, and so on). Moreover, the sexual residue lies at the basis of the feminine cult in various religions and also of its opposite, the censure of carnal sin, as well as behind the tolerance of, and respectively, the ban on prostitution. Finally Pareto detected it, under disguise, even in the moralistic literature.[75] Essential from the point of view of the residue is the ensemble of the philosophical, literary, moral and journalistic writings that dwell on sexuality.

No extensive commentaries need to be added to this theory of residues. However, one detail should not be overlooked, namely that residues may act in correlation and that those of the first two classes in particular may intervene concomitantly. As a matter of fact, in the rest of the TREATISE, especially in the part dealing with politics, Pareto insisted on the residues of the first two classes at the exclusion of almost all the others. For him they determined the fundamental opposition between creativity, the spirit of expansion or renewal, on the one hand, and the spirit of stability, preservation and order, on the other. Moreover, he came to draw some conclusions regarding the history of philosophy which even nowadays may not seem wholly arbitrary, though they cannot be contested particularly when formulated in the following way: 'The residues of the 2nd class were stronger by far among the Romans than among the Greeks.'[76] Or when he tried to convince his reader that Athens in Antiquity or France at the beginning of this century were rather rich in residues of the first class, while Sparta or the 18th-century Prussia, in residues of the second class. Speaking even more generally, one may say that the theory of residues served Pareto especially as backdrop for evincing the latent elements of human action, though obviously in a sense quite different from that of psychoanalysis. It also had a deeper meaning. On the one hand, Pareto tried to show that mankind needs residues in order to justify non-logical actions, since no society would be able to survive which would organize itself only in keeping with the principles of logical actions, or of the logical-experimental method, and in consequence on the basis of science. There, where he was accused of attaching too much importance to irrationality, he only saw a factor of equilibrium. On the other hand, as Raymond Aron underlined, '...the classification of residues and derivations is a doctrine of the human nature as it becomes manifest in social life. The different classes of residues correspond to the groups of sentiments that act in every society and throughout history. In Pareto's opinion, the classes of residues vary little. In other words, man, so defined, does not change fundamentally. That man does not change in depth is another way of affirming the thesis of the approximate persistence of the classes of residues.'[77]

B. The Theory of Derivations

The human being is instinct and reason. If logic is the most accomplished of the rational activities, the residues, diffuse and powerful sentiments, on the other hand, are the expression of instincts. Actually, the logical activity is also determined by a residue (fifth genus of the first class), but reason tries to dominate the residues, without however succeeding to master them in reality. This effort on the part of reason results into derivations, instead. The latter designate the apparent logic that the human being tries to give to the acts which are prompted by an impulse of residual origin. By all this it should be understood that the publicly avowed reasons for our acts are, generally speaking, not those that are actually at play. The derivations dissimulate the genuine motives under a whole apparatus of justifications or ideologies. In other words, they substitute authentical logic, which is demonstrative, by a justifying logic, or a logic of sentiments, to borrow the expression coined by Théodore Ribot, and which Pareto took over readily. 'People allow themselves to be persuaded particularly by sentiments (residues); consequently, we may foresee, and experience has confirmed it, too, that derivations gather their force not from logical-experimental considerations, or at least not exclusively from them, but also from sentiments. In the derivations, the main core is made up a residue or a certain number of residues. Other secondary residues cluster around this core. All this aggregate is brought into being by a powerful force, and as soon as it is formed, it is kept together by the same force which consists in the need of logical or pseudo-logical developments, experienced by the human being and made manifest by the residues of the 1,5 genus.'[78] (The 1,5 genus is the fifth of the first class, which Pareto called 'the need of logical developments.') More explicitly: 'A sentiment is expressed by a residue; if the latter serves afterwards to explain, justify, or demonstrate, then it is a derivation.'[79] Thus one is face to face with a derivation whenever, for instance, private interest is concealed under the appearance of a claim in the name of general welfare, or whenever a politician talks of his political performance as a public duty in order to disguise his own instinct of power. In Pareto's opinion, most of the political, moral and religious doctrines are derivations.

Nevertheless, not all human actions give rise to derivations. As a matter of fact, Pareto excluded the purely instinctive acts as well as the strictly logical actions: derivations '...are absent at the two extremes.'[80] Thus, '...the animal that does not reason but performs instinctive acts only, is devoid of derivations. To the contrary, the human being experiences the need to reason and among other things to spread a veil over his instincts and his sentiments: thus very seldom does he go without any trace of derivations since he cannot do without residues.'[81] On the other hand, the purely logical action is free of derivations, because it does not need justifications: 'In matters of social life, the actual theories are made up of residues and derivations. The residues are manifestations of sentiments. The derivations comprise logical reasonings, sophisms, manifestations of sentiments deliberately used as sources of derivations: they are manifestations of man's need to reason.'[82] It goes without saying then that the contents of a derivation are not entirely false logically, that is, pseudological. A derivation may contain instinctual elements, in keeping with the residue in which it is grounded, alongside of purely logical elements, and still others, of an experimental nature.

Characteristic of a derivation is that: a) it is more pondering than strictly logical. Whence it tends to stir countless debates and endless controversies. It presents itself as the most important element of an action, whereas it only disguises the residue which alone is fundamental. According to Pareto, the theologians, the metaphysicians, the reformers, and the intellectuals tend to assign the first place to the derivations. 'In their opinion, the residues are axioms or dogmas and the aim is simply to take a logical argument to its conclusion. As they usually do not agree on the derivation, they keep quarrelling to death and imagine they can alter social facts by exposing the sophism of a derivation. They delude themselves and do not realize that their disputes are incomprehensible to most people.'[83] One thinks of having done away with a derivation only to let it reappear under a different disguise: 'Generally speaking, the only effect obtained by eliminating a derivation is to have it replaced by another, drawn out of an inexhaustible armory.'[84] The task of the sociologist is not to give in to these appearances and spectacular disputes, but to look for the residue which they conceal; b. it is subtle: 'The derivations are generally of a resilient nature.'[85] They are capable of adjusting to circumstances, turning everything to their advantage, of being contradictory or incoherent, sinuous or tortuous, shifting or dogmatically rigid, because they disregard logical rigour, and their aim is to persuade or justify and not to demonstrate. Unlike the residues which are almost unchangeable, the derivations vary and diversify with the circumstances: 'The derivations change, the residues rest the same.'[86] They play on the resources of language.

These observations are equally apt in the case of debaters and theoreticians as in the case of recipients and respondents, because derivations are accepted or rejected for presumably logical-experimental reasons. In reality it is the sentiment that compels one to act one way or another. Said differently, it was Pareto's opinion that the socialist or the pacifist, whether in control or still militant, act as a general rule by derivation and under the influence of the residue. And so do their opponents. Alongside ideologies, some allegedly scientific theories are subject to the same rule and are dealing with derivations while claiming all the time to be discussing ideas logically. 'Those who take it upon themselves to examine social phenomena usually do not go beyond their manifest activity; they stop at the derivations and do not fathom the causes of the particular activity and so reach down to the residues. In this way, the history of social institutions has become a history of derivations, and often the history of groundless dissertations. One thinks of having compiled the history of religions while in fact one has written a history of theologies; a history of political institutions, while putting together a history of political theories.'[87] Consequently, in Pareto's eyes a science that does not conform to the rules of the logical-experimental method and which overlooks the residues is phoney: it is merely a system of derivations.

The derivations may be examined from various points of view. One is that of the relation of the derivations to logic, in order to find out whether the reasoning is correct, and the extent of its correctness whenever one is confronted by a syllogism. However, this kind of analysis is incumbent on logicians, and is not the concern of sociologists. Derivations may also be analyzed from the point of view of their relation to empirical reality. It is along this line that Pareto advanced in the first chapters of the TREATISE, when he tried to determine the experimental value of various allegedly scientific theories by means of the inductive method. Although interesting in themselves, these approaches are only auxiliary to the sociologist. The latter's task lies in the examination of the social phenomenon with the only aim of uncovering uniformities among social facts. It is not his concern to examine them with any practical aim in mind, as for example, in order to persuade the public or to offer recommendations to the militants. 'As soon as the logician discovers the error in a given argument, as soon as he uncovers a sophism, his work is over. On the other hand, the sociologist's work starts only then: he must find the reasons why sophisms are accepted, why they are persuasive. Those sophisms which are just logical subtleties are of little importance to him if at all, because their impact on people is minimal. On the contrary, the sophisms, or even the well-built arguments which are accepted by a great many people are his main concern. Logic wants to find out why an argument is faulty, whereas sociology, why the same argument is so often consented to.'[88] To sum up, the problem that was confronting Pareto was that of working out a sociology of ideologies. Instead of doing just that, he ended once more with a classification. It is true that it contains the essence of such a theory, in the same way as his typology of residues does. This time, however, he outlined four classes of derivations, that is, four main sources which are resorted to, whether unawares or not, in order to lend the appearance of logic to justifications prompted by sentiments. Pareto divided these four classes into genera, without any further subdivision as had been the case with the residues.

The First Class:
Assertion

An idea or a theory hold simply because someone stated it; then it is picked up and acquiesced in. That is how one comes to believe in a fact presented in a newspaper, for the simple reason that the journalist made up a story. In the same way one accepts proverbs, sayings and precepts of all kinds. One joins the army, or goes to college after graduation from high school, because that is in general what one does. The assertion assumes an absolute value, namely that of an axiom or a doctrine. 'The affirmation may consist of a simple narrative or an index of experimental uniformities; but often enough it is stated in a way which makes one unsure whether it conveys empirical facts alone or is a combination of the two genera.'[89] Pareto distinguished three genera within this class:

- Experimental facts or imaginary facts. The assertion refers to experience. Obviously, if the fact is of the logical-experimental order, there is no derivation. The latter intervenes only when the reference to experience is perfunctory. The journalist gives his reader to understand that his article about China, for instance, is based on unquestionable evidence, or on solid and genuine documents. 'The simple assertion has little or no demonstrative value, but quite often it has a great persuasive force.'[90] This is the case on which Pareto insisted, namely that of recurrent assertion, a technique readily used by all the propaganda machines, irrespective of their sources. Through the sheer repetition of an idea, one ends by believing in it: '...through simple repetition, an assertion often ends by acquiring a force of its own; it becomes a motive; it assumes the character of a derivation.'[91] The assertion may also be reinforced by others of the same genus, as for instance, the introduction of a political measure as democratic, humane, progressive, and so on. Finally, an arbitrary or imaginary assertion may be inserted into a group of experimentally controllable statements with the result of undermining the consent reached as soon as the validity of the other propositions has been assessed.

- Sentiments. The assertion originates in sentiment and is accepted by those who share the same sentiment. For a party activist the subjective statement made by one of the leaders easily turns into an objective fact. One may equally obtain adherence by sentiment, that is to say, by consent following the utterance of a statement with confidence, firmness and with the tone of conviction.

- The mixture of facts with sentiments. This genus is easily understood and needs no commentary.

The Second Class:
Authority

The argument for authority takes a good many forms. Among other things, Pareto noted that it often happens that because an individual exerts political power, an analogous authority is conferred upon his declarations in matter of esthetics, for instance. Likewise, if the person is a physicist, the same scientific validity is granted to his political statements. Pareto showed that this kind of authority may be enjoyed by a person, a custom, or an idea, whence the different genera:

- The authority of an individual or of several people. In yonder times, one used to submit to the authority of the poets. More recently, the latter have been replaced by other people. As the Ancient Greeks found all they wanted in Homer, Pareto would argue, the Romans, in Virgil, the Germans of previous decades, in Goethe, nowadays it is 'Marx has said' that prevails. At the basis of this derivation lies the residue of veneration.

- The authority of tradition, customs or habits. 'The wisdom of the elders,' Pareto remarked, has yielded the place to a new formula: 'the party traditions.' The authority of the Bible has been replaced by the authority of other writings. In Pareto's opinion, the argumentation has remained the same, despite the apparent obsolescence of the customs, because as he pointed out, each association, each group, builds up a tradition of its own as a frame of reference.

- The authority of a divine being or of a personification. Thus Pareto remarked that to the authority of the supernatural in the formula 'God's will' other abstract notions have been substituted, such as Democracy, Progress, Nation or Science.

The Third Class:
Agreement with Sentiments or with Principles

It focusses on the general tendency of elevating a sentiment to the rank of a principle. 'Often the agreement is limited to the author of the particular derivation, or the individual who accepts it. Nevertheless, it is presented as an agreement with the sentiments of everybody, or of the greatest number, or of the people in the street, and so on. Then these sentiments detach themselves from the person who experiences them and becomes principles.'[92] This class subsumes a very large number of genera:

- Sentiments. Pareto remarked that firstly one raises the general consent to the rank of principle and then one presents one's own beliefs as confirmed by this general consent. That is how theologians have often tried to prove the existence of God. In the same manner one invokes the authority of the 'right reason', 'the human spirit', 'the expert opinion,' and so on.

- The individual interest. 'One of the procedures most widely used...consists in confusing the two interests by means of derivations, in affirming their identity and in maintaining that by promoting the welfare of the collectivity, one also caters for one's own well-being.'[93] In this context, Pareto examined at length Bentham's thesis on the identity of the maximum well-being of the individual with the maximum welfare of mankind.

- The collective interest. 'If the interest is real and if the individual performs actions logically, in view of this interest, there is no room for derivation: we simply have logical actions which are meant to attain a result expected by the agent...But most often the objective aim differs from the subjective, and in such cases one is confronted by non-logical actions that are justified by derivations. This genus of derivations is widely employed by those who want to obtain something for themselves but claim to want it for the collectivity. Some politicians want something for themselves, while publicly demanding it for their party, their county or their nation.'[94] Pareto went on to show that in the same way union members publicize their claims on behalf of the proletariat, and the industrialists, on the other hand, in the name of the public interest or even in the name of the working classes.

- Juridical paradigms. Certain moral or legal relations become so familiar that in the end they turn into a mental attitude, an outlook, with an absolute value. That is how, Pareto pointed out, the ideas of contract or of peace have come to be regarded nowadays, namely as having a quasi-mandatory quality. By such words, one hopes to conjure the future, as in the Middle Ages it was believed that by putting the rats on trial, an end was put to their invasion.

- Metaphysical paradigms. Pareto noted that they are derivations mainly at the disposal of intellectuals and cultured people: they justify their acts by their invocation of such concepts as Mankind, Solidarity, Justice, Equality, and so on. Here, too, he insisted particularly on Kant's notion of the categorical imperative raised to the status of Absolute Duty. The notion of divine right has been so much fought against that one is no longer aware that it has merely been replaced by another notion, of the same nature, namely the will of the people. Pareto drew the conclusion that in the long run any political régime comes to justify its legitimacy by means of an argumentation involving the notion of divine right.

- Supernatural entities. It is a justifying means better adapted to the needs of people with little education. They contain no trace of the categorical imperative, but are imbued with the spirit of the God of the Ten Commandments, inspiring fear and respect.

The Fourth Class:
Verbal Proofs

It is to this class of derivations that Pareto alloted the largest number of pages, actually a whole chapter, in the TREATISE. There, he examined the digressions and the ruses of language, the subtleties, the ambiguities and the artifices of the rhetorical style. 'This class, he went on to say, is made up of verbal derivations obtained through the use of terms with an indeterminate, doubtful, equivocal sense, and which are not in agreement with reality. Were one to lend this category a broader sense, it would include almost all the derivations that do not correspond to reality. Thus it would include almost all the derivations, and there would make no sense to add a fourth class.'[95] At times, one is content with a purely formal logic. At other times, one switches by captious means from the object to the term, or the other way round, from the term to the object. With regard to such cases, too, Pareto preferred not to insist on generalities, but instead to move on to the genera:

- Indetermined terms designating a real object, and an in-determined object corresponding to a term. Pareto showed that numerous arguments are of the sorites type which makes it possible to play on the imprecision of a notion in order to give the impression of logic. It is in this way that all positive qualities may be attributed to socialism as soon as one gives up defining the concept. Actually definition puts an end to indeterminateness.

- Term designating an object, and which at the same time stirs additional or accessory sentiments that in turn induce the selection of a term. In Pareto's opinion, the same terms change their meaning in keeping with one's sentimental attachment to a philosophy or a political camp. Thus one should call false democracy that which the opponents regard as true. Wherever an orthodox believer remains faithful to his creed, his attitude is described as perseverance, but the same attitude in a heretic would be described as pig-headedness. Pareto went on to show that one may be either a parricide or the avenger of the honour of one's mother, all depending on the circumstances. In time of war, the same intelligence agent would be called an informer in one camp, and a spy, in the other. An established government that executes an anarchist who has attempted the lives of several people, is as a consequence a criminal in the eyes of the revolutionaries. On the other hand, a revolutionary who is already in office and who would perform the same operation would claim that he has sacrificed a criminal for the cause of the people. The police is a protective body for those in power, whereas for the opposition it is an oppressive tool of those in power. However, as soon as the opposition seizes power, it changes its perspective and presents the police once more as a protective organ.

- Term with several meanings, and several objects designated by one and the same term. Pareto examined several instances belonging to this genus, and particularly the terms 'peace,' 'history' and 'nature.' I shall not follow him closely in this matter because his explanations are unfortunately long-winded. I shall content myself with giving the gist of his discussion instead. After all what is the use of reviewing here the meaning attached to the word 'nature' from Aristotle and up to Rousseau? The word 'peace' may have several meanings, depending on whether it refers to a present state of things or to an aspiration. Accordingly, the policy pursued by a government would be qualified either as war-mongering or as pacifist. That depends on which of the two conditions one favours. One may play even on the word 'history' by confusing its meaning with that of the utopian and philosophical concept of the interpretation of the future. By pointing to this alternative,

Pareto pointed to still another aspect of this matter: one may pass from the object to the word by calling the wicked and the imaginary beings devils or, the other way round, one may switch from word to object and declare that given the existence of the word 'devil' it must correspond to a real object.

- Metaphors, allegories, analogies. These three procedures, and particularly analogy, may be very useful as heuristical means. Nonetheless, Pareto warned, one should not draw conclusions from them in the manner of pseudologic which identifies the analogous only. In fact an analogy that is valid only in regard to certain aspects and characteristic features cannot be extended to all the phenomena as a whole. Whenever the opponents of capital punishment refer to the execution of a criminal by calling it an assassination by legal means, for instance, they misuse the metaphor by mixing up two distinctive phenomena. The same applies in the case of the metaphor which tries to describe private property as theft. Indeed the reader is impressed by such procedures, yet they have no scientific value at all.

- Doubtful, indeterminate terms that do not correspond to anything concrete. Each age has its fashionable terms that are indifferently applied to the solution of whichever problem. There are sociologists who have said everything as soon as they affirm that the situation under consideration may be traced back to the question of the nexus of production. Others employ the term 'alienation' in the same way. Pareto chose as an illustration the word 'outdistance' which was in fashion in his time.

As happened with his theory of residues, Pareto's theory of derivations could not help the anger of certain of his readers either. Actually one does not feel flattered to read that the exposé which one considers coherent and the ideas in it both lack logic. On the other hand, one would readily accept that the demonstration of such truths be made at the expense of politicians, given the fact that the ironic dissection of their speeches is common enough, owing mostly to the media. However Pareto himself went farther than that. On the basis of his logical-experimental method, he showed that all philosophical systems without exception, be they purely metaphysical or, like Marxism, allegedly scientific, do not reason otherwise, and that as a result they are all susceptible of the same criticism. To make matters worse, he ruthlessly assaulted the vanity of certain authors by his statement that a doctrine which passes for progressive, humanitarian, liberating, and which is almost unanimously acknowledged as such, is but a derivation. When traced to its latent residue, as Pareto explained, it appears as an expression that differs in no way from an old superstition or from one of the retrograde doctrines which it ridicules. The impenitent moralism which is generally inherent in the intellectuals' outlook was subjected to a forceful blow when on top of it all Pareto insisted on the social utility of this pseudologic. What he said is that society would be unable to survive if it were perfectly rational and coherent and if the conduct of its population were logical as it is claimed to be, or if the latter would conform to the conditions of the logical-experimental method. In fact, Pareto underlined, the success of a doctrine does not depend either on its logical validity or its scientific content, but only on sentiment, that is to say, on its emotive capacity: 'If one wants to acquire knowledge, the logical-experimental method is the only one of value in this pursuit; if one wants action instead, then one should better allow oneself to be guided by sentiments.'[96] The blow is unsparing, all the more because by its means, namely that of the theory of residues and derivations, Pareto had made holes in the propaganda machine before its race in the aftermath of the 1914-1919 war. He was a wrecker of illusions. Two quotations would suffice to illustrate it. 'Other derivations very much in use are the verbal derivations. For example, in France during the Restoration, everything that the ruling party found unpleasant was called "revolutionary" and it was enough of a condemnation. Today one speaks of "reactionary" and with as much of an implicit accusation. In this manner, the sentiments of the party or the sect (residues of sociability, fourth class) are put into action.'[97] The other excerpt reads as follows: 'The knowledge of the incorrectness of Marx's theory of surplus-value is as insignificant in assessing the social value of Marxism as is the knowledge of the effects of baptism upon the original sin in assessing the social value of Christianism. In other words it has little import if any.'[98]

C. The Correlation Between Residues and Derivations

'Now that we have got a general theory, we may again concern ourselves with the subject-matter already examined directly.'[99] These are Pareto's words as he wrote them in the chapter dealing with the properties of residues and derivations. It has already been noted that at the beginning of the chapter on residues, designated at that stage by the letter (a), Pareto was on the look out for the elements of this theory. Eventually the objective was attained: the residues and the derivations are the conditions that make non-logical actions intelligible and as a result they, the non-logical actions, may be easily explained, as easily as the logical actions. Thus a general theory of society became possible after it had been rendered necessary by the resistance the economic activity and the logical actions had encountered in real life. Said differently, the prospect of a sociology that would allow of scientific investigation was quite feasable, in spite of all difficulties. Nevertheless, before embarking upon the new project, Pareto thought it indispensable to examine the various correlations between residues and derivations. The longest chapter in the TREATISE is taken by this aspect of the problem.

The residues, to which no objective existence should be attributed (and Pareto insisted on that point), are elements that determine the social equilibrium.[100] Yet they remain latent. Only the derivations are directly observable. To Pareto's regrets, sociology had to stick to what could be empirically asserted without venturing into the lower depths. Notwithstanding, one should not infer from it that the direct link between a derivation and the residue that conditions it can be traced easily. The problem is more complex than it seems. In the first place, one has to debunk the ruses of pseudologic which often enough conceals the genuine processes involved, and in consequence, the actual residue in question. Thus, for instance, whoever pays exclusive attention to the derivations will subsequently find considerable differences among various religions. However, as soon as one is able to identify the residue, one also realizes that they are mere variants of the same content.[101] Thus, '...superstitions believed dead and buried have on the contrary been transformed and subsist in a different guise.'[102] As Pareto pointed out, the quest for the residue would help to understand the reason why derivations that are seemingly opposite or even contradictory are actually drawn from one and the same source. Whence the possibility of establishing correspondences and connections which may astound at first sight, but which are preeminently suggestive and meaningful to the sociologist. Here is an example: 'The catholic processions have almost disappeared, but they have been replaced by the social and political "rallies" and "demonstrations." '[103] This is so because the residues change very slowly, whereas the derivations are extremely variable,so much so that one tends to regard each as representing an improvement upon the other. Looked at from the perspective of the residue, on the other hand, it appears as a matter of form alone. Likewise, the need of uniformity remains constant, although each time it is directed to different phenomena at the derivation level. By the various aspects which they tackle, Pareto's analyses are a contribution to a theory of simulation.

Like any other hypothesis, Pareto would argue, the residues offer but an approximate knowledge of reality. That is why their relations with the derivations must be considered in the light shed by the principles of mutual dependence and of multiple causation. To a certain degree this type of analysis may be likened to that implicit in historical materialism which in turn makes use of the principle of the interaction of infrastructure and superstructure. Notwithstanding, there is a fundamental difference between the two approaches, because in the case of Pareto's analysis, the economic aspect cannot be isolated from the rest of the social phenomena.The relation with them is of mutual dependence, and besides, '...a one-way relationship between cause and effect cannot be made to replace a great number of intertwining, analogous relationships.'[104] To affirm that in the last instance there is only one cause at play is, in Pareto's opinion, characterstic of those theories that exceed the limits of experience and as a result cease to be scientific in order to become metaphysical instead. Pareto warned those intent on using the explanatory model of residues and derivations to remember that whenever one talks of '...the action of the residues upon other social factors, we are concentrating on one part of the phenomenon only; there is yet another, made up not only of the impact of all these factors upon the residues, but also of the mutual

actions of all these phenomema.'[105] For the same reasons the
relationship between residue and derivation is that of interaction: 'We have seen that the residues are more stable than
the derivations, and that is the reason why we may consider
them, in part, "the cause" of derivations. Yet we should not
forget the secondary action of the derivations which sometimes
may be "the cause" of residues even though in a subordinate
way.'[106]The mutual action of the two concepts may be summarized
as follows:'The residues may act on: a) other residues, and b)
derivations. Likewise, the derivations may act on: c) residues
and d) other derivations.'[107] One should not exclude the possibility that derivations may originate in contradictory
residues (for example, those of the first and the second
classes), and that the derivations might be in strong disac-
cord. The case is quite frequent among intellectuals who
make the most of their pseudological resourcefulness to recon-
cile them apparently. Quite the opposite is the case of those
people who in general are content to attune their derivations
to their sentiments.

One must dwell more on the action of the derivations upon the
residues. 'It is this action alone that accounts for the
importance of derivations in the determination of the social
equilibrium. A derivation which only gives free rein to the
human need of logic and which does not change into sentiments,
or otherwise does not reinforce the sentiments, has little or
no impact upon the social equilibrium. It is but another
derivation.'[108]Whence, '...generally speaking a derivation is
accepted less for its persuasive power and more because it
gives a clear expression to the dim ideas that people already
hold. This is by and large the main process. As soon as the
derivation is accepted, it increases the force and the vitality
of sentiments which, in this way find an outlet for their
expression.'[109]Pareto showed that most often one wastes one's
time trying to demonstrate the non-logical character of an
action. Only a person reasoning logically, in the full sense
of the word, accepts to be shown his errors. On the other
hand, to combat an non-logical action, it is more suitable
to oppose sentiments to sentiments.[110] In such cases, too, one
should not be too full of hopes. it may happen and quite
often it does that the logical refutation of an absurd argument reinforces the latter, especially whenever it is prompted

by strong sentiments.[111] This is more likely to happen, because most of the time a derivation supports another derivation. From all this Pareto concluded that silence is often an excellent means of depriving a derivation or an absurd argument of its force.

One may wonder how people do in fact attain positive results despite their acting in a non-logical way most of the time. Pareto did not overlook that question. He even remarked that human societies would have been destroyed a long time ago, had non-logical reasoning not been attuned to the facts of life one way or the other.[112] Nevertheless, he dispatched the question rather simply by rejecting the Darwinian solution and implicitly by putting his own conception of human nature to work, instead. If actions are non-logical, which does not mean illogical, he argued, they are structured, nonetheless, and contain logical elements, too. The residues and the derivations are not accidents, because after all, human nature consists of instinct and reason at the same time. It is with the participation of the two that actions occur and find their place in between the two extremes, namely that of total alogism and that of perfect logic, respectively. In their unfolding, actions take into account both instinct and logic, that is to say that they correct themselves whenever the results appear nefarious: 'One takes care that a residue which strays from experience may be corrected by a derivation which strays from logic, so that the conclusion may be nearer the empirical facts of experience.'[113]

4. THE SOCIAL EQUILIBRIUM

Earlier, while talking about Pareto the economist, one was made aware of the fact that he regarded the equilibrium model as a valid blueprint of his sociological approach, too. He began to back down only when challenged by the difficulty of determining the variables inherent in the social equilibrium. The discovery of the residues and the derivations enabled him to solve the problem in part. Although these concepts are, as Pareto admitted himself, more literary than mathematical, and so quite imprecise, they may serve as approximations for an analysis of the global society. As already said, it is very likely that in the beginning Pareto became interested in sociology in order to help economists to make more sense of the concrete resistances encountered by their theories in everyday social life. By shifting his attention to sociology, the optics of his research changed, too. His image of society expanded and his awareness of the scope of sociology increased without however contradicting the previous results of his research. Instead of considering sociology from the point of view of the economist, he went out of his way to look at economics from the standpoint of the sociologist. That is to say that he tried to integrate economy alongside the other social activities into his own sociology. This conversion was openly acknowledged in the TREATISE, in a chapter entitled 'The General Form of Society.' In it he admitted that the analysis of very many economic facts cannot be pursued without the help of sociology.[114] By carrying over his equilibrium blueprint, Pareto found himself in the position to declare that the analogy between the economic and the social equilibria is so sweeping that the various states of the economic system may be regarded as particular cases of the general states of the sociological system.[115] In other words, Pareto remained faithful to his erstwhile intuition about the concept of equilibrium. However, instead of considering things essentially from the point of view of the economic equilibrium as in the COURS or the MANUAL, he contemplated them primarily from the point of view of the social equilibrium. In the process, the economic equilibrium came to be seen as one of the aspects of the more general social equilibrium. Quite probably this shift may be attributed to Pareto's increasing awareness of the importance of non-logical actions in society. There will always be interpreters of his works who will oppose his economic theory to his sociological theory in the same way as some interpreters of Kant's writings think that there is a breach in the latter's work between his CRITIQUE OF PURE REASON, on the one hand, and his CRITIQUE OF PRACTICAL REASON, on the other. To such critics Pareto would have replied by observing that creation does not follow the strict rules of logic, because the latter cannot depart from its original conditions without cancelling itself.

Thus what needs to be stressed is that the concept of equilibrium is fundamental to the understanding of his economic and sociological thinking. The concepts of residue and derivation were worked out for the very purpose of building up a theory of social equilibrium. A closer look at the latter is appropriate at this point. The equilibrium is not a synthesis which in Pareto's opinion is characteristic of action. It is action that coordinates the various intervening factors along its course. Science is analytic, and so it is from an analytical standpoint that one has to account for the equilibrium. After all one deals with a scientific notion meant to help explain the general form of society. If the equilibrium is not a synthesis, then it should be regarded as a system. However, the term 'system' is not to be understood here in its philosophical sense, namely that of a group of ideas mentally conceived in keeping with a predetermined order, but rather in its scientific sense, of a theory based on elements or variables, and on uniformities. Pareto himself mentioned the solar system as an example when he was defining his notion of social system: 'Whatever the number of the elements under consideration, our supposition is that they constitute a system which we call the "social system," and we assume the task of examining the nature and properties of the system. It changes its form and character with time. So when we say social system we understand this system as it is at a precise moment, together with the successive transformations it has undergone in a determined time and space.'[116] Thus what interested Pareto was less the equilibrium as such than the state of equilibrium with its variations. He made that clear himself: 'If we wish to reason with some precision, then we must determine that state in which we wish to consider the social system, the form of which changes continuously. The real state, static or dynamic, of the system is considered in keeping with its conditions.'[117] Looked at under its static aspect, the social system is characterized by the heterogeneity of the elements that determine the state of equilibrium. On the other hand, when considered under its dynamic aspect, it is characterized by the undulatory movement of the social phenomena. Whence the double viewpoint from which Pareto's theory of society needs to be examined.

A. Social Heterogeneity

It is highly probable that his efforts to standardize some

of the variables in pure economics and particularly his research concerning the distribution of wealth led Pareto by
contrast to realize the heterogeneous character of society.
Social heterogeneity does not mean that society is in a permanent state of conflict, otherwise the concept of equilibrium
would make no sense. Rather it means that the relative stability
is the result of diverse and discrepant elements as well as of
concurring and often antagonistic forces. As Pareto came to
see it, the rivalry of these forces conditions the social
development and, given the circumstances, may stir trouble and
bring about revolutions. Thus the social equilibrium is always
precarious.[118] It is more in the way of a compromise or an
accommodation than a harmonization by synthesis. In this
light, the uniformities which the sociologist may uncover
have nothing in common with the regularities of social action.
Most often these regularities are divergent, in keeping with
the social groups and classes involved. Pareto realized that
willpower does not conform to purely logical intelligence
because the strength of instincts keeps the dynamism of reason
at bay. Accordingly, the sociologist can but describe or try
to understand the social heterogeneity, without in the process
being able to reduce it. Nor did Pareto think that it was the
sociologist's task to do so, because it would have exceeded
the limits of the logical experimental science. Pareto's image
of society is that of an arena in which a perpetual play of
actions and reactions goes on, and which on an epistemological
plane is translated by the necessity to take into account the
mutual dependence of phenomena and to conceive of social
relations in terms of multiple causality. Pareto employed
a graphic formula to describe the relative impotence of logic:
'...there where it would prevail, any reaction would become
impossible, for the simple reason that there would be no
action either.'[119] Thus finally the core is reached of the
problems posed by Pareto in the course of his investigations:
logic and action are realities that are in no way commensurable.
That is not to say that he disparaged the rational and exalted
the irrational instead. He only made a statement of fact without emitting any value judgment at the same time. Indeed,
Pareto ridiculed those who believed that they could settle
social problems rationally, but he did so because they ignored
this fundamental fact.

The idea that society is not homogeneous, reiterated time and again in the TREATISE, is already recognizable in the MANUAL. 'Human society is not homogeneous; it is made up of elements that differ more or less not only in virtue of such obvious traits as sex, age, physical force, health and so on, but also of less noticeable features, though no less important, as the moral and intellectual qualities, diligence, courage, and so on.' [120] Without hesitation he drew from that a conclusion of fundamental importance to social analysis, and which would eventually condition his idea of politics, too. The equalitarian revendication, he concluded, corresponds to a subjective aim, in other words, it is a derivation, and there is no way that it might be achieved objectively: 'The assertion that people are objectively equal is so absurd that it is not worth refuting. On the other hand, the subjective idea of equality among people is a fact of great importance and acts forcefully to bring about the changes undergone by society.' [121] Said differently, equalitarianism is the expression of a residue: the need of uniformity.

The factors involved in the social equilibrium are many and varied. Some of them have a direct impact, while others act only accessorily, and still others are short-lived because they are inherent in a definite time and space. Generally speaking: 'The form of society is determined by all the elements that act upon it, and in its turn reacts upon these elements. In consequence, one may say that a mutual determination is taking place.' [122] It is certain, for instance, that the development of a society is partially determined by the action exerted upon it by the other societies, but also by its own past history. Pareto was content to take notice of these factors, and did not insist on them. Instead, he dwelt longer on four determinants that seemed to him particularly important. Firstly, the material, physical, biological and geographical elements of such categories as climate, soil, fauna and flora, race, and so on. Pareto called them 'external circumstances.' Secondly, the residues and the derivations. Thirdly, the interests, and finally the force and the ruse. His commentary on the first type of determinants is quite brief. He acknowledged their significance, but denied them any exhaustive explanatory value in the manner of the theories of the habitat and the like, that were in circulation in the nineteenth century. Made up of vague generalities, those theories never stated the nature of the influence exerted by those factors. The race factor has provoked the most divergent explanations without however enabling anybody to draw scientifically useful conclusions. The second type of factors (the residues and the derivations) have already been dwelt upon at length. There is no need to return to them here, save perhaps to stress that Pareto regarded them as **the** sociological factor par excellence. The force and the ruse will be discussed later on, while examining Pareto's political thinking. Here I shall attempt to clarify what is left, namely the idea of the role of interests.

This latter notion is problematic, because it has led many of his interpreters, and in particular Sorokin and Guy Perrin, to reproach him either an alleged failure to distinguish between residues and interest,[123] or the absence of any analytical curiosity concerning the latter's role. They accuse him of being too laconic and superficial when listing it among the essential factors of the social equilibrium.[124] As my purpose here is to examine Pareto's thinking and not to refute certain of its interpretations, I shall concentrate on the ellucidation of Pareto's concept alone. It would take too much space to list and quote all the texts which show that each time he spoke of the variables of the social system, Pareto mentioned the concept of interest without fail. Indeed, the economic sector was the area of choice, which does not mean the exclusive area in any way. Having discussed the notion of interest at length, particularly in his economic works, Pareto did not think it necessary to explain the concept once more in his sociological writings.[125] That is why he simply listed it as one of the important factors of the social equilibrium. Thus: 'It is only elliptically, in order to make a long story short, that we say, for instance, that the residues, in addition to appetites, interests, and so on, play a main part in the determination of the social equilibrium.'[126] Or, elsewhere: 'The sentiments and the interests are the main determinants of these actions, and in certain cases, the sentiments get the upper hand of the interests.'[127] For the most part, Pareto acknowledged that interests were as important as the sentiments in the determination of the social equilibrium, and that both could generate derivations. There is however a difference between them. If sentiments led only seldom to logical actions, that is not the case of the interests, particularly in economy. Nevertheless, they both intervene in other activities such as politics, for instance. Thus, Pareto argued that interests should be added to the residues as means of government. 'Sometimes they may open the only way available to the modification of the residues. It is also convenient to note that the interests alone, not covered by sentiments, are a strong means of action on those people who have the residues of the instinct of combinations to a high degree, in other words, a great many members of the ruling class. Nevertheless, alone, that is without the sentiments, their effectiveness is low whenever they come to act upon individuals whose residues of the persistence of aggregates are predominant. It is the latter people who form the great majority of the ruled class.'[128] This quotation shows how mistaken are those who have grasped Pareto's notion of interest only in its economic sense. In order to understand Pareto's concept one must allow it a broader scope.

Notwithstanding, the concept of interest, confined to the sphere of pure economics, should not be confused with the notion of interest as a variable of the social equilibrium. In its economic sense, the concept of interest represents the search for maximum satisfaction or ophelimity, and as such, together with tastes, aspirations and desires, it is one of the data of pure economics. It is under this aspect that Pareto opposed it to the residue. It is the purely economic notion of interest that is the basis of logical reasoning, in the same way as taste. This is what may be inferred from a paragraph already referred to. After having made clear that the residues correspond to certain instincts but not to all of them, Pareto added: 'In our quest we have been able to find only the instincts that generate arguments, and those concealed by arguments. Thus left out are all the simple appetites, the tastes, the dispositions, and at the level of social facts, that very important class, called the interests.'[129] In its general sense, the interest is no longer a simple given that serves as premise to logical reasoning. Besides, not unlike the residue, it may lay the ground for pseudological or non-logical actions. In that case it designates the conscious representation of an objective, whether political, economic, religious, or other which one wants to attain. Thus in this new acceptation, it is amenable to analysis, in the same way as the residue or the sentiment. 'Individuals and collectivities are compelled by instinct and reason to appropriate the material assets that are useful to them, or which simply make life more agreeable, and to seek considerations and honours. These tendencies may as a whole be named interests.'[130] If need be, the interest may in this case be easily assimilated to the residue of the fifth class. However, it is more convenient to tackle it separately, because of its capital role in the determination of the social equilibrium.[131] Pareto summarized the whole matter himself as follows: '...the form of society is determined not only by external circumstances, but also by the sentiments, interests and logical-experimental reasonings that aim at the satisfaction of sentiments and interests; in a subordinate way it is also determined by derivations that express and sometimes reinforce the sentiments and interests which in certain cases serve as means of propaganda.'[132] Each time Pareto dwelt on non-logical actions and social equilibrium in his works, he would associate the sentiment and the interest in order to stress the idea that they reflected the influence of other factors such as habitat or the past history of a particular society, besides their being essential components of the social system. Already in the MANUAL the following could be read: 'Thus one may turn to sentiments, and interests in order to make people act and proceed along a desired pathway.'[133] Likewise, in his last important work, THE TRANSFORMATION OF DEMOCRACY, one reads: 'When the sentiments, the tastes, the interests, the styles of action have changed, the premises of our reasoning would change, too, but not before that.'[134] These are only some of the instances, and they are quite a few, to be found in those writings, not to mention MYTHES ET IDÉOLOGIES, or for that matter the very TREATISE.

Thus there is no ground to affirm that Pareto spoke of interest only occasionally. It suffices to recall that he also discussed it extensively under another name, that of social utility. Apparently, this aspect of the problem has eluded the sagacity of some of his critics. We have already discussed the basic distinction which he made between ophelimity and utility. Let me recall briefly the characteristic traits of ophelimity. This term defines the process by which the maximum satisfaction of a taste or a given interest is sought. There is no need to wonder about the formation of the particular taste, or about its soundness. On the other hand, the economic subject with his hierarchy of preferences is to be taken into consideration as one tries to work out the logical action by assessing the most adequate means necessary to obtain the maximum satisfaction. As a result, ophelimity is verifiable by means of the logical-experimental method, and is even measurable. In short, an individual acts logically whenever given an interest, he seeks maximum ophelimity. Utility, on the other hand, is a vaguer and more complex notion because it is con-concerned with what each individual or collectivity regard as profitable or suitable to either, respectively. In this sense an object is not useful unless an individual or a group have decided that it is profitable to them in keeping with a more or less arbitrary norm. Is it really useful? What one regards as useful another would think noxious, and possibly on grounds as firm. Is it advantageous to seek wealth alone, or would it be better to give up and instead lead a more austere life ? What is more useful to a nation: military glory? Economic prosperity? Artistic fame? However formulated, the question is by far more difficult to solve than that raised by ophelimity in economics. Leaving other distinctions aside, and concentrating instead on those which he considered truly indispensable, Pareto worked out the following genera:

  a) Utility to the individual:

      - a_1: direct utility;

      - a_2: indirect utility, obtained because the individual belongs to a collectivity;

      - a_3: utility to an individual in relation to the utilities to other individuals.

  b) Utility to a given collectivity:

      - b_1: direct utility to the collectivity considered separately from other collectivities;

      - b_2: indirect utility, obtained by the influence exerted by other collectivities;

      - b_3: utility to a collectivity, in relation to the utilities of other collectivities.

'Far from agreeing among themselves, the various utilities are often in obvious opposition.'[135] Besides, what a person considers useful subjectively would not appear as such in the eyes of the neutral observer, free of passion or prejudice.

After all, there is also a difference between maximum utility for a collectivity, on the one hand, and the maximum utility to a collectivity, on the other. In the former case, it is a matter of threshold; in the latter case, it is a question of choice. In a particular society, and given a certain interest, say, public welfare, a threshold not to be exceeded may be established by means of logical-experimental reasoning. Above it utility ceases to be a public good and turns into a pre-judice shared by most of the members of that society. Let us suppose, Pareto would argue, that power '...acts logically and solely with the purpose of obtaining a certain utility. That happens quite seldom, but it is not necessary to concern ourselves with this fact here, because we deal with a hypo-thetical, theoretical case and not with a real, practical situation. In that case, the public authority must necessarily compare the different utilities; yet, for the time being, we need not go into the criteria for this comparison.'[136] The max-imum utility to the collectivity lies in finding the balance which would make it possible to guarantee the maximum utility to the collectivity without endangering the utility to the individuals composing it. On the other hand, the maximum util-ity for a collectivity depends on the choice made by the ruling power from a wide range of possible ends: military strength, economic prosperity, social justice, or all together. Whereas in the former case it was possible to introduce a certain homogeneity, in the latter, a choice is involved between heterogeneous elements. As this is a matter of values, it cannot be determined by logical-experimental reasoning. Every-thing comes to depend on the more or less arbitrary norm in the name of which a certain objective is chosen instead of another. Pareto went on to remark that the great number of possible and sometimes antagonistic ends is an index of the unsurmountable heterogeneity of social life. Moreover, inside the same collectivity, the groups pursue ends that are dif-ferent, nay divergent: one wishes to promote peace, another, revolution, still a third, a national objective, and so on.

What is useful to the one is not so to the other.

All the above considerations and others, which could be adduced besides, show that Pareto's concept of utility is equivocal and that in general it is not amenable to definition because 'the useful' depends every time on the end that is pursued. There is no utility valid for everybody or for every collectivity. It is there that the breach lies between the purely economic concept and the sociological concept. In the area of pure economics, if an interest is given, then it is possible to determine the logical conduct which assures the maximum satisfaction, that is to say, its ophelimity. In sociology, on the other hand, one does not reason with a given interest in mind, but in keeping with the simultaneous presence of divergent interests. 'Pure economics...have chosen a single norm, say, the satisfaction of the individual, and conclude that he, the individual, is the sole judge of this satisfaction. It is in this way that the economic utility, or ophelimity, has been defined. On the other hand, if the simple problem of seeking what is most profitable to an individual is raised without taking his own judgment into account, then all of a sudden one faces the need of a norm which in itself is arbitrary.'[137] There is an additional difficulty. Society is not a simple sum of individuals. Moreover, in order to know the utility to a collectivity it is not enough to add up the individual ophelimities, because they vary in their implicit hierarchy of preferences and may even be antagonistic. 'If the utilities of individuals are uniform quantities and in consequence they could be compared and added up, our study would present no difficulty, at least theoretically. The utilities of various individuals would be added to obtain the utility of the collectivity which they form together... However, to talk of such a sum of utilities is senseless, there is none. It is impossible even to imagine it.'[138] The opposition of utilities translates the opposition of interests. Not only are interests hardly reconciliable, but they are also covered by derivations in the same way as the sentiments, whence the similarity which Pareto found between these two notions. 'From that we should conclude that it is impossible to resolve the problems which consider various heterogeneous utilities simultaneously. Likewise, in order to tackle these heterogeneous utilities some kind of hypothesis must be accepted that renders them comparable. Whenever such a hypothesis is missing, which happens often, it is absolutely idle to dwell on these problems. One deals simply with a derivation that conceals certain sentiments. In consequence, one should concentrate on them alone, without paying too much attention to their cover.'[139]

Notwithstanding, the analysis of interests suffices to show that society is fundamentally heterogeneous, because the utilities are divergent by virtue of the divergency of ends pursued by the human being. The latter may well wish to attain divergent and even antagonistic values. Several consequences derive from this. In the first place, and on an epistemological plane, mathematics are no longer as easily applicable as in pure economics, in order to determine the social equilibrium, because the quantities involved are not uniform. Secondly, on an analytical plane, if in certain conditions, like those of pure economics, it is true that interest may give rise to logical actions, in real life, on the other hand, it is a source of non-logical actions. There it covers itself with derivations such as the sentiment, for instance. Said differently, the interest is a determining quantity in the context of ophelimity, but not in that of social utility. Moreover, if the other variables are taken into consideration, such as the sentiment, the external circumstances or the force, the social heterogeneity becomes even more manifest. Because of this heterogeneity, there is only one way left by which to explain society rationally: by the means of the equilibrium between the elements which perpetually act and react upon each other. Thanks to it, Pareto had no difficulty in integrating the class-division of society and the class-struggle into his system, though on two conditions. One, that the division is regarded as inherent in society, that is to say, it would persist as long as society, and two, that no social class should be considered homogeneous, '...in the sense that there are always rivalries within each of them.'[140] As a result the rational explanation of society does not mean that society itself is rational.

Although Pareto refrained from making any value-judgment, there is no doubt that this theory of social equilibrium based on social heterogeneity sheds light on some of the positions

which he took outside the area of social investigation. Actually, in his opinion, the social heterogeneity is unsurmountable. Furthermore, all the theories are idle that are held to
be capable of a solution in the sense of bringing about harmony
within the whole by cutting its elements down to measure. That
would not be possible, Pareto concluded, unless all behaviour
becomes perfectly logical. Whence his hostility to socialism
which is grounded in such a hope. 'Moreover one must point to
the end that society is supposed to attain by means of logical-
experimental reasoning. The humanitarians and the positivists
should not take offence when told that a society exclusively
determined by reason does not exist and cannot exist either.
Not because of the prejudices that might prevent people from
following the promptings of "reason." Rather because the
data of the problem which one wants to solve by means of
logical-experimental reasoning are lacking.'[141]

B. The Undulatory Movement of Social Facts

While no society can ever be entirely determined by reason,
Pareto conceded, nevertheless, it may be admitted that there
is a slow progress in the sense of an increase in number of
logical actions to the extent the residues themselves undergo
a change of their own. 'To sum up, the opinion which attributes
an ever greater part to "reason" in human activity is not
mistaken. However, this proposition is indefinite like all
those which literature substitutes to scientific theories.'[142]
According to Pareto, the progress of reason does not occur in a
linear and continuous way, but rather rhythmically or period-
ically. Whence some reservations which he admitted to, as
soon as he made the above observations public. On the one
side, progress may be witnessed in certain sectors of human
activity, but not in all by any means: it goes on uncontested
in science, the arts, and economy, but not in politics. On the
other side, the average or statistical course need not be
mistaken for the real course of things. There are phases of
development, stagnation and regression, as also of expansion
and decadence. The dynamics of social movements seem to conform
to this law of oscillations. In Pareto's eyes this tendency
appeared to be confirmed by historical facts. Athens, Sparta
and Rome, to quote some of his examples taken from Antiquity,
each of them knew a period of development, enrichment and

power, followed by another, of crisis and decadence. Indeed, these oscillations were of varying duration, but their occurrence seemed to Pareto unquestionable. He was prone to notice them in all societies, and with regard to almost all the social facts.

It is in connection with the economic crises that Pareto first formulated his theory. 'The manifestations of the human activity do not reveal a continuous progress. Generally they assume the shape of an undulated curve.'[143] He made haste to extend his concept of periodical motion to other social phenomena: 'The crisis is but a particular case of the law of rhythm which affects all social phenomena.'[144] That is from the MANUAL. It was in the SYSTÈMES that he expressed his conviction most explicitly: 'For causes partially unknown, but some of which seem to belong to human psychology, the moral and religious movement is rhythmic in the manner of the economic movement. The rhythm of the latter generates the economic crises which in our times have been carefully studied and are understood quite well. The rhythm of the former movement, however, has often gone unnoticed. Nonetheless it suffices to scrutinize history in order to recognize it quite distinctly.'[145] This rather long quotation sheds light on the question under discussion. As a matter of fact, his thinking is not as clear-cut and concise in the TREATISE, despite the additional details made available by Pareto. It would be out of place here, however, to quote the many examples from which he took the elements for his theory. They cover the Reformation, the circulation of the élites, private property, and so on.

In Pareto's thinking, periodicity acquires three different meanings at least. Either one and the same social phenomenon gets through an ascending or descending phase, as for example, Athens' power expansion, then its decay. Then, two opposite phases succeed one another rhythmically in time, as for instance, a period of ardent faith is followed by a period of skepticism which in turn is followed by a new period of faith, and so on, on the understanding that it is not the same faith throughout (in the first phase the faith might be religious whereas in the second, the faith could be social). Or, one and the same type of phenomena reappears time and again under different aspects in the course of history. An example is the renewal of élites which are each time recruited from other social groups. Indeed folklore has been able to work out a notion of the periodicity of social facts by analogy with the rhythm of natural phenomena (alternance of drought and fertility, the phases of the moon, and so on). Likewise, the idea of undulatory motion led to dogmatic and a priori reasoning, as well as to hasty generalizations. Nevertheless, Pareto thought himself capable of grounding his theory on facts and of making use of the explication by means of the alternance of the residues of the first and the second classes, respectively (in other words, the instinct of combinations and the persistence of aggregates, as he called them). As a result, the residues, like the derivations, became liable to the law of oscillations in the same manner as the social phenomena.[146] On the premise of the relative identity of human nature through time, Pareto concluded that the rhythmic movement is permanent and moreover that it operates changes of form only, and not of content. However, it was only in the TRANSFORMATION that he expressed the implications of the persistence of content most explicitly: 'If one remains at the experimental level and events are examined as facts leaving beliefs aside, one soon finds out that eras are new in form alone, whereas their substance registers points of correspondence on the slope of the continuous curve of motion. Looking back upon the course of history, one finds out that there had been a christian faith before Christ, a moslem creed before Muhammad, a "democracy" before the French Revolution, and a bolshevism before Lenin's revolution.'[147]

The oscillations may vary according to amplitude, duration and intensity. In that light, Pareto distinguished among the main and the secondary or accidental oscillations that are mistaken for simple repetitions, the oscillations of short, medium and long durations, and finally the strong and the feeble oscillations. Although useful to research, this classification makes no contribution to the understanding of the undulatory phenomena. Instead, more relevant are Pareto's observations on the confusion that may arise between this classification and the notion of causality. 'The oscillations of the various parts of the social phenomena are in relation of mutual dependence, in the same way as the parts themselves. If one insists on using the fallacious term "cause," one may

say that the descending period is the "cause" of the ascending
it is followed by, and the other way round. However, one must
understand that only in the sense that the ascending period
is indissolubly linked to the descending period that precedes
it, and the other way round; that by and large the different
periods are merely manifestations of a single and unique
state of things, and that through observation, one finds
out that they succeed one another in such a way as to acquire
the quality of an experimental uniformity.'[148] Said differently,
the undulations are not independent of one another, but rather
mutually determined, and furthermore, form cycles of mutual
dependence. Thus one must be wary of causal imputation. Pareto
went on to show that in the days of the Emperors Hadrian and
Marc-Aurelius, the curve of the prevalence of intellectuals and
of rationalism peaked, but then, under Emperor Commodius, it
turned contrariwise. In Pareto's opinion, it would be mistaken
to attribute this change of rhythm to Commodius' 'vices' because the descending curve which accompanied his rule was a
natural reaction explained by the fact that in '...the social
lower depths matured the rich harvest of faith which made itself manifest in the pagan philosophy that followed, in the
Mithra cult and similar others, and finally in Christianism.'[149] For some good reasons, he warned, one should refrain
from drawing the hasty conclusion that a decline of the religious form of expression is accompanied by a decline in the
religious sentiment itself. By losing its intensity in a
particular form, it may make itself manifest in another. On
the other hand, whenever a phenomenon attains its highest
intensity, it is the oscillation in the opposite sense that
becomes imminent. Whence, Pareto pointed out, the error of
explaining social phenomena in terms of a purely linear causality. 'An institution, a social fact, which is observed at a
given time, may be, though not necessarily, the direct transformation of another institution and of another fact. In
general, the evolution does not follow a direct line, and the
commonality of certain elements should not be mistaken for
their lineage.'[150]

C. The Individual and Society

The phenomena of equilibrium and oscillation facilitate the
understanding of the relations between the individual and

society. Durkheim's concept of society was an abstract entity in Pareto's eyes: it did not exist in real life. Such a concept was of no use to the logical-experimental science. Society is but an aggregate of individuals. Pareto publicized that idea in the COURS for the first time: 'Human society appears to us as a vast aggregate of molecules which render services, consume, produce and economize; and of the centres or glands where savings are turned into capital, and one kind of goods into another.'[151] This idea of society is reproduced in the TREATISE where, after having defined the economic system, Pareto wrote: 'The social system is by far the more complicated. Even if we want to simplify it as much as possible, without committing serious errors, we need to regard it as composed of particular molecules, containing particular residues and particular derivations, as also certain interests and tendencies. These molecules, subject to numerous connections, accomplish logical and non-logical actions.'[152] It is precisely because society is an aggregate that, in Pareto's opinion, it cannot be explained otherwise but by resorting to the notion of equilibrium. Does it mean that it is but a collection or sum of individuals? Pareto's stand on this matter is very clear, and he made his readers aware of it time and again.

Pareto placed the instinct of sociability among the residues from which it may be inferred that society responds to a need of the human nature. It is in the MANUAL that he defined his position on the matter most explicitly. If it is true that the moral and religious sentiments contribute to the preservation of society, nonetheless, they presuppose, in Pareto's opinion, a more primitive sentiment of goodwill: 'A society in which each individual would hate his fellow-man would obviously not subsist, but disintegrate. There is a minimum of goodwill and mutual sympathy necessary to the members of each society, which enable them to resist the violence perpetrated by other societies, and that by coming to each other's assistance. Above this minimum, the feelings of affection may vary more or less.'[153] Despite the goodwill, society remains the field of opposite forces, some tending to union and uniformity, others, to division and discrimination, or to use the terms employed by Pareto in the TRANSFORMATION, some forces are centripetal, and others are centrifugal. Either one tends to prevail according to circumstances, whence the heterogeneity and the undulatory motion of societies. In the last instance, Pareto saw it as a question of rivalry between the first two classes of residues. It is obvious that if the need of uniformity were as powerful in the case of each individual as to prevent the deviation of any single one of them from the existing uniform-ities in the society in which they live, that society would have no internal cause of dissolution. Nor would it have any cause of change, either in the sense of the augmentation or the reduction of the utility of individuals or of society. To the contrary, if the need of uniformity were lacking, society would not survive and the individual would be on his own, as the felines, the birds of prey and other animals.'[154] The equilib-rium theory is the only scientific one because in his eyes it conformed to factual observation. Thus Pareto discarded as two of a pair the **theology** of social immobilism and that of the social change.[155]

It was the image of this great number of concurrent and opposite human actions, which form the texture of social rela-tions, that made Pareto refuse to regard society as a meta-physical entity, transcending the individuals. Systematically, the individual cannot be opposed to society, in the same way as one cannot research the social or the individual origins of particular aspirations other than in an idle effort. 'It is vain to try to find out whether moral sentiments have an individual or a social origin. The individual who does not live in society is an extraordinary human being almost, if not totally, unknown to us. Likewise, apart from people, society is an abstraction which has no correspondent in real life. As a result, all the observable sentiments of the human being living in society are individual from a certain point of view and social from another. The social metaphysics which serve as backdrop to that kind of research are mere social metaphysics which tend to defend certain doctrine a priori.'[156] The problem of the relationship between the individual and society was the subject-matter of the paper delivered by Pareto at the Inter-national Congress of Philosophy at Geneva in 1904.[157] His thesis may be summarized as follows: the concepts of society and the individual are both precise and vague at one and the same time, given the vantage point from which they are considered.

At first sight, the concept of the individual seems more precise because it refers to a living being that can be identified and observed, while that of society appears vague and abstract. Looked at from a different angle, it is the individual that appears fictitious and society that becomes a precise concept, because there is no individual to live outside society and as a result the individual per se does not exist. Thus we are faced by a contradiction. 'On the one side, there is the banal and often repeated remark that society is simply a juxtaposition of individuals who by their very living in society acquire new characteristic features,'[158] and on the other side, the human being as pure individual cannot be observed anywhere. This contradiction is insoluble because '...were we able to observe isolated human beings and human beings living in society, then we would have got all the means to know in what lies the difference between them, and be able to separate the individual from the social. However, the first term of the comparison is missing altogether, and it is only the second which is known to us.'[159] In order to shun the difficulty, Pareto showed, the specialists in the social sciences invented illusory solutions in accord with their sentiments, such as the theory of social contract, of solidarity, that of moral, religious and intellectual unity of mankind, as well as the theory of the majority which can crush the minority in the name of the interest of the greatest number, or still, that of the natural and innate individual rights which must be protected by society. All these are but pseudo-logical and non-scientific derivations. What is observable, in Pareto's opinion, is that the individuals that make up a society have both common and opposite interests.[160] Whence, society is but an equilibrium between these forces which affect both the individual and society. It is this solution that Pareto adopted in his SYSTÈMES when commenting on Herbert Spencer: '...Spencer has wisely noticed that the characteristic traits of an aggregate are the result of the characteristic features made manifest by its parts. The objections raised against this proposition do not seem grounded at all. They refer to the fact that the features of an aggregate are not the sum of those of the parts, that they do not result from the simple juxtaposition of the latter. That is pefectly true; but the resultant of several things is not necessarily the

total of their sum. If a body is attracted by two forces represented in scope and direction by two straight lines which
concur at one point, it moves as if it were attracted by a
force represented in scope and direction by the diagonal line
of the parallelogram drawn upon the first two straight lines.
Can it be objected that this force is not their resultant, because it is not equal to their sum? Nobody denies that the
people making up a crowd think and act otherwise than they do
when taken individually, but it is no less true that the
characteristics of the crowd result from the characteristics
of its parts...The economic and political system of a people
is after all the resultant of the characteristics of that
people. Yet this manner of speaking is not utterly accurate,
because in its turn the system also intervenes and modifies
the characteristics. There is a sequence of actions and reactions there, that is to say, a system of equilibrium between
various forces rather than a phenomenon reducible to a cause
and the effects of that cause.'[161]

The theory of residues, that of the social equilibrium and
also his conception of the relationship between the individual
and society show clearly that Pareto was not seeking to build
up an anthropology. Indeed, his idea of the human nature be-
trays an anthropological orientation, but his sociological
analysis precludes it precisely because it makes of the residue
a working hypothesis and refrains from assimilating it to the
sentiment or the instinct.

IV

THE POLITICAL SCIENTIST

Erstwhile Pareto had been publicly known as an economist, then the sociologist took the upper hand. Towards the end of his life, he focussed almost all his attention on the analysis of the political phenomenon. He set his mind on seeking to understand the concept of democracy and the reasons of the bourgeois decline. Without question, he had made politics his concern since his youth and had even intended to enter its arena. Furthermore, the last two chapters of the TREATISE contain long analyses of some of the political aspects of society. Nevertheless, after he had left the University of Lausanne, and during his retirement, he toned down his socio-logical research and showed increased preference for political analysis. Pareto's last important work, THE TRANSFORMATION OF DEMOCRACY, published in 1921, is evidence of that shift. It may even be said that he embarked upon a political career at the end of his life: he was asked to represent Mussolini's government on one of the commissions of the League of Nations, and on the eve of his death he was nominated senator of the Italian Kingdom.

He tried to examine politics along the pathway followed earlier by the economist and the sociologist. In other words, he stuck to facts strictly and did not seek to work out any reforming or redeeming theory. Likewise, by separating politics from morality, he adopted a Machiavellian stand. Actually, he had always advocated that line of approach: the validity of an analysis need not be confused with the social utility of a theory. 'If empirical facts seem to allow me to draw from them the conclusion that our bourgeoisie advances to its ruin, I do not expect to qualify that process as "good" or "bad." Nor would I make any pronouncement of the sort about the analogous process brought about by the Crusades, and which was the ruin of the feudal seigneurs. I would not exort the bourgeoisie to change its ways, either, or preach in favour of the reform of habits, tastes and prejudices; and less than ever would I

give reason to believe that I set aside a couple of prescrip-
tions to cure the sickness of the bourgeoisie, or if you wish,
the illness from which the whole society is suffering. On the
contrary, I openly state that such a remedy, provided it
exists, which I doubt, is entirely unknown to me. I am like
the physician who recognizes the symptoms of tuberculosis in
his patient without knowing how to cure it.[1] The scientist
had no choice but to give up making value-judgments. He was
content to acknowledge what was out there and refrained from
making any suggestion about what it should be like. After all,
one could not be sure whether a historical event was good or
bad, unless one had special knowledge of the absolute: 'The
prospcriptions of the triumvirs at Rome, the Terror during the
French Revolution and the terror of the Bolshevists, are
they "good" or "bad"? The sentiment, the faith, the judgment
derived from a priori concepts, metaphysical or otherwise,
have the power to rcsolve this question, but not the logical-
experimental science.'[2]

Is there a better government? Such a question is idle talk to
the political scientist '...not only because of the vagueness
of the term "better," but also because it presupposes an
impossible event, that by which movement comes to a halt the
moment it reaches the state called "better".'[3] For the same
reasons he refused to state whether a measure or its consequences were just, praiseworthy, good, morally necessary, or
merely useful. 'Sparta denied citizenship to foreigners;on the
other hand, Rome conferred it indirectly by counting the
free men among the citizens. How could these measures be
judged? 1. In the light of the so-called human equality,
of man's immortal rights, and of humanity? 2. In regard to the
economic, social and political consequences? These are two
different questions that have nothing in common.'[4]

Obviously Pareto did not miss the opportunity to speak his
mind in private, and sometimes even in public,about the events
he was witnessing. To those who would like to sample the
caustic taste of his private opinions I recommend Pareto's own
diary.[5]

1. THE ELITES AND THE CLASSES

No theory of the state can be found in Pareto's writings. His opinion was that the notion of the state was a mere abstraction. Instead, one comes across a theory of the political aspect of society. He started from the observation which anybody could have made about the division of any given society into two layers: 'A higher layer to which usually the rulers belong, and a lower layer, made up of the ruled.'[6] In Pareto's mind this is a general and unquestionable fact, despite the derivations which try to disguise it by means of all kinds of theories affirming what it should be. No scientific reasoning on politics is possible if this fundamental aspect of social heterogeneity is overlooked. It means that '...society appears to us as a heterogeneous mass, hierarchically organized. This hierarchy is always there, with the possible exception of the savage peoples that live in a state of dispersion akin to the animals.'[7] In any case, '...the human societies cannot subsist without hierarchies.'[8] The higher layer is numerically smaller than the lower. It represents a minority even in the democratic régimes. This minority may be designated by means of various terms: oligarchy, aristocracy, and so on. Pareto, however, showed a preference for the term 'élite.' Under this aspect, the social heterogeneity is characterized by the élite-mass opposition which is a determinant of the social equilibrium. Nevertheless, it was only occasionally that Pareto showed an interest in the mass. His analyses focus mainly on the composition and the movement of élites.

There are as many élites as human activities. Referring to the law of the distribution of wealth, in his attempt to generalize it, Pareto thought that the distribution of people in categories by other criteria such as intelligence, aptitude for mathematics, musical, poetic or literary talent, moral character, and so on, would yield curves more or less similar to that arrived at for the distribution of wealth. 'The latter is a curve resulting from a fairly large number of characteristic features, good or bad, which as a whole faciliate the success of the individual in pursuit of wealth or anxious to keep it as soon as he acquired it. The same individuals do not occupy the same positions in the same hypothetically drawn diagrams.'[9] There are artistic, scientific, religious, as well as erotic élites, in the same way as there are political and economic élites. Thus in the light of Pareto's proposition, Krupp belongs to the economic aristocracy in the same way as a famous chess-player or an athlete belong to the sports élite, or the mistress of a monarch belongs to the erotic élite. He warned his readers about how important it was not to estimate the worth of élites according to the categories of good and evil. 'The choice of élites is affected by the current social forms. The élites have nothing absolute about them; there may be an élite of highwaymen as well as an élite of saints.'[10] There is an élite among the industrial workers, and the trade-unions cultivate it.[11]

Societies are recognized by their élites and nothing affects their character and their development more than the types of élite which they produce. Sociology points still to another fact: no élite lasts for ever. Élites too are subject to the law of oscillations. This is explained by the phenomenon of selection which is unavoidable, given the hierarchical character of societies. According to him, this selection operates in virtue of multiple criteria that vary with the type of activity: military victory, political intrigue, ability to manoeuvre, special talents, and so on. In rest, the selection is a factor essential to the social equilibrium because, in general, it secures stability in movement. Indeed, the higher class is more often than not the richest. Nonetheless, because one and the same élite does not keep the same place eternally, it does not remain perpetually rich, either. 'There is a fact of extreme importance to social physiology, namely that aristocracies do not last. All of them are stricken by a more or less rapid decline. Here we need not look for the causes of this fact, it is enough to become aware of it, not only in the case of élites that are perpetuated by heredity but also, though to a lesser degree, in the case of those that are recruited by co-optation. For the warring élites, warfare is a powerful cause of extinction, which fact has always been known. One has felt tempted even to take it for the only cause of the disappearance of the élites. However, that is not quite so. Even in the conditions of the fullest peace, the circulation of the élites goes on, and those very élites which suffer no loss from warfare do disappear eventually, and sometimes quite promptly. It is not exclusively a matter of extinction by an excess in the number of deaths over that of births, but also of the degeneration of the elements composing the élites. Thus aristocracies cannot survive unless they discard these elements and bring new ones in.'[12] Indeed, whenever it meets with obstacles in its drive to get a place in the sunlight, an aristocracy in the ascendant destroys wealth and structures, yet at the same time it represents the force of reconstruction that enables society to develop. 'Nowadays the circulation of élites grants access to the ruling class to a larger number of people who destroy wealth. At the same time, however, it lets in a relatively greater number of producers of wealth, too.'[13] Thus the élite is shaken by internal motions tending to replace the degenerate elements by others, more competent.

A. The Circulation of Élites

The circulation of the élites made Pareto famous, together with his law of the distribution of wealth and his theory of residues and derivations. It is one of the masterpieces among Pareto's theoretical constructs. In the previous section it has already been said that each society has an élite, and as a consequence the structure of each society is hierarchical. In order to cope with the ever present challenges, élites cannot remain unchanged. The older élite needs to agree to renew itself by the infusion of new blood or by relinquishing its place to another, more dynamic élite, and that sometimes through violent means. In general, the new élites have their origin in the lower classes and climb the social hierarchy of ranks because they have the will to succeed and also that enterprising spirit which an élite in power tends to lose when intent to enjoy its privileges. Pareto saw the circulation of élites at work throughout history. 'One may imagine a society with a stable hierarchy, but such a society would have nothing real about it. In all human societies, even in those organized by castes, the hierarchy ends by renewing itself. The difference among societies lies in the following: that this change may be more or less slow, or more or less fast. The fact so often recalled that aristocracies disappear is made evident by the whole history of our societies. It is a fact known from times immemorial...The history of human societies is by and large the history of the succession of aristocracies.' [14]

The circulation of élites is a fundamental sociological fact. No social hierarchy remains the same indefinitely. As heterogeneity is the condition for social equilibrium, it is momentous that this heterogeneity is maintained by the circulation of the élites, as a factor that facilitates the mixing of the various groups of the population.[15] Pareto took the case of Rome as an illustration. Rome appears to have been devouring élites and to have been able to maintain all its might thanks to this perpetual renewal. After having exhausted the rural classes, it forced the provincial élites to make their contribution, and finally turned to the Barbarians until the moment it succumbed, unable to renew its élites any longer.[16] It would be incorrect to think that prosperity is the result of hierarchical rigidity, though the inconveniences inherent in too rapid a change of élites may be as serious.

'One may say so far that everywhere the prosperity of nations depends on a certain ratio between the old and the new rich. The absolute preponderance of the former renders societies immobile and halts all progress. On the other hand, the preponderance of the latter is linked to societal instability and allows only ephemeral progress.' [17]

Indeed, as soon as it is installed and acquires its privileges, every élite tends to close upon itself, yet generally speaking, this is to its detriment.

The phenomenon of the circulation of the élites is often concealed by various facts. On the one hand, no attention is paid to it, as the movement is often slow and so one becomes aware of it only afterwards, after the fact. On the other hand, historians tend to take only spectacular events into consideration, such as rebellions, revolutions, dictatorships, and are content to describe them instead of embarking upon an in-depth analysis. Actually, Pareto pointed out, those events are generally the symptoms of a change of élites, which occurs in a disguised form. Relatedly, he warned against the attraction exerted by ideologies, because the circulation of the élites is carried out in the name of multiple derivations. In other words, the new élite in power conceals its determination to climb upwards behind a whole mythology or theology of ideal

revendications and noble ends such as freedom, universal suffrage, equality, social justice, and so on, to mention only
those in circulation in Pareto's life-time. Like Sorel, though
without making them the core of his analyses, Pareto attached
considerable importance to myths. All the more so, as he
realized that generally people are sensitive in the extreme to
everything that looks like a moral claim. However, he was
anxious to see that sociologists were not taken in by those
justifications, and treat as legal tender what was but camouflage for a will to power. 'One cannot make any sense of
these events unless a distinction is made between form and
content. The content is the movement of the circulation of the
élites, the form is that prevalent in the society in which the
movement occurs. It would assume the form of a dispute among
the literati in Ancient China, a political struggle in Republican Rome, a religious controversy in the Western Middle
Ages, a social strife nowadays. The malcontent who lived in the
Middle Ages would have expressed his need of reform through
religious claims and taken his arguments from the Gospels. Were
he our contemporary, he would express the same need by means
of socialist theories and take his arguments from Marx.'[18]

Not without insight, Pareto observed that the same ideals
that are a strength for the ascending élite become a weakness
in the case of the élite in place, whenever the latter accepts
them out of sentimentality. In general, the élite in power
allows itself to be contaminated by the new ideas, but they do
not have for it the value of a myth capable of rallying forces.
Rather they turn into humanitarianism which paralyses the
élite's actions. Pareto took for a sign of decline the fact that
in his days the bourgeoisie accepted the various objectives
promoted by socialism in a way not unlike the nobles of yore
who used to dig their graves by sympathizing with the ideals
of the bourgeoisie. Thus the élite in power endangers its
own life by becoming the object of ethical sensitivity. 'A
symptom that almost always announces the decline of an aristocracy is the invasion of humanitarian sentiments and the
affected squeamishness which renders it incapable of defending
its positions.'[19] In other words, when a bourgeois becomes
socialist, he deserves to be swept away by the new élite because he ceases to be himself. 'Any élite which is not ready

to fight in defence of its position is in full decline, it has nothing left to do but relinquish its place to another élite endowed with those virile qualities which it lacks. It is sheer day-dreaming if it thinks that the humanitarian principles which it has proclaimed would be applied to it: the victors will fill its ears with the implacable *vae victis* . The blade of the guillotine was being sharpened in the wings while the French ruling classes were practising their "sensibility" at the end of the last century. At elegant suppers, that idle and frivolous society, that lived like a parasite in the country, was talking of delivering the world from "superstition and crushing the infamous" without suspecting that itself would be crushed.'[20]

Contrary to the claims of some of his critics, Pareto did not overlook the economic factor in the process of the circulation of the élites. He went so far as to show that the economic factor is used either as a means of defence against the ascent of the new élite, or as a weapon by the latter. He only refused to consider it an exclusive or even a preferable explanation of the circulation of élites. His reason was mostly that economy might be turned into a pretext for derivations as well. Consequently, the circulation of the élites, too, needs to be related to the residues, in the sense that the residues of the ascending élite are stronger than those of the élites losing speed. Nonetheless, it should not be conluded from it that Pareto held the ascending élite to be intrinsically superior to that which it was in the process of dislodging. As soon as it takes its place, the new élite will be torn between the partisans of consolidation and the supporters of change who are intent on prolonging the intervening transformations by incessant innovations. It becomes evident that Pareto regarded the transition from one élite to another as a transition from one social equilibrium to another. In his opinion, the social equilibrium has to conciliate forces in order to maintain itself, as its predecessor had done. The circulation of élites is an endless process: none would emerge irrevocably victorious, because no élite, once in power, is sheltered from new claims and innovative incursions. Socialism would not escape that fate, either. According to Pareto: 'The weakening of the spirit of resistance on the part of the higher classes, and even more, the consistent effort they make unawares in order to speed up their own undoing is one of the most interesting phenomena of our age. Nonetheless, it is far from exceptional. History has already provided more than one example and would probably furnish many more, as long as the circulation of the élites goes on, that is as far as our foresight may stretch into the future.'[21] Pareto resumed this idea with even more pregnancy in the TREATISE: 'Aristocracies do not last. Whatever the causes, it is unquestionable that after a while they disappear. History is a graveyard of aristocracies.'[22]

B. The Ruling Élite

The higher layer in turn is divided into two categories: 'We set apart those who directly or indirectly play a noteworthy role in government; they form the ruling élite.The rest is made up of the non-governing élite.'[23] Practically, Pareto concerned himself with the former alone. In his opinion, the ruling élite is not only an aristocracy but also an 'oligarchy' most of the times. While running the business of the country, the ruling élite works for itself, either by reinforcing its structures in order to increase its own power, or by increasing the wealth of its members individually.Historically this oligarchy assumes various forms: parliament, ruling committee of a political party, and so on. Although these groupings are less apparent under a tyrannical or despotic régime, they are still there, in spite of everything. In fact, besides the personalities that fulfill the official functions, one should count in its ranks those who act in the wings, so to speak, and whose advice is often efficacious. The ruling élite may in turn be subdivided into two sub-categories: '(A) the individuals who resolutely aim at ideal ends and who strictly follow certain of their rules of conduct; (B) the individuals whose aim is to work for their own interest and for that of their clients; they may be further divided into two groups: (B-a) the individuals who are content to enjoy the power and the honours and who leave the material advantages to their clients; and (B-b) the individuals who seek the material advantages, generally money, for themselves and also for their clients.'[24] In the case of the members of the A sub-category, it is the second-class residues that are prevalent. Generally speaking, they are honest, but also fanatical and sectarian.

On the other hand, it is the residues of the first class which prevail in the case of the B subcategory, and for that reason its members are more capable of governing than the former whom they use 'as ballast and for the apparent honesty they lend to their party.'[25] Those in the B-a group are generally considered honest and as a result may play the role of guarantors as do the A's. Those in the B-b group are regarded as dishonest, although more often than not they cost their own countries less than those in the B-a group, the personal honesty of whom often covers various cases of corruption and spoliation.

In Pareto's eyes, the ruling class is no more homogeneous than the higher layer in general or than society as a whole, for that matter. Sociologically speaking, he argued, it would be inaccurate to attribute to it fully thought-out schemes, as party programmes try to make people believe: 'The tendency to personify abstractions, or even to give them the appearance of objective reality is so strong that many people conceive of the ruling class as a living being, or at least, a concrete unit endowed with a unique will, and believe that by taking logical measures it implements its party programme.'[26] Pareto illustrated this heterogeneity by the opposition of the rentiers (R) to the speculators (S), which no doubt is peculiar to the capitalist countries, but which may be found under a different guise in the socialist countries as well. As a matter of fact, he made it clear that despite some common features there is no identity between those whom he called the rentiers and the conservatives, nor for that matter, between the speculators and the progressives or revolutionaries. Likewise, he warned that this distinction should not be made only from an economic point of view alone.[27] The difference between these two categories is rather a matter of residues. Actually, in the case of the (R), the second-class type is predominant, while the first class type becomes prevalent in the case of the (S). 'By and large, the former category is conservative, hostile to novelties, which it always fears a little, patriotic and also nationalistic. The latter category is, on the contrary, innovative, seeking everywhere the chance for a good operation, internationalistic because everywhere it can find a place to exert its dilligence; after all, money has no fatherland. The former category consists of the "rooted," while in the latter one finds the "uprooted"...The extreme types are rare, those in the middle, quite common.'[28] On the one side, there are the cautious individuals, inhibited and inner-oriented, who do not court adventure and avoid taking risks; they have a narrow horizon and tenacious prejudices. On the other, there are the audacious beings, the conquerors, the exhuberant fighters, ready to accept novelties, never discouraged, prone to become either socialists or anarchists, depending which of the two trends has the chance of seizing power.[29] The two types are to be found in every higher layer, with the consequence that the policy pursued by a country changes with the prevalence of one or the other. Notwithstanding, '...both categories fulfill functions of diverse utility in society. The (S) category is above all a source of change and of economic and social progress. The (R) category is, on the contrary, a strong stabilizing element which in a great many cases avoids the dangers of the adventurous movevements of the (S) category. A society in which the individuals of the (R) category dominate almost exclusively stands still, like petrified. A society in which the individuals of the (S) category are predominant lacks stability. Said differently, it is in a state of unstable equilibrium which may be destroyed by a slight accident that may occur inside or outside that society.'[30] Or, as Pareto said elsewhere, in the former case a country may run the risk of suffering economically, and in the latter, politically.[31] The opposition between these two categories of the élite may turn into outright conflict.

The unity of the ruling classes is a myth. The élites fight each other; they reflect the social heterogeneity. What Pareto seems to have been interested in was rather the manner in which they compete for the favours of the lower classes, that is to say, the ruled. This manner never changes because it is almost always a matter of the so-called relationship between clients and proprietors. Undoubtedly, the ruling class acts in the light of derivations and in consequence on the basis of residues, as already seen. However, it becomes quite remarkable by the ways it exploits the derivations either in order to seize power, or in order to preserve it. First of all, it appeals to the ruled class institutionally: 'In order to maintain itself in power, the ruling class employs members of the governed class. In keeping with the two ways in which power is secured, the ruling class may be divided into two categories. One category resorts to force, that is soldiers, police, agents, the bravi of past centuries. The other category makes use of the artifice; from the Roman politicians and their clienteles, and up to our contemporary politicians.'[32] Another means consists in building up an economic prosperity, but in Pareto's opinion this alternative is far from sure. It is more worthwhile to act upon the ideas. Not without a tinge of cynicism did Pareto remark that the stirring up of moral ideas is particularly efficacious. 'The ethical point of view is what impresses people most. Thus the political or religious enemy is generally accused, rightly or wrongly, of having infringed the moral norms.'[33] It is by means of moral justifications that universal suffrage and equality are made legitimate. One goes even farther and invokes the law, the public good. How much it has been written about the Legal State *(Rechtsstaat)* and which Pareto ironically called 'the ethical state'! Often freedom-fighting is but '...a mere struggle waged by two competing élites.'[34] There is also the derivation which exploits the prestige enjoyed by truth. Each faction or party engaged in battle present their particular stand as the only true one: 'All the revolutionaries successively proclaim that the past revolutions managed only to dupe the people: it is only that which they themselves envisage that is the true revolution. "All the historical movements," the Communist Party Manifesto read in 1848, "have so far been minority movements which benefited minorities only. The proletarian movement is the spontaneous movement of the huge majority to profit the huge majority." Unfortunately, this **true** revolution which ought to bring to people unmixed happiness is but a deceiving mirage which never turns real; it resembles the golden age of the millenia: ever waited for, ever vanishing in the mist of the future, and always deluding its faithful the very moment they think they have seized it.'[35] Actually Pareto was constant to the idea that revolution is one of the means of replacing an oligarchy by another.

C. The Social Classes

Unless the Marxist theory of social classes is regarded as the final say in the matter, with a few minor corrections here and there, Pareto's idea of social classes need not be rejected for the sole reason that it departs from Marx's theory on certain points. The worst criticism that could be levelled at Pareto in this respect is a complete disregard for the economic factor. For Pareto, the concept of class represented a complex phenomenon, like all the aggregates, while economy was only one element among many. 'Different traits fit into the social classes. Sometimes it is birth, a common origin, real or presumed, certain religious practices, the same type of occupation, and so on. Wealth is no doubt one of the main causes of social differentiation into classes. The rich tend to flock together in the same way as the middle class and the poor.'[36] Nor did Pareto deny class consciousness, but could not admit it as sufficient condition for the definition of a class, given the gap between the objective and the subjective facts. 'The socialists have realized that one should not consider absolute wealth alone, but also relative wealth, that is to say, one must also take into account the value people attach to this wealth, by not limiting oneself to the objective fact but by paying attention also to the subjective fact. They are right. Happiness and misfortune are mainly subjective things. It is true that there is a certain melting point where the objective and the subjective facts merge, but before reaching that point there is a wide margin within which there is no perfect correspondence between the subjective facts of happiness and misfortune, on the one hand, and the objective fact, represented by a larger or smaller amount of wealth, on the other.'[37]

Like any other group, the class is an aggregate and as such it is heterogeneous. The social classes are in fact divided within themselves not only by virtue of the divergence of interests, but also owing to the different residues that animate their members. It is true of the working class, because there is a social hierarchy in the world of labour, too. It is also true of the capitalists themselves. 'Under the name of capitalists one has mixed up, and continues to do so, the persons who derive an income from their real estate and their savings, on the one hand, and the entrepreneurs, on the other. This confusion makes it hard to understand the economic phenomenon, and even harder to grasp the social phenomenon. In reality, these two categories of capitalists have interests

that are often divergent, and sometimes even opposed. They
may be more opposed than are the interests of the so-called
capitalist classes, on the one side, and the "proletarians,"
on the other side.'[38]

Pareto remarked that the rigid class segregation is a theoretical view which may be promoted for political reasons. He
pointed to the fact that consistent and unavoidable exchanges
and relations exist among classes in social real life. 'The
social classes are not separated entirely, not even in the
countries where the caste system prevails, and...in the modern
civilized nations an intensive circulation takes place among
the different classes.'[39] Only an ideology of a theological   type
may dissociate what mixes more or less indistinctly in social
life. In fact, Pareto concluded, the rivalry among classes
is conditioned by the competition among the élites, that is
to say, an élite gets the backing of a class in order to weaken
or defeat another élite which becomes the defender of another
class, in reaction to it, or in virtue of its economic situation. 'No social class is homogeneous; rivalries are always in
the midst of each, and any party which takes shape in this way
may seek its support among the lower classes. This is a very
general phenomenon. Almost all the leaders of revolutions
have been dissident members of an élite.'[40] It is by reference
to a derivation that one would qualify as 'deviant' or 'revi-
sionist' any person who strays from the line one follows:
a resurgence of medieval heresies. According to Pareto, the
sociological reality shows that socialism is similarly divided
and amenable to different interptretations as is Islam or
Christianity. Is the proletariat a homogeneous reality? Observation reveals that several parties claim a proletarian origin
and that in spite of it they fight each other outrageously.
Furthermore, he remarked that there are socialist sects as
there are Christian sects and that orthodoxy is each time
defined as the idea of the strongest. Pareto went on to admit
that among the socialists there are people of good faith,
genuinely convinced, as there are others who only seek their
interest. If the revolution is pure, the revolutionaries
are not. Moreover, he observed: 'De Tocqueville has very
well remarked that the revolution had merely used the methods
of the Ancien Régime. Actually, the new social classes that

have come to power in some countries grant themselves the
priveleges previously enjoyed by the earlier dominating classes. Under the Ancien Régime, those members of the gentry that
abused the villeins were seldom punished; under the new régime
that privilege has been transferred to the striking workers
who can with impunity or on derisive penalties mishandle
and sometimes even kill the workers who want to keep on working.'[41]

Pareto found no difficulty in accepting the notion of class
struggle. On this point he agreed with the Marxists, yet
his interpretation of the notion is different. 'The class
struggle, to which Marx drew one's attention in particular, is
a real fact, and its traces are to be found on each page of
history. Notwithstanding, it does not take place between
two classes only, between the proletarians and the "capitalists": it is encountered in an infinite number of groups which
have different interests, and above all among the élites which
contend for power.'[42] Each time it is the élite in power that
is interested in denying this struggle in order to'...distract
the attention of the subjected class from this matter and so
spare its own members' capacity to resist. In fact the class
that is in power has already obtained everything that the class
struggle could offer it. The only thing left to it to do
is to preserve what it has acquired and prevent others from
despoiling it of its assets in the way it might have dispos-
sessed the class it has replaced.'[43] The class struggle has
little chance of ever disappearing because it is an aspect of
the permanent struggle between élites, between those in power
and those aspiring to it. The seizure of power by a class
relying on the proletariat would not put an end to the class
struggle, because other élites will set the proletariat in
motion in order to dislodge it. Thus Pareto concluded that the
possibility of eliminating the conflict between labour and
capital is simply an illusion. Only by means of pseudological
reasoning alone can such an expectation be justified. 'The
class struggle is only a form of life struggle. The so-called
"conflict between labour and capital" is just a form of the
class struggle. During the Middle Ages one might have thought
that had the religious conflicts disappeared, society would
have been pacified. Those religious conflicts were but an

instance of class struggle. They have disappeared partially and been replaced by socialist conflicts. Let us suppose that collectivism were already established, and let us suppose that "capitalism" has ceased to exist, it is clear then that it could no longer be in conflict with labour; but that would be only one form of the class struggle to disappear, other forms would take its place. Conflicts would emerge among different categories of workers in the socialist state, between the "intellectuals" and the "non-intellectuals," between different types of politicians, between the latter and those whom they manage, between the innovators and the conservatives.'[44] To sum up, the struggle between élites takes as pretext either the economic contentions or the religious rivalries, or still other rivalries, in keeping with circumstances and historical periods. While being fundamentally right, Marx made the mistake of believing that economy alone is the ground of class struggle, and it was that belief that projected him into utopia.

2. THE FORCE AND THE RUSE

Force is one of the essential variables of any social equilibrium. Notwithstanding, Pareto paid no attention to it earlier in his research. It was only gradually, while building up his sociology that he realized its importance. Perhaps he had in the first place to overcome what had been left in him of the pacifism of his youth. It is also possible that he turned to this new factor after having become aware of the inability of economics to solve social problems. Nonetheless, the reasons which led him to reflect on the social importance of force do not matter as much as the meaning he came to attach to the term. Let us examine his notion. Eventually force came to be regarded by Pareto as a determinant in the suppression of the decay of a society, and in consequence, as an incomparable civilizing factor. The refusal to resort to force does, in Pareto's eyes, explain not only the collapse of régimes such as that of the French monarchy at the end of the 18th century, but also the decadence of civilizations whenever humanitarianism hinders its use. Moreover, it stimulates innovations and favours social stability, essential conditions of the social equilibrium. Indeed, law is decisive in the regulation of society, but it '...started through the efforts of isolated individuals. Nowadays it fulfills its function by means of collective force, but it is always force.'[45] The classical opposition between force and law belongs to the order of dissimulations by derivation. 'As usual, all these derivations are deprived of any precise meaning. All governments make use of force, and all claim to be grounded on reason. Actually, with or without universal suffrage, it is always an oligarchy which rules and knows how to give to the popular will the expression it desires.'[46] Pareto's formulations may be quite shocking to those who think by means of derivations and who consider them more important than the residues. It was his opinion not to take that detail into consideration as long as the task of sociology was to analyse facts, to describe what was effectively going on in the different societies, without masking the roughness of real life and without taking into account the justifications; after all, each and every political régime claims its wish to be that of bringing happiness to the people. 'The question whether one should use force in society, whether it is advantageous or not, has no sense, because force is used both by those intent on preserving certain uniformities and those who want to transgress them. The violence of the latter is directed against the violence of the former. As a matter of fact, whoever favours the ruling class and declares his disapproval of the use of force does in reality object to the use of force by the dissidents who in turn want to evade the rules of uniformity. Whenever he speaks in favour of the use of force what he actually does is to approve of its use by the authorities in order to constrain the dissidents.'[47] The stylistic dullness of this quotation does not diminish Pareto's sociological insight: those who theoretically are opposed to force end by using it, or by supporting its use, in practice.

Thus it is an implacable and ineluctable fact that affirms itself unsparingly and has been confirmed by experience all through history: every society makes use of force even when it is on the defensive. So far no science has been able to change that, or at least to check the use of force. For centuries, the best intentions went the same way. More than in any other walk of social life, one must be on guard here against any illusion. More often than not, the régimes that claim to put an end to violence are those which make the most lavish use of it. Pareto's law reads as follows: 'The living being which shies away from meting blow for blow and from shedding the blood of the opponent, by that very attitude places himself at the mercy of that adversary. The sheep has always found a wolf ready to devour it, and if for the time being it is not in danger, this is so simply because man reserves it for his own consumption. Any nation which is horrified by the sight of blood to the point of not knowing how to defend itself would become the prey of some other war-like people sooner or later. It seems that no square foot of land on our globe has been left unconquered by the sword and that its inhabitants have not kept it without resorting to force. Were the Negroes stronger than the Europeans, it would be the Negroes to share out Europe among themselves, and not the Europeans, Africa. The "right" which self-proclaimed "civilized" nations claim for themselves, namely that to the conquest of other peoples whom they call "uncivilized" is altogether ridiculous. In other words, this right is but force. As long as the Europeans are stronger than the Chinese, the former would impose their will on the latter; but as soon as the Chinese become stronger than the Europeans, the roles would be reversed. It is not at all sure whether humanitarian declamations may ever be opposed with any chance of success to an army.'[48] The best institutions, rules or laws remain dead letter unless they are backed by force. The lesson is bitter, but it has never been proven a lie. In Pareto's opinion, the sword is more powerful in politics than the truth. Numerous religions owe their existence to force. 'It is to the sword of the princes that the Reformation owes its victory in Germany; had it not received their backing it would have ended like the heresy of the Albigenses.'[49] Like it or not, force is protection. A tottering political force gives free course to blind violence. In any case, neither justice nor peace are served by the attempts to do away with force.'If the ruling class does not know how, does not want to, or cannot make use of force to reprimand the transgression of uniformities in private life, then the anarchical action of the ruled would make up for the defficiency. It is a well known fact in history that private vengeance disappears or reappears as the public power takes upon itself or relinquishes the task to punish misdeeds.' [50]

Thus one cannot simultaneously be a partisan of the class struggle and a promoter of humanitarianism without becoming guilty of the contradiction implicit in the derivations. Such an attitude is non-logical, to say the least.The replacement of an élite by another shows that the balance of force was favourable to the triumphant élite. That does not mean, and Pareto insisted on it, that the cause which the successful élite had been promoting was more just.[51] A minority which decides to make use of force has every chance to emerge victorious, provided the adversary hesitates to employ the same means. In this way, Pareto placed force on the same footing as the economic condition and the life-style in his definition of a social class. In no way can a class make itself heard unless it represents a force or is capable of influencing the existing balance of force. 'A social class is heeded only by virtue of the force it possesses. If it does not take care of its own interests, how can it think that the other classes, its rivals, would do that for it? History shows us that only those people capable of defending their freedom have been able to preserve it. All the others were deprived of it. Moreover, even when they had been allowed to keep it through the mercy or out of the disdain of the strong, they had not made any use of that freedom. If the British bourgeoisie preserves its freedom,that is because it has got the force to defend it; without that force it would lose its freedom.'[52] This paragraph can be understood only in the light of Pareto's theory about the social equilibrium. It is ridiculous to wish to impose freedom upon those who do not want it, because love of freedom implies in the first place readiness to defend it, otherwise all is but pretence. Those who give up the struggle for their freedom acknowledge their willingness to accept an equilibrium imposed by an alien force. Yet Pareto went even farther. The social equilibrium is made up of the will to freedom, equality, but also of the pursuit of certain interests, as well as the need of force. As a consequence and from the point of view of the social equilibrium, freedom for the sake of freedom is as vain as the attempt to demand that an interest be granted as one's due in the name of that very interest. By its own nature the equilibrium demands a compromise to be reached among the will to freedom, the claim of equality, the concern for justice, and the intervention of force. The term 'equilibrium' becomes meaningless as soon as it is made to designate an exclusive aspiration or factor. A society that knows liberty alone is as absurd as a society that is grounded solely on economy or religion. Said differently, the social equilibrium rejects the exclusivity of any one element or ideal, because it itself is the outcome of concurring and sometimes even diverging elements and aspirations. That is also the reason why Pareto did not accept the idea of force for the sake of force, either. It is a mistake to take his insistence on the necessity of force simply as an eulogy on it. His hostility was directed against the humanitarians, as he called them, because they disconsidered reality and overlooked the fact that force was inevitable. One cannot do without it. Pareto dismissed both humanitarianism and cynicism simultaneously because they are exclusivistic attitudes. On the other hand, his merit lies in the recognition of the importance of force, without for that matter giving in to the cult of force.

Actually force is not a means by which all the problems and all the difficulties may be solved. It cannot be resorted to unrestrictedly. Rather each case needs to be considered on its own merits, and then the adequacy of the use of force needs to be deliberated in each particular instance; force should be employed accordingly. It is not only weakness in those holding positions of power that breeds anarchy, but also the excessive and too frequent use of violence.[53] By its arbitrary intent to settle everything through force, despotism is a form of anarchy. On the other hand, a balanced society is equipped with juridical and institutional mechanisms the role of which is precisely that of regulating problems normally without the use of force. In other words, stability does not result from the presence of force alone. The importance of derivations also needs to be acknowledged. Pareto kept insisting on the fact that they may become useful to the extent a society does not display logical actions alone and the conduct of people and even of rulers is manifestly non-logical. The derivations are incompatible with the reckless, inopportune and disproportionate use of force. Pareto disapproved of those theories which condemn force off hand, and equally so of the justifications by force, as also of its indiscriminate application.

As force is one of the normal means of government action and an essential factor of the social equilibrium, the refusal to apply force in the name of humanitarian principles is to assume a false position. The moment the government in question declines to employ it, others will resort to it in its place and in the most irregular circumstances. That is just what the discriminative justifications of force show: 'A small number of dreamers reproach in general terms the use of force by no matter whom; but these theories either are without effect or undermine the resistance of the rulers, leaving free room for the violence of the ruled.' [54] In other words, the theory of non-violence is specious, not only because it does not distinguish between force and violence (as will be seen further on), but also because it is an indirect means of encouraging social disorder. Generally, it benefits the 'dissidents' who do not hesitate to resort to blind force whenever the government in power allows itself to be influenced by the humanitarianism of such a principle. For the same reasons the cowardly use of force needs also to be deplored. Pareto observed that it had become a current phenomenon. In his opinion, it endangers the social equilibrium because it forbids the use of force against groups, while accepting it only as a means to punish individual or private offences. Pareto returned to this idea time and again. Yet nowhere else did he express it so precisely as in the following passage: 'For instance, one draws a considerable distinction between the individual who kills or robs on his own account, on the one hand, and the individual who commits the same acts with the intention of making himself useful to his party, on the other. By and large, among civilized nations the former are extradited whereas the extradition of the latter is declined. Likewise an increasing tolerance is shown to offences committed during strikes or other economic, social or political conflicts. One always tends to show a passive resistance to the aggressors by forbidding to the agents of public force to make use of their weapons otherwise than in cases of extreme necessity. Such cases hardly ever occur in practical life, because as long as the agents are alive it is maintained that the necessity is not extreme. It is altogether futile to acknowledge this condition of extreme necessity the moment the agents are killed and as a result can no longer carry out the sanction of using arms. Repression by means of law courts is growing softer.'[55]

There are limits to the use of force. If one wishes to do justice to Pareto's concept, then the temperate use of force which he favoured needs to be taken into consideration. Relatedly, three points must be kept in mind. Firstly, that there is no identity between force and violence. Far from necessarily being the expression of force, violence is more often than not a sign of weakness. 'Violence should not be mistaken for force. Violence often goes hand in hand with weakness. One sees individuals and classes that have lost the force to maintain themselves in power render themselves loathsome by the violence with which they strike right and left. The strong strike only when it is absolutely necessary, but then nothing prevents them. Trajan was strong, but not violent; Caligula was violent but weak.'[56] The main complaint which Pareto raised against the bourgeoisie, in decline because of so much humanitarianism, is that of misunderstanding the virtues of force and so indirectly preparing the ground for blind and disorderly violence. 'The big mistake of the present age is to believe that one can rule the people by sheer reason and without the use of force which is, contrary to what is believed, the basis of social organization. It is quite strange to notice that the antipathy which the contemporary bourgeoisie nurses for force gives free scope to violence as a consequence. As soon as they are sure that they will go unpunished, criminals and rebels do almost everything they want. The most peaceful individuals are pushed to join unions and resort to threats and violence by governments that leave only this outlet open to them to defend their own interests.'[57] No doubt that these lines were written by Pareto under the influence of the wave of anarchical assassination attempts which rolled over Europe round the year 1900. Nonetheless, he gave them a more general meaning. Irrespective of circumstances, violence raises a theoretical problem, namely that of its justification. 'On the one side we have theories which condemn the use of force by the ruled in any condition, and on the other, we have theories that disapprove of its use by the rulers.'[58] Actually, one is confronted by derivations which for moral or interest-related reasons try to justify violence in the name of principles. In political matters, on the other hand, one deals essentially with a sort of casuistry. That is to say, one weighs the most convenient measures possible to be taken in particular circumstances. In this light, Pareto thought that violence could serve as a last resort in order to redress a compromised situation. Otherwise, he saw in it a way to replace an inept and bankrupt élite, incapable of maintaining the social equilibrium, by a more dynamic and enterprising élite, able to guide society.

Pareto was neither an anti-revolutionary nor a counterrevolutionary, yet he refused to pay tribute to the revolutionary mythology and to romanticism. He rejected the doctrine of revolution for the sake of revolution, and the doctrine of change for the sake of change, in the same way as he castigated the doctrine of the use of force for the sake of force, and the doctrine of freedom for the sake of freedom, and of equality for the sake of equality. The social equilibrium does not rest on exclusive theoretical elements, rather it is based on factors that act concomitantly. 'Sometimes wars and revolutions are useful, which does not mean always.'[59] Pareto did not believe in the ideal aims of revolutions, because they were unattainable. The only benefit they could bring was, in his opinion, the substitution of the weak and feeble élite by another, more dynamic. Together with Georges Sorel, he remarked with some irony that revolutionary idealism claims to transform the world, whereas in fact it does not even manage to change individual habits.[60] According to Pareto, modern revolutions are but a mode of élite selection, which replaces the ancient military or religious rivalry by the economic and social rivalry. The content of the problem remains the same, only the forms change. Said differently, revolutionary violence is not justified as such. In more general terms, the justification of violence by means of violence is a false problem, because all violence represents a provisional state which aspires to the status of legal force. Pure violence is animalistic, because in the case of the human being the derivations intervene, seeking to legitimate it. This legitimacy rests on the substitution of a weak link that unsettles the social equilibrium by a force capable of maintaining it. 'Whoever makes use of illegal violence does not desire anything better than to be able to transform it into legal violence.'[61]

The second point that should be taken into consideration derives from the need of the ruling class to obtain a minimum of consent from the governed: 'Throughout history, consent and force appear as the means by which to rule.'[62] Only in the extreme and highly improbable case of unanimous consent can those in power do without force. Although even then one should not sit rocking oneself in illusions. Consent does not mean participation or popular representation; the latter two may exist in the absence of consent. They may even break up the consensus by introducing useless divisions and conflicts. At any rate, even in the case of popular representation, it is a minority that rules. 'With a very small number of short-lived exceptions, in all other cases one encounters a small ruling class which keeps itself in power partially by force and partially by the consent of the governed class which is by far the more numerous.'[63] According to Pareto, the best way of obtaining the consent is not by acting violently upon the residues, but as the Romans did, by making the best of those present. 'Rome was to a high degree endowed with the skill of making the most of the residues; that is why it could assimilate a great number of peoples that surrounded it in Latium, in Italy, in the Mediterranean basin.'[64] To exploit the residues means also to play with the derivations. To a large extent it is also a question of ruse.

Thus one arrives at the third point which is also the most important in the last instance. Adhering to the Machiavellian principle, the ruling class must be capable of alternating force by ruse, or at least count in its ranks elements capable of acting respectively as lions and as foxes. It is unwise to use force all the time; one must know how to apply the other method, too, the method of deceit. 'In order to prevent or resist violence, the ruling class resorts to ruse, fraud, corruption, or to put it briefly, from a lion the government turns into a fox. Faced by the threat of violence, the ruling class lowers its head, but gives in only seemingly, whereas in fact it braces itself to circumvent the obstacle which it cannot overcome openly.'[65] As experience shows, it is not always good to extend open resistance to the 'dissidents.' Sometimes it is worthwhile to show more subtlety and make use of an armory of artifices. Thus it is more practical for a ruling class to include members that act in accordance with the residues of the first class, but who know also to put to good use their instinct of combinations in order to counterbalance the rashness and the impetuosity of those who act according to the residues of the second class. It is generally '...more difficult to dispossess a ruling class that knows how to make use of ruse, fraud and corruption in a competent manner. It becomes very difficult, indeed, whenever the ruling class manages to co-opt the greatest number of those who have the same gifts from among the ruled class, who know the tricks and as a result could become leaders of those willing to resort to violence. The ruled class, which in this way is deprived of guidance, talent and organization, is almost always incapable of building up anything lasting.'[66]

Historical evidence induced Pareto to argue that the régimes in which the residues of the first class were prevalent alternated with those in which the residues of the second class were predominant, although more often than not a mixture of residues of both classes might be the rule. Both methods are efficacious. Among the régimes the élites of which showed a penchant for the residues of the second class Pareto quoted Sparta and the Republic of Venice. Among those with a preponderance of the residues of the first class, he listed Athens, the Roman Republic, but also the theocratic governments and as a result those régimes which nowadays rely mostly on a particular ideology. Pareto claimed that in the former case the circulation of the élite is rather slow, whereas it is much faster in the latter. Nonetheless, he did not advocate the one-sided exploitation of ruse, and that not because the foxes show little courage in general, but because they lack faith, they are not elevated by any ideal which is indispensable as soon as one wants to obtain the lasting consent of the ruled. Besides, there is the question of equilibrium. Without force, the ruse is ultimately powerless. 'There is a genuine contest between the ruse and the force. In order to come to the conclusion that it is never useful to oppose force to deceit under any circumstances, it is necessary in the first place to demonstrate that the use of deceit is always and without exception more effectual than that of force. Let us assume that in a certain country there is a ruling class A which assimilates the best elements of the whole population, as far as ruse is concerned. In such conditions, the ruled class B is deprived of these elements to a large extent, and because of that can nourish but little hope, if any, of ever defeating the class A, as long as ruse alone is resorted to, in the struggle between them. Were the A group to add force to it, then its domination would be perpetual. Yet that happens only in a very small number of cases. Most of the times, those who make use of deceit are less capable of violence and their disability grows the more they resort to ruse, and the other way round. It follows that if the camp A accumulated people that are better at employing deceit, then the party B by necessity accumulates people that are more able to use violence. In this manner, and provided the movement goes on, the equilibrium becomes unstable, because the A's are helped by ruse but lack the courage to employ force and also the necessary instruments to do so. On the other hand, those in group B have both the courage and the equipment, but lack the skill to use it. If the latter find leaders who do have that skill, and history shows that usually they get such leaders from among the defectors from camp A, then they get everything they need to emerge victorious and chase the A's from office. History offers countless examples ranging from the most distant past and up to the present.'[67] To sum up, the two means of politics are force and the ruse, and it depends on the circumstances and the acumen of the ruling class to use one rather than the other, or better still, to combine the two.[68]

3. POLITICS AND DECLINE

Two aspects of this problem will be left unanswered. The first refers to the influence exerted on Pareto by another Machiavellian, Gaetano Mosca. Pareto never denied that influence categorically, as far as I know, but rather chose to assume a haughty and disdainful attitude whenever asked about it. It is left to the scholars to assess the importance of the influence and to spell out its essential points. The second aspect is relative to the doctrines that Pareto fought against: socialism, parliamentarism, democratism, humanitarianism. He himself was teaching that they were derivations and that it would be a mistake to attach too much importance to them. The rest of this chapter will be taken instead by a systematic review of his basic ideas on the political phenomenon. Pareto himself never managed to give them a coherent and consistent form.

Politics should be understood in the light of their objective. Following Hobbes closely, Pareto defined this objective as the **protection** of a collectivity as people or as nation. This is merely a modern rendition of the age-old idea of politics, expressed by the adage: *salus populi suprema lex esto*. In order to provide this protection it matters little whether one resorts to force or to ruse, since the essential is to be able to guarantee it effectively. From all this it follows that :

- Politics are not a personal matter, and in consequence they are not concerned with problems of personal conscience and individual morality. Rather their concern is the mass of people, the crowd. Whence Pareto's hostility to all those who in the name of private scruples give priority to individual conscience over the salvation of the collectivity. He did not have a poor understanding of the legitimacy of the hesitations prompted by one's conscience, or of the individual-social dialectic from a sociological point of view. Yet he refused to mistake the plane of personal exigencies for that of collective necessities, given the fact that the individual is only a fiction outside society, and society in turn, an abstraction if isolated from the individuals. In other words, individual perfection is one thing, the protection of collectivity, another. 'Were the ruling body to develop in the midst of a people composed of perfect beings, then the most honest and moral means would also be the most efficacious to use in order to subsist and prosper; but as it develops in the midst of imperfect human beings, it must resort to means suitable to these people and necessarily embodying a mixture of good and evil.'[69]

- Concrete action prevails against speculations about an ideal society, all the more so, as the individual members of a collectivity are far from being in agreement on those ideals. Said differently, in any particular situation the purity of principles must yield to the needs of real life. It is not the invidual comfort that is at play in politics. 'Social life makes it impossible to accept all the logical consequences of the principles which one would like to observe; thus one must find the means by which to interpret those principles in such a way that their consequences woult not impair the conditions of real life too much.'[70] That is not at all to say that the principles should be discarded. On the contrary, Pareto underlined their significance which is directive and not immediately active. 'An organization that reproduces law and justice only is merely an ideal conception similar to that of a soul without a body. The real organizations are altogether unlike that.'[71] The role of the state is not to be ethical but political. Before being a **Legal State**, it simply needs to be a state. The error of many theoreticians is to demand the most in conditions in which not even the least is achieved, and it is unfortunate that so often they despise the least in the name of the most. 'Whenever the terms "Ethical State" serve only to designate a metaphysical entity that exists in imagination alone, they may be permitted to attribute to it all the qualities they wish. On the other hand, whenever by these terms it is to be understood something real, as for instance, the public centres of power in their totality, then one is confronted by an organism which contributes to the good or the bad qualities of the aggregate, which in turn may act in order to reinforce the former as much as the latter.'[72]

Politics are a contest between the pressure exerted by social necessities (that is, difficulties that arise from the cohabitation of the members of a collectivity and the problems that emerge from the co-existence of nations), on the one side, and the will to materialize different ideal and practical aspirations, on the other. This contest gives rise to internal and external conflicts, depending whether the aspirations are stronger than the patience indispensable to resolve the difficulties and the problems arising from concrete situations. Whence the working out of derivations or ideologies the purpose of which is either to legitimize the power in place or to justify the demands put forth by the candidates to power. As Busino remarks, at the end of his life Pareto came to the conclusion that the central concept of politics is that of power which some try to preserve while others try to seize.[73]

Thus the forces which enter the competition are conditioned by the unavoidable social stratification, that is to say, the existence of the élites and of social classes. It is important to the competing élites to obtain the adherence of the ruled by means of ideologies, in order to reach their separate ends. In this way the élite in power might keep its position, or the aspiring élite might snatch it. This is the kernel of Pareto's political thinking. It is also the starting point for the clarification of the other aspects of the political life.

a) Under the influence of Marxism the class struggle has assumed the form of a radical opposition between the bourgeoisie and the proletariat nowadays. This means that an élite, largely originating in the lower classes but the leaders of which are of bourgeois stock ('...almost all the revolutions have had dissident members of an élite for leaders'[74]) would try to impose its will in the name of the proletariat. Nevertheless it is not the proletariat that would rule, but an oligarchical minority which would speak on its behalf. Society would remain divided between the ruling and the ruled classes. This process is more likely to happen as the bourgeoisie and its régime, which Pareto called 'plutocratic democracy,' are in full decline. Indeed, Pareto argued, its élite tries to save itself by adhering to the humanitarian ideals of non-violence, peace with justice, and so on, and by coaxing the proletariat with promises of social justice. Yet '...all this would have some effect only upon a timid, feeble and degenerate bourgeoisie, like all the élites in decline, and none at all upon the members of the new "élite," upon the partisans of a Lenin, for instance.'[75] Anyhow, '...of the two forces present in society, it is the popular force that is the greater nowadays; that is why the bourgeois state is shaking in its shoes and its power is turning into dust. The demagogical plutocracy witnesses the weakening of its first term and the strengthening of its second; it prepares new oscillations for itself the scope and the time-span of which cannot be predicted.'[76] Notwithstanding, and as already said, the change would be limited to the substitution of a declining élite by another, more dynamic, and without for that matter bringing about any basic change in politics.

b) No doubt the new élite sets upon abolishing privileges

and upon putting an end to the abuses of the former élite. However, being itself an oligarchic minority, it would equally work to its own advantage, to consolidate its new position, and so would engender new abuses. Pareto concluded that it is not equality that the élites of socialism will set up; they would rather seek to acquire the privileges that go with the higher class. In order to justify their action they would turn to spoliation, they would strip the former ruling class in order to satisfy their own clients and their supporters. 'Everywhere and at all times, past history and present-day observations point to people divided into groups, each of which generally acquires economic assets partly through its own productive efforts and partly by despoiling other groups which in turn despoil them.'[77] As far as the present is concerned, one has even come out with a hypocritically easy method of operation: 'Lately one has got the idea of plundering not against the law, but with the help of the law.'[78] New combinations may be devised but politics cannot be created anew and altogether different from what it was before. In Pareto's opinion, the revolutionary ideal remains an ideal, because the concrete historical revolution would operate the way Sylla acted in favour of his troops. One only invents new theories justifying procedures that do not change in the least.

c) Because he did not believe in the possibility of achieving ideal ends for the simple reason that they were ideal and not empirical, Pareto was the opponent of utopias. He did not dismiss them off hand, rather the opposite, as shown in his LES SYSTÈMES SOCIALISTES, which consists mostly of a close scrutiny of utopias. Utopia is grounded on the belief that man and society can be transformed, that man can be turned into a being altogether different from what he has been, whereas in reality the means for such a transformation are lacking. On the other hand, ideology takes stock of the qualities and shortcomings of living people in order to manipulate them politically. Said differently, in Pareto's opinion, utopia thinks that it is capable of modifying the content, whereas ideology changes the forms in view of a precise objective, apt to be achieved empirically. Thus, by invoking experience and logic, Pareto sent the utopians back to their fantastic theoretical speculations. Yet, he remarked: 'The twenty-three hundred years or so that separate us from the glorious age of the Athenian democracy are comparatively nothing in the history of mankind. That is true, and if one concludes from it that we know nothing about what man would be like in ten thousand years' time, for instance, this conclusion would be perfectly legitimate. There is nothing else we can do but keep silent about it and admit our perfect ignorance, in all sincerity.'[79] In general, utopias rest on sophisms reached by association of ideas: '...almost all false arguments.'[80] On the other hand, Pareto insisted upon the importance of ideologies, and actually he was one of the first non-Marxist sociologists to recognize their significance in society. 'Ideology is part and parcel of the character of the civilized human being. To wish to ban these sentiments and this **ideology** and everything related to it altogether is to repeat in full the error of those who think that man can do without religion entirely and can replace it by some simple scientific notions.'[81] In the last instance, ideologies are theologies in disguise, and accordingly, as persistent. They make it possible to lend meaning to life and action, no matter whether they are false or deceptive, because '...in their present wretchedness, people like to find solace in imaginary worlds which they forge for themselves.'[82] At the same time, ideologies make possible the explanation of the unexpected, the strange and the complex. Notwithstanding, Pareto openly derided the derivations which ideologies are surrounded with. While taking as a case the attempt on the life of Empress Elisabeth of Austria by the anarchist Lucheni, Pareto noted that the socialists '...made haste to declare that the anarchists were a product of the capitalist society exclusively. Nobody would be astonished. It is widely understood that the infamous capital is the only source of the ills and crimes of our "bourgeois society." It is simply in virtue of the rhetorical device called repetition that by listing each of those ills and crimes one is reminded once more that they are caused by the infamous and abominable capital.'[83] In the same context Pareto also noted that the reactionaries, on the other hand, put the blame on 'the new ideas,' although he added humorously:'I am astonished that the vegetarians have not been as quick to seize the chance to preach in favour of their saint! Although it is probable that morals would grow mellower, on condition that everybody were forced to feed on vegetables alone. Starting from that premise and with the little skill needed to insert the sorites and project an enthymeme, it may easily be proven that the crime committed by Lucheni is due to the use of meat as foodstuff.'[84] Nevertheless, ideology is unavoidable because the non-logical action is preponderant. Ideology makes it possible to imprint a universal dimension on a particular claim, that is to say, ideology legitimates it by invoking all kinds of worthy principles. Thus it is normal that an élite seeking to attain power takes advantage of it even if it does not believe in it: success would add credit to the particular derivation. In politics one needs scapegoats, and while serving as a stimulus to action, ideology also faciliates the manufacture of scapegoats.

d) Politics are full of contrasts, that is contradictions. An élite violently denounces the abuses perpetrated by the opponents in power, but as soon as it seizes that power, the same élite commits others in its turn and that without delay. It accuses the dislodged élite of having oppressed the people, and embarks upon the same road as soon as it can. Both sides claim to struggle solely in the service of law, justice, peace and freedom. The contradictions are manifest both in internal and in foreign politics. In his diary, Pareto set side by side two speeches made almost at the same time by Llyod George, the British Prime Minister, and von Arnim, the Chairman of the German Lower House, respectively, and in which the two speakers were equally claiming to fight for freedom until victory.[85] Before WWI, whoever had been ignorant of the German culture had been taken for a barbarian; after that war, whoever showed admiration for German culture was regarded as a barbarian.[86] Stranger still, each nation thought itself entrusted with the noblest missions: 'Each people claims to have its own mission, handed over to it by one does not know whom, and for which no evidence is supplied.'[87] Whence Pareto's conclusion: 'Nothing is more aggressive than a mission. From this point of view only the so-called vital interests stand comparison.'[88] The socialists have the mission of leading the proletariat to victory, the liberals, to develop democracy the world over, and so on. Each élite claims to act in the name of the people, but the latter is not privy to the decision-making process:

it is always a minority or even one man that decide. The art of politics does not consist in producing derivations as much as in acting upon the residues which lend consistency to ideologies. As Machiavelli would have said: one should make believe. 'There where the residues are strong and kept that way by a skilful government which knows how to make use of them, the population readily accepts the burden of war preparations. On the other hand, there where the residues are weak or weakened by a government solely concerned with certain material interests without casting a glance towards the future, the people turns down the burden of national defence.'[89]

e) Politics are less a matter of principles and doctrine and more of circumstances, the main of which serve basically to wrest the consent and the adherence of the ruled. That does not mean the practice of blind and narrow-minded politics, but rather the skilful exploitation of circumstances to consolidate those in power and secure the protection of the members of the collectivity. Whence the fundamental role which Pareto assigned to experience, since to that end the knowledge of certain mechanisms becomes necessary. 'A great many of the socialist arguments rest on the proposition that given the identity of the qualities inherent in the ruled and the ruling, no abuse and no oppression are possible. We understand that this proposition could have appeared at least probable before one could have had the experience of governments resulting from the universal suffrage. However, after that experience, the possibility of abuse or oppression should not be contested there where everyone is ruled and ruling simultaneously. Between the ruled, representing a unit, and the ruling who have but a minimal percentage of sovereignty, a certain mechanism intervenes by necessity.'[90]

The fact that in politics most people develop passionate attachments on the basis of derivations need not prevent the sociologist or the political scientist from trying to find out the nature of politics behind the ideological disguises. In the first place, they have to understand that politics do not need to dissemble in order to act efficiently, but also that the scientist should not be taken in by the statements made by the politicians. Whenever the derivations and the ideologies are pierced through, and actions are compared stripped of their justifying glitter, then one realizes that politics remain practically the same. Whatever the party or the régime, they all proclaim the beginning of a new political life, juster, cleaner, in one word, unprecedented, and despite their experience, the ruled keep on believing them. Is there a paradox? Not at all. Given the fact that most actions are non-logical, they can only subsist on non-logical arguments, be they sophisms, myths, theories that exceed experience, or ideologies. Under the words, one must look for the reality which they conceal, because, for instance, one may call hegemony by another name, say, zone of influence, but the fact of domination persists. Notwithstanding, Pareto stressed that the sociologists would be mistaken to lose patience when confronted by such procedures as they are normal and unavoidable. They are part of the essence of politics, as Pareto himself admitted. In other words, a scientist who would like to practise politics on the basis of science would make a bad politician.

Thus Pareto acknowledged the importance of political parties and régimes, but was less concerned with these problems than the majority of his contemporaries. He showed a keener interest in revealing the substance of politics from under its formal covers. It seemed to him idle to ask which was **the best form of political régime**, although that question became topical again, with the substitution of the traditional political explanation by the economic explanation of régimes, under the influence of Marxism. In fact, such explanations kept giving priority to forms, and as a result, to derivations. On that Pareto used to remark: '...the study of the forms of political régimes belongs to a special sociology,'[91] and not to general sociology which has as object of analysis the main and general factors inherent in the social equilibrium.

While examining their contents, one soon becomes aware that politics too conform to the law of oscillations. In political science this phenomenon is known as decline. Thus Pareto reactualized a notion which has been momentous in the political science of the Ancient Greeks, but which seems to have lost its importance since the Age of Enlightment. It is wishful thinking to believe that what mankind once produced best could be improved upon consistently through time in the direction of rational perfection, while allegedly retrograde elements would become obsolete. Pareto broke with that tradition by showing that from the logical-experimental point of view what is regarded as progressive is but the result of a subjective judgment of an era, and it might not appear as such to a later age. Likewise, what has been regarded as retrograde at one time might get a new lease of life at another. Indeed, all social phenomena are subject to change. Pareto returned to this point many a time. However this change, as he saw it, is not linear, nor is it continuous as presupposed by the theory of progress. It might consist of an alternation. Pareto did not oppose a concept of decadence that states the progressive degradation of mankind as a continuous fall to the idea of evolution grounded on the premise that the phenomena presumed progressive follow a definite course of development and perfection. Rather he believed that all social phenomena might disappear only to emerge anew in a different form. A period of development may be followed by a period of recession; a predominant, individualistic outlook may be succeeded by an outlook in which the idea of the State is prevalent, and so on. In reality, even this interpretation does not do justice to Pareto's concept of decline. Actually, his philosophy is not that of the eternal return; his conception is not cyclical but rhythmic, to use his own words.

Pareto's theory of decline has a twofold meaning: on the one side, that of a tidal evolution, the ebb and the flow of a social movement, and on the other, that of a resurgence at a later time. Pareto's thinking would be distorted, were this twofold meaning taken apart. Let us get an example. A new political régime asserts itself, is institutionalized and develops as long as the élite that supports it remains dynamic and is not frustrated by the opposition offered by another, more aggressive, élite. Generally speaking, an élite which gets out of breath as it declines is relieved by another which sets up a new régime and which in turn may get out of breath and leave the place for a third régime to be installed. What is worth remembering is that in virtue of the principle of mutual dependence, the decline of an élite is accompanied by the ascent of another. Thus the progressive undoing of the bourgeoisie is accompanied by the surge of socialism. Whereas the bourgeoisie destroys itself through its 'squeamishness, the working class ignores these queer rituals of "humanitarian" religions and allows a new élite to emerge from its ranks, in the wings, so to speak. If it acknowledges them, it does so with disdain. It feels its forces grow with every passing day, and full of sap and vigour, it has no use of such pacifiers.'[92] Notwithstanding, this decline of the bourgeoisie and of the ideas that it represented during its high tide does not mean at all that they will be wiped out without a trace. They may reappear under a different and often unexpected form in keeping with the new derivations which would accompany them. Thus Pareto drew the comparison between Christianity, a religion with universalistic tendencies, and socialism which is a new universalistic theology. The latter, like the former, divides itself into rival sects that are at each other's throat. Socialism is not one and the same thing as Christianity; but the sectarianism which is characteristic of the one would become manifest in the other, too. Put differently, the decline of a régime or of an idea is inversely related to the ascent of another régime or another idea. The worn-out idea or régime may eventually surface again in a different form and possibly bring about the decline of the idea or the régime they have been dislodged by. In the decline of Athens, it was the disintegration of the democratic idea that one was witnessing. Later on, it found renewed vigour elsewhere. One used to believe in the final disappearance of tyranny. Yet it has reappeared in the form of modern dictatorships that contribute to the decline of democracy. Politics remain essentially the same, although they display various faces which show themselves one after another with different looks, all along history, provided the oscillations are more or less long-lived and more or less intense, as the case may be.

As already underlined more than once, Pareto became aware of the decline of the bourgeoisie and admitted willy-nilly that socialism increasingly stood a good chance. Despite all that, he gave no credit to the latter doctrine, not because at heart he remained an economist with liberal leanings, but rather because politically the socialist élite appeared to him torn by doubts and hesitations that risked to lead it to excesses which had nothing revolutionary about them. On reading his later writings, it soon becomes obvious that

Pareto stopped describing social and political life simply in terms of the ascent of an élite and the decline of another. Occasionally, he even expressed admiration for the socialists' energy, though he doubted their abilities.[93] Briefly, the actual situation is more complex than the TREATISE describes it. Whatever the case, Pareto cannot be denied a certain perspicacity. He was foreseeing that together with the decline of the bourgeoisie, a few ideas would also disintegrate, as for instance, the notion of liberal democracy and the idea of individual rights. Without going any farther, it seems that in his opinion the decay of liberalism was due more to the plutocratic system which was its consequence, rather than to the attacks launched by socialism. Said differently, for reasons that have to do with their own logic or that of the system, the élites harm themselves more than they are harmed by their opponents, with the result that their feebleness makes for the strength of their rivals. Likewise, it must be admitted that he foresaw the subsequent tide of the movements of violence, the dictatorships and the increasing etatism, and in particular the economic etatism. An élite which tried to rule mostly by ruse was replaced by an élite readier to resort to force.

Pareto's doubts about socialism are also explained by the fact, already pointed out by Roberto Michels, that he suspected its strong instinct of organization to be apt to evolve along the line of a bureaucratic society. He was ready to compare his own time with that at the end of the Roman Empire which brought into existence the Byzantine régime in the East. There, a bureaucratic organization of the social life was supported by a relative prosperity: 'It is easy to see that we move along a curve similar to that already covered by the Roman society after the establishment of the Empire, when a period of prosperity was followed by decline.'[94] Very significantly, the TREATISE concludes with the hesitating forecast of the prospects in store in the twentieth century, after a period of prosperity not unlike that of the Roman Empire, namely the prospects of a crystallized society. 'Almost a century ago, during the ascending period of freedom, one was condemning the restrictive and fossilized institutions of the Byzantine Empire. Nowadays, when we find ourselves in the descending age of freedom and of the ascent of **organization**, one admires and praises the same institutions. It is proclaimed that the European nations owe considerable gratitude to the Byzantine Empire which saved them from the Moslem invasion, and it is forgotten that the brave warriors of Western Europe did alone defeat and chase the Arabs and the Turks away many times and that they had become masters of Constantinople long before the Asian peoples. Byzantium makes us see the direction of the curve which our societies are on the point of following. Whoever admires this future is necessarily led to admire that past, and the other way round.[95] Nevertheless, the ultimate question was that of finding out whether socialism was not already a decadent doctrine of the conditions of decline, given the fact that its élites were above all seeking to work out plans by which to oppose bourgeois combinations. In such a situation, the genuine renewal would come from somewhere else, from a doctrine capable of bringing together socialism and the residues of the second class. At least it seems to me that Pareto's last writings do not exclude this interpretation.

V

PHILOSOPHER AGAINST THE GRAIN

As Raymond Aron has said, Pareto was a non-philosopher. He might have even wished to build up an anti-philosophy by taking the risk of working out a general theory of society within the strict limits of experience and without the intervention of any philosophical notion. In any case, he never ceased to repeat that he had no philosophical preoccupation whatsoever. Nonetheless, he failed in this endeavour whatever his intentions were in this respect. As a matter of fact, he made permanent use of philosophical categories, such as the concepts of form and content, but he never clarified them scientifically. Nor did he become aware of the philosophical premises of his thinking, as for example, the identity of human nature through time, or the philosophical dimension of historical interpretation, in an enlightening way. Finally, many a page of his writings exhude philosophy and even several philosophies or philosophical systems: nominalism, naturalism, positivism, rationalism, and so on. He did acknowledge the nominalism, but with certain reservations. 'It may be said that we reach the extreme limit of nominalism, provided that one deprives this term of its metaphysical accessories.'[1] Is it possible to use a philosophical doctrine by precisely depriving it of its metaphysical implications? It is difficult to do philosophy without philosophy. Actually Pareto gives the impression of having confused philosophy in general with metaphysics, and of having ignored the positive contributions of epistemology, for instance. Despite it all, he was familiar with the philosophers, and some of his critical observations show that he had read them attentively. Thus one may wonder whether his aggressiveness towards philosophy did not lie in a peculiar inability of his to think deliberately in philosophical categories, for which he had undergone no previous training. Perhaps his manner of thinking, with its strong analytical tendency, prevented him from thinking synthetically, the latter being the characteristic trait by which genuine philosophers are recognized generally.

In my opinion the greatest number of critical shafts levelled at him, and some of them are justified as already shown,
have been generated by the philosophical weakness of his
work. The shortcomings of his character aside, what interests
me here is his theoretical thinking alone. Unless one is
content simply with an exegetical criticism of his writings, a
detailed, paragraph-by-paragraph examination of his writings
is less likely to account for his lapses than his philosophical
stand and his general outlook. It is quite strange that an
author who advocates the logical-experimental method so vehe-
mently and by means of examples gives proof of so little logic
in the exposition of his ideas and of so much incoherence in
the composition of his work, in general. I suspect that those
shortcomings may be imputed to the absence in his case of a
philosophical thinking capable of synthesizing his reflections.
Despite all that, the positions which he took were quite original. Yet, in the absence of a reflective and epistemological
elaboration, they remained scattered and fragmentary. He
never managed to establish a link which could have allowed them
scope and would have revealed their significance. Thus in his
writings a great number of elements may be found belonging to
a philosophy which he did not know how, or had not the wish,
to work out conceptually. Here are some examples. Sometimes,
by assuming a provoking tone, he boasted an undeniably positivistic attitude with his demand that sociology should limit
itself strictly to the logical-experimental method. Notwithstanding, he avoided the narrow scientism of those who hold
valid only what can be explained scientifically. His works are
free of the scientific superstition, so current in the intellectual circles of his time. Did he not maintain that the
kind of conduct which would always conform to science would be
absurd ? On the other hand, a naturalist orientation makes
itself undeniably felt in his writings, but he knew better
than Marx to avoid the danger of substantive naturalism. His
had only an epistemological significance. The idea that conscience is but a reflection of the material conditions cannot
be encountered in his writings. Nor did he uphold any idea
about the autonomy of the spirit. His assertions remained
scientifically cautious. Likewise, his rationalism cannot be

contested, yet it did not allow of hasty conclusions: after all he warned his readers against the rationalistic aberrations which deny the forces of the irrational. It is simply false to say that Pareto was the author of such a concept like the 'profound irrationalism.' Why interpret in a deprecating and unfavourably one-sided manner the importance which he attached to non-logical actions and to derivations, while empirically they are so common? Does one need only to point out the play of the irrational in human actions in order to be taken for a supporter of the irrational? Pareto made a discovery, but he did not place it on a pedestal. Unfortunately his opponents show less scientific restraint when they exalt the rational alone.

To sum up, one witnesses a nominalism wary of words, a positivism which takes its measures to ward off scientism, a naturalism confined to methodology, and a rationalism which gives its due to the irrational. Several philosophical streams run across each other in his work, yet Pareto gave them a meaning that was unlike the currently accepted. Unfortunately he did not submit them to any analysis as would have been expected, in order to give them greater conceptual precision. In other words, the variety of stands he took has nothing contradictory in itself. It only suffers from the absence of that philosophical elaboration which would have enabled him to overcome his epistemological dispersion and achieve more coherence and unity in his own thinking. His undertaking, that of logically explaining the derivations and the irrational implicit in them (to use Raymond Aron's phrases), was not lacking in courage. He took the risk. His attempt left room for blots, gaps, mistakes and other shortcomings. Nonetheless, he contributed to the clarification of the process implicit in human action, and of the incoherent aspects of social relations in a telling and equally profound way. If nothing else, the notion of the 'non-logical' is quite remarkable in itself, a heuristic tool by which sociology could profit to a larger extent. He broke new ground which, in his own words,represents an approximation of reality alongside institutional analysis and the study of external conditions, such as economic, geographical and the like. It is true, the tool is quite delicate and its handling incurs the risk of psychologism which Pareto avoided by working out the notion of residue and setting it apart from the notions of instinct and sentiment. Like most scientific concepts, that of residue has only an instrumental value.

Max Weber has underlined the paradox implicit in action by showing that more often than not the end-result contradicts the original intention. On his part, Pareto tried to supply an explanation by means of the notions of residue and derivation. He let it to be seen that the gap between the avowed aim and the actual unfolding of the action is due to the non-logical, without the agent being necessarily of bad faith. To the contrary, Pareto acknowledged that most of the times the agent acts in good faith, the partisans of the ruse excepting. He did not make much of that gap, or at least no more than Weber made of his paradox, although he was fully aware of it and tried to examine it sociologically. Thus one should think twice before attributing him a philosophy in virtue of which 'the irrationalism imputed to the structure of action would gradually change into an irrationalism of principle.'[2] Likewise, one should know better than turning him into the author of a theory of violence which defines the true climate of his philosophy of history. For sure Pareto laughed at the partisans of progress but never did he deny the progress of science. He even nourished the idea that sociology had already made considerable progress. On this matter his declarations were so numerous that it is not worth insisting. It was the philosophy of progress which he rejected, that is to say, the idea that more would necessarily mean better, or in other words, the illusion of a progressive perfection of mankind as a whole. Here it is superfluous to recall that distinction which he made between force and violence, or his idea of force. What should be said is that despite his efforts Pareto could not set himself free from philosophy. In this regard, he deluded himself. Indeed there is a philosophy in his works, yet it is not the one imputed to him by Guy Perrin and others.

It is a truism of philosophy to affirm that the anti-metaphysical attitude of certain authors such as Compte or Marx contains metaphysical elements, though not deliberately, and that anti-philosophical declarations reveal a hidden philosophy. There is no reason why one should not be ironical

at Pareto's expense on this account, when he himself complain-
ed so much about and even denigrated the philosophers. Once
this point is made, the next is to bring to light Pareto's
latent philosophy in the most coherent way possible and at the
same time by resisting any tendency of overshooting the mark.
There are other sociologists who have raised the same problem,
Max Weber among them, although Weber was less sarcastic about
philosophy but equally intolerant: privately he kept saying
that logic was the only worthwhile thing in philosophy.

Without expounding on the possible similarities between
Weber and Pareto, nonetheless it may be noticed that while both
of them were non-philosophers, their thinking was not so wide
apart as one is bound to believe. Points in common are not
lacking:

a) They shared a common disdain for literateurs in the
realm of science. This is a minor point and its value is
polemical so I would not insist on it.

b) Both posed the question of action in terms of rationality
or logic, and were struck by the part played by the irrational
in human conduct. If their topic is analogous in this matter
as in others, their problematic, on the other hand, is divergent at times. Both had started from the model of economic
action (both, by the way, had taught political economy before
sociology) in order to define the logical or the rational
actions in their finality, respectively. Nonetheless, their
formulas do not coincide. In fact, Weber's rational action
refers to the co-ordination between the means and the end.
Pareto's logical action requires in addition that the agent
does not exceed the experimental conditions present at the
start. According to Pareto, an action which is rational in its
finality is still non-logical in the Paretian sense. On the
other hand, for Weber an action may be rational in relation to
a value, a category which Pareto excluded from what he considered logical conduct. Furthermore, whereas Pareto worked out a
dichotomy and placed the logical actions on one side, and
the non-logical actions (including those purely illogical) on
the other side, Weber elaborated an outright typology that
distinguishes alongside the action which is irrational in its
finality and the action which is rational in relation to a

value, the action grounded on affectivity and finally, the tradition-oriented action. Although Pareto did not deny any social worth to logical action (the general who heeds the omens, in which he does not believe, in order to bolster up the morale of his troops, behaves logically), he did not consider logical the action which is rational in relation to a value. Here the difference between the two sociologists rests on the fact that Pareto referred to logical reasoning while Weber to reason in general and not to any particular kind of reasoning. As for the irrational to which both of them assigned a large part in human life, it lent a tragic element to life in Weber's writings. That element however was practically absent in Pareto's, no doubt because the latter did not think in terms of destiny. Nevertheless, both of them were intrigued by the irony of consequences, in the sense that it seldom happens that the wished-for end is in agreement with the actual result of one's action. Perhaps Pareto's concept enjoys the advantage of seizing action in its internal unfolding, to the extent of his insistence on the deep-going motivations, the residues and the derivations. On the other hand, Weber's idea is subtler and more discriminating.

c) Each of them worked out a sociology of ideologies: Pareto did it in terms of derivations, whereas Weber, in terms of convictions. Nonetheless, both were respectful of that kind of conduct that remained consistent to its beliefs. Both were liberal and equally skeptical about the future of democracy, though both believed in the chances of socialism to succeed. However, Pareto seems to have been more critical of the latter since in his opinion its supporters were recruited particularly from among those people whose prevailing residues were of the first class. While giving ideology its due, both were of the opinion that the analysis of the political phenomenon had to exclude any moral considerations. From this point of view both were Machiavellians.

d) In regard to methodology, their ideas are strikingly similar. Both of them were the theoreticians of plural causality and both demanded that axiological neutrality should be conformed to in factual analysis. It is for those very reasons that both were opposed to Marxism, although challenging it. For both, each phenomenon had to be analyzed in its characteristic conditions, and if need be, with reference to an ideal model (which Pareto, unlike Weber, did not expound theoretically). Both were against interpretations that would exceed the original data and presuppositions. Thus both rejected the reduction of phenomena to an economic cause alone, which in the last instance was the decisive factor for Marx, despite his infrastructure-superstructure dialectic. They both shared the same exactness in matters of objectivity, though Pareto's stand was even more intransigent, no doubt in the absence of any in-depth reflection upon the Kantian epistemology. Pareto stuck solely to facts within the logical-experimental framework, whereas Weber forbade only the value-judgment of a subjective nature. In consequence, Weber availed himself of the possibility of integrating values into his research in the form of value orientations, while Pareto refused in principle to have anything to do with valuations, whatever their order. On this point, too, Weber's position was more discriminating as he sought to develop his theory epistemologically.

e) More astonishing still is the identity of the philosophical and even theological basis of their thinking, or put differently, its shared polytheism. One may recall the famous passage from his lecture 'Science as a Vocation,' in which Weber was saying that the categories of true, good and beautiful were not identical, that they could contradict each other, and even enter into conflict.[3] One may also recall the paragraph in 'Politics as a Vocation' where he opposed Förster's thesis, namely that from good comes only good, but from evil only evil follows.[4] Weber held that thesis to be unproblematic and contrary to historical evidence, and even more so to the experience of daily life. Furthermore, he sharply remarked that it was the opposite thesis that lay at the basis of all the world religions. The same idea may be encountered in Pareto's works where he wrote that a thing might be true without being useful, and the other way round, and that what is rationally absurd may be socially useful: 'The experimental truth of a theory and its social utility are two different things. An experimentally true theory may be useful (or noxious) to society, in the same way as an experimentally false theory.'[5] Pareto became even more explicit when he referred to mythology: 'A theory need not correspond to objective facts and be instead wholly fantastic from this viewpoint, yet still reflect subjective things of great importance to society. Whoever sees the social importance of mythology also wants it to be true. Whoever denies it reality also denies it any social importance.'[6] Like Weber, Pareto thought that from evil and falsity happy consequences may follow, and the other way round, namely that good may give way to disagreeable and unreasonable consequences: 'The work of the Church concerning magic is altogether absurd, and all these stories about devils are ridiculously childish. All said and done, there are people who draw from these premises the conclusion that Church religion is also absurd and that as a result is harmful to society. Can we accept this opinion? First of all it should be noted that this judgment does not refer to the Catholic faith alone, but is applied to all the other religions and even to all the metaphysical systems. In short, it is applied to everything that is not logical-experimental science. However, it is impossible to accept this conclusion and consider absurd most of the history of human societies until the present time'[7] Numerous gods and demons continue to be active in this world of ours and give social facts their distinct character. It is strange to discover that Weber and Pareto resorted to one and the same example to illustrate this thesis, namely the opposition of the German culture to the French or Latin culture. 'I do not know,' Weber said, 'how one should go about deciding the value of the French culture compared with the German culture scientifically; because there, too, different gods fight each other and no doubt for ever. Things do not happen differently from what went on in the ancient world that was still under the spell of gods and demons; nowadays they acquire a different meaning. The Greeks used to offer sacrifices in turn to Aphrodite, then to Appolo, and above all to each of the city gods; at present we are doing the same, though our conduct has broken the spell and stripped itself of the myth which nonetheless lives in us still. It is fate that holds sway over the the gods and not a science whatever that is. All that is given to us to understand is the meaning of the divine for a particular society, or what one or the other society regard as divine.'[8] On the other hand, Pareto wrote: 'It is useless to talk sense, and jokes alone are appropriate in such situations when people are lacking so much in intelligence and knowledge

not to see that whoever wants to burn those people whose opinion differs from the reputedly orthodox about, say, the mystery
of the holy trinity is simply a criminal. Likewise, whoever
wants, without any idea of civilization, to gaol all those who
do not agree that the German "civilization" is inferior by far
to the Latin "civilization," or the other way round, doubt the
superiority of the German *Kultur* over the Latin civilization
is no better, either, though he can no longer burn them at the
stake. The sanctity of different "civilizations" or of different "fatherlands" does not vary greatly from that of countless
deities which various peoples enjoyed adorning their pantheons
with. These beliefs may be useful from the social viewpoint -
and within certain limits they are, indeed - but this does not
render them harmless as soon as they exceed those limits, nor
easier to grasp from the experimental viewpoint.'9 It may be
added that both Weber's text and Pareto's were written in the
same year, 1918.

Pareto gave expression to his polytheism in most of his
writings, but nowhere with such perspicacious concision as in
the following lines: 'To the principle of Evil one opposes the
principle of Good which formerly was called the True Religion
and nowadays is named Science. It also surrounds itself by
secondary deities, such as Democracy, Humanitarianism, Pacifism, Truth, Justice and all the entities which may deserve
the epithet progressive. As the angels of light fight the
angels of darkness, these deities fight the so called reaction-
ry entities, defend poor mankind and save it from the ambushes
laid by these demons.'10 It should not be concluded from this
quotation that Pareto condemned the struggle between the
deities and the entities. His writings show that the opposite
is true. Content with it, Pareto took pleasure in denigrating
the modern intellectuals, unaware as they were of what was at
stake and of their offering sacrifices to polytheism. No doubt
that theology suited his 'heathen' temperament which was
that of an exacting scientist and a lover of life, all in one,
and which surfaces in his book LE MYTHE VERTUISTE. It also
explains his hostility towards Protestantism and its puritan
morals, as well as his tolerance of Catholicism, more pagan
because it was more sensitive to the pleasant aspects of life
such as pomp and festivals and to certain delectations shroud-

ed in mystery by the sacraments. Likewise, his world outlook
was not tragic at all. He loved the fantastic, laughter and
all the pleasures of life but without depravations. Under
such circumstances one may understand the association which he
made between decadence and self-contempt. 'As already seen,
the weakening of the so-called manly sentiments without which
one cannot go on in the struggle for life is one of the symptoms of decline. Another is the development of depraved tastes
and strange pleasures. Among the latter there is one which used
to appear in the midst of our race at least, during the ages
of decadence. It is the experience of acute voluptuousness in
humiliating oneself, degrading oneself, ridiculing the class
to which one belongs, turning into a laughing stock everything
that until then had been thought respectable. The Romans in
the period of decadence debased themselves to the level of
histrions.'[11]

A world inhabited by multiple deities means implicitly that
each notion has its proper value and significance which need
not be mixed up. Love is not the same thing as peace, politics
is not morality, and science is not religion. Thus Pareto
criticized those doctrines which mistake science for religion,
or further still, those doctrines which reduce all phenomena
to a unique source or cause, such as Marxism, for instance,
and finally those which attribute all qualities to one kind
of social system only, as for example, socialism, and all
the evils to another, namely capitalism. There is also a false
polytheism which believes that one deity can solve the problems
of another, or that at least fulfills the other's function.
It is in this latter sense that the religion of Progress
is polytheist whenever it is held to bring well-being, peace
and justice, too. The same may be said about socialism whenever it claims to be able to put an end to all wars, to crime,
prostitution, ignorance and idleness, or about science whenever
it is believed that it can promote democracy, social justice
and solidarity among peoples.

To sum up, Pareto's philosophy is a break philosophy, in
the sense that following the order of things, it severs what
various theologies and metaphysics regarded as one. The logical action is one thing, the non-logical, another. The same
goes for sentiment and reason, for instinct and reflection. It

does not deny the possibility of any relation between these notions. It only stresses that these relations are neither necessary nor final. On the contrary, they are dependent on ideologies, on derivations, and because of that they may be either longer lasting or merely provisional, yet always contingent. For the same reason they may assume the most varied forms, sometimes strange and queer, other times contra- dictory or conflictual, and on occasion, obvious and in agree- ment. Despite all possible converging relations, analogies and similitudes, art is not science and neither of these activities can replace the other. Likewise, experience is not metaphysics, and science is not theology: 'One understands that Christian philosophy seeks the origins of natural law in the will of God. Were it content with that, then one would be presented with a theory that is strictly theological. Remarkable, however, is that it wants to secure for itself the help of metaphysics and perhaps even of empiricism, which once more confirms the hypothesis that the form of apparently similar theories does not depend on their content but rather on the concepts that are favoured by the societies in which they prevail. Most people loathe the prospect of being content with theology alone, and in order to placate them, the support of metaphysics and experience is sought and brought to bear.'[12] Pareto demanded that each time a term is used in science, it should be defined in order to avoid such misunderstandings and false assertions. In other words, it is a question of seizing a phenomenon in the context of its determining factors, without reducing it to those of another reality, be it theological or economic. Besides, it is a matter of employing appropriate concepts and defined terms instead of vague and imprecise notions. On the other hand, practical action results from a choice, and as such is the consequence of an indecision. It follows from it that action needs the imprecision of words.

In Pareto's opinion, man's unity resides in man himself, in his nature and in each of his particular activities. One can- not find it either in economy, science or in religion, because despite their will to unify the other activities under their concepts, each of them is only an expression or manifestation. As such they cannot account for existence which is always something more than all these activities put together. Moreover, they are the signs of an existential reality which they are incapable of replacing. Unfortunately, hostile as he was towards metaphysics and philosophy, Pareto never thought of defining or even hinting at what he understood by existence, and remained content to suggest that human nature continues to be practically identical to itself through time. If at all, the human nature alters only slowly and imperceptibly. To put it more accurately, Pareto referred all human activities to a content of which they are its forms only: 'Under the most diverse appearances, a common content lies hidden...they are varied metamorphoses of one and the same thing.'[13]Or still: 'We cannot affect the content of a phenomenon, and all our efforts can at best slightly alter some of the forms.'[14] His analysis never went beyond the logical coherence of theories which account for those forms and which try to translate the content or to express it one way or another. Under this aspect, his philosophy may be regarded as a critique of discourse. Even so, Pareto narrowed the confines of his thinking quite drastically by his lack of interest in values and significations. He was content solely to appraise the validity of logical relations established by discourse in order to check whether they exceed experience, whether they conform to the original premises, or whether they introduce elements that are alien to them. Whence the multitude of quoted examples the purpose of which is to verify whether theories exceed experience, whether they are pseudo-scientific,whether the reasoning behind them is logical or non-logical. They are also evidence of his interest in chain-syllogism, the enthymeme and other kinds of reasoning inherent in perverted logic.

Pareto's theory of oscillations, which is a theory of change, expresses this relative permanence of human nature in time. Only forms are altered through oscillations, in the sense that once the curve reaches its peak, a contrariwise movement intervenes. Accordingly, old forms may even disappear for a long time, before reappearing in a different garb. History reflects this alternate movement which is rhythmic and not cyclical, or said differently, a movement that is far from regular since it implies discontinuities. That is why Pareto did not agree to the thesis defended by Ferrari in the latter's TEORIA DEI PERIODI POLITICI. The regularity of oscillations which Ferrari was claiming to have discovered in history exceeded the boundaries of empirical observation. 'His main fault,' Pareto wrote, 'which is common to other authors in similar cases, springs from his wish to submit facts to inflexible rules of an illusory precision.'[15] With regard to Vico, Pareto was harder on him in the TREATISE than in FATTI E TEORIE, or in TRANSFORMATION. In the first of these works, he simply rejected Vico's thesis on the ground of its 'metaphysics,' of its being no better than the imaginary theories of Plato's.[16] Later on, he grew wiser, and in the TRANSFORMATION conceded that it accounted for one aspect of reality only: 'In a general manner while examining the history of different lands and ages, one would come across periods that have been considered and equally named feudal by means of synecdoche, that is to say, by taking the part for the whole. One would notice that they developed and then declined, or in other words, that dynamic phenomena were involved, and more precisely, oscillations. That is what is true in Vico's theory about the "return" of fiefs; but he was mistaken in bestowing identical forms upon different oscillations, as well as in details for which he appealed to imagination and so took us beyond the experimental field.'[17] What made Pareto unconfortable in regard to Vico's theory was that the oscillation was too perfectly cyclical.[18]

Ultimately history does not repeat itself. It reflects the movement of forms which are variable, and consequently it expresses oscillations that are never identical to themselves in time. Not only they do not reappear regularly, but also each time they are dependent on the new conditions in which mankind finds itself. Moreover, the oscillations are only apparent: 'Let us examine the oscillations of the residues in the population as a whole; it follows that the oscillations in the intellectual part, made up of literati, philosophers, pseudo-scientists, and scientists, have only the value of indices, they do not mean anything in themselves. They must be accepted by the rest of the population before the oscillations may become indicators of sentiments.'[19] Thus this theory of oscillations should not be relied upon to forecast the future, which was what Vico had done. Besides, he had offered an imaginary construction of cyles rather than an approximation of facts.

In short, the undulatory theory is no more than a hypothesis apparently confirmed by a certain number of facts, though without the validity of a logical-experimental uniformity. Thus despite the analogies drawn between the contemporary age and that of the decadent Roman Empire, Pareto argued, the form which the new oscillation will assume cannot be forecast because of its dependence on the present moral and intellectual conditions which are different from those of the Roman Empire. 'History never repeats itself, and it is not at all probable, unless one believes in the "yellow menace," that the new period of prosperity would come out of another barbarian invasion. It is less unlikely that it would emerge from an internal revolution which would grant the power to individuals with a large stock of residues of the second class, who know how to, can, and will make use of force. Yet these distant and uncertain prospects belong to the realm of phantasy more than to that of the empirical science.'[20] There is no doubt that on this point Pareto's thinking was hesitant, and would be wrong to attribute his caution to a certain incoherence in his reasoning. Such speculations exceed the limits of experience, and he was the first to admit it, unlike those who present their convictions as facts. This undulatory theory may be taken for Pareto's philosophy of history, provided that one keeps in mind the fact that he never presented it as the truth-core of history but only as a hypothesis facilitating an additional approximation. At any rate, the explanation of change by means of intervals and oscillations is no less rational than that which has for premise a linear and continued progress.

Pareto did not accept the theory of the eternal return and of *ricorsi*, because in the light of his experience he grasped a slow and precarious ascent of minds towards reason. In fact, progress is possible to the extent the residues themselves are not absolutely unchangeable, but subject to the imperceptible alteration in time, though in different ways, according to different societies.[21] Pareto acknowledged it even more clearly when he stated in the already quoted text that there was some truth in the idea that the part played by reason was on the increase.[22] He insisted that it was corroborated by facts. Obviously this paragraph may be interpreted in the sense of a progressive rationalization of life, which does not necessarily imply an axiological progress.Pareto is not at all clear about the way he wanted to be understood on this point. That however is of little importance, because as soon as progress is possible one can no longer accept the idea of the eternal return, which allows for progress only between cycles, since the moment the peak is attained, mankind relapses to its beginnings. It is also correct to say that Pareto refused to express any opinion of progress only because he found the notion equivocal, which does not mean that he denied any kind of progress.[23] He was particularly concerned not to be taken for one of the high priests of the god Progress. Whatever his intentions, he conceded that mankind has a chance to develop in the direction of greater rationality, but that it is a precarious chance, because indeterminate, despite the declarations to the contrary made by the humanitarians. Belief may lead to a certain subjective attitude, but it has nothing in common with the objective and verifiable truth. It would simply be convenient not to spoil the fragile chance with the fraudulent claims made by the progressives.

It is this chance that Pareto wanted to preserve. The supporters of ideological rationalism do not understand that. They run the risk of throwing mankind into terror by not acquiescing in the part played by the irrational. The latter is part of the human nature, made up as it is of instinct and reason. Man remains an animal. By ignoring or underestimating this fact, they leave everything open to violence. They even prepare that violence. In fact, force, which is reason and equilibrium, cannot but give in before the arbitrariness and the savagery of that kind of violence which, if need be, would assume the looks of rationality. This is in my opinion what Pareto was afraid of: reason at its highest becomes confused with the unleashed instinct. Supreme rationality is a call to arms addressed to the barbarians. More than that: Pareto rejected the utopias for the best of worlds, because human history, the history of mankind as lived until now by the various peoples would be but a parody and a fraud if it were to be believed that the human being could be thoroughly changed and that as a result would cease to be what he has always been, as soon as he gains access to a social system (or a counter-society, to use a more recent term) in which justice, peace, freedom, equality and well-being reign at last in a harmony that would identify all these notions. If utopia were true, society as given to us would be but an aberation and the violence which wants to change it would have every right to act. But who is to consider historical society perverse? The utopians, in other words, the high priests of progress and reason. Let us suppose that they were right. All the generations which did not experience the glorious moment of the new society would be damned generations. We the living and those who lived before us become the accursed of the earth. Hell would be a reality, it would be the whole history of mankind until the utopian's second coming. Pareto had neither that heart nor that temperament which would have made him regard himself as damned. He believed in a life fraught with possibilities. Likewise, he was incapable of accepting to become the slave of one possibility alone. Freedom which would be identical for everybody would be the freedom of a tyrannical society.'It was not long ago that in several countries the law would punish the author who by his writings would prejudice the principle of individual property. It is possible that in the same countries, in a near future, the law would punish the author who would be as defiant as to speak ill of collective property. Nowadays one may talk of both freely.'[24] In the name of various ideologies and of all sorts of derivations, there are people who still claim that Pareto lacked in foresight. Is utopia not a derivation, too?

About private property, he said that its survival is due to the continuous onslaughts it is subject to.[25] I suspect that this observation may be extended to his concept of freedom and even to everything that the human being finds worth fighting for. Basically the utopias and the rationalism of progress would force man to betray man. Considering all the shortcomings imputed to Pareto, one should admit in spite of it all to a clear-sightedness that was his: 'In general, people desire freedom and fear constraint. The former term is associated with pleasant images, the latter with unpleasant ones. In order to make people accept constraint, it would be practical to call it freedom.'[26] All modern dictatorships claim to free the human being. Nowadays slavery is voluntary.

NOTES

CHAPTER ONE

1.   See in particular Talcott Parsons' book, THE STRUCTURE OF SOCIAL ACTION. A STUDY IN SOCIAL THEORY WITH SPECIAL REFERENCE TO A GROUP OF RECENT EUROPEAN WRITERS, Part II, chapters 5, 6 and 7. New York: McGraw Hill Book Co., 1937.

2.   Originally published in Italian in 1916 as TRATTATO DI SOCIOLOGIA GENERALE by G. Barbera of Florence. The American edition bears the double title of MIND AND SOCIETY. A TREATISE ON GENERAL SOCIOLOGY. For more details see the Select Bibliography. Like all the titles of Pareto's book-form writings mentioned in this study, it will be used in the shortened version, i. e., the TREATISE.

3.   His first substantial effort to introduce Pareto to the French public, the short study, VILFREDO PARETO, SA VIE ET SONT OEUVRE, published by Payot of Paris five years after Pareto's death, was translated into English and published by the Sociological Press of Minneapolis in the same year, under the title THE WORK OF VILFREDO PARETO.

4.   'La Sociologie de Pareto' in ZEITSCHRIFT FÜR SOZIALFOR-SCHUNG, Vol. VI, 1937, No.3, pp. 489-521.

5. Gurvitch, Georges, ÉTUDES SUR LES CLASSES SOCIALES, Paris: Éditions Gonthier, 1966, p. 137.

6.   Perrin, Guy, SOCIOLOGIE DE PARETO, Paris: Presses Univer-sitaires de France, 1966.

7.   It was published by Payot of Paris in 1925. However, it was another compendium, in Italian, edited by Giulio Farina and published in 1920 by G. Barbera of Florence that was translated into English and published by the University of Minnesota Press. For more details see the Select Bibliography.

8.   The complete original title is TRASFORMAZIONE DELLA DEMO-CRATIA. It is a collection of articles firstly printed in RIVISTA DI MILANO, in the Spring and Summer of 1921, and published in book-form by Corbaccio of Milan later in the same year. For the American edition see the Select Bibliography.

The references in this study relate to the French version, published as Volume XIII of OEUVRES COMPLÈTES DE VILFREDO PARETO, edited by Giovanni Busino, and published by Droz of Geneva in 1970.

9. Originally published in French as LE MYTHE VERTUISTE ET LA LITTÉRATURE IMMORALE. ÉTUDES SUR LE DEVENIR SOCIAL, under the imprint of V.M. Rivière of Paris in 1911. Another edition was published in 1914. References here relate to the 1971 edition, published as Vol.XV of OEUVRES COMPLÈTES.

10. Gurvitch, Georges, LE CONCEPT DE CLASSES SOCIALES DE MARX À NOS JOURS, Paris: Centre de Documentation Universitaire, 1954, p. 72.

11. The issue of July 1923, pp. 1059-1063. For a sample of the way Pareto approached the phenomenon of Fascism in Italy the reader is also referred to the Appendix C at the end of the present book.

12. Aron, Raymond, 'Préface' to a new reprint of the French version of the TREATISE, published by Droz of Geneva and Paris in 1968, p. IX.

13. TRANSFORMATION, p. 6.

14. TREATISE, § 69.

15. Ibid., § 73.

16. Ibid., § 1081.

17. Quoted by Giovanni Busino in his INTRODUCTION À UNE HIS-TOIRE DE LA SOCIOLOGIE DE PARETO, Geneva-Paris: Droz, 1968, p. 13.

18. Quoted by Busino, op. cit., pp. 6-9.

19. See Pareto, Vilfredo, LIBRE-ÉCHANGISME, PROTECTIONISME ET SOCIALISME, published as Vol. IV of OEUVRES COMPLÈTES, Geneva: Droz, 1965, p. 15.

20. Ibid., p. 49.

21. Ibid., p. 82.

22. Ibid., p. 225.

23. The former was published as Vol. VI of Pareto's OEUVRES COMPLÈTES by Droz of Geneva in 1966. The latter was brought out by UTET of Turin in the same year.

24. Quoted by Busino, op. cit., p. 42.

25. Pareto, MYTHE VERTUISTE, loc. cit., p. 23.

CHAPTER TWO

1. Originally published in Italian under the title MANUALE D'ECONOMIA POLITICA by the Società Editrice Libraria in Milan, in 1907. For the American edition see the Select Bibliography.

2. The whole title is COURS D'ÉCONOMIE POLITIQUE PROFESSÉ À L'UNIVERSITÉ DE LAUSANNE. It was first published in its original French version in two volumes by F. Rouge of Lausanne and Pichon of Paris, between 1896 and 1897. No translation in English is available. The edition referred to in the present study is that published as Vol. 1 of Pareto's OEUVRES COMPLÈTES in 1964.

3. Published in the original French in two volumes by Giard & Brière of Paris in 1902. So far no English translation is available. The edition referred to here is that reprinted as Vol. V of Pareto's OEUVRES COMPLÈTES in 1965.

4. Perroux, François. L'ÉCONOMIE DU XXe SIÈCLE, 3rd ed., Paris: Presses Universitaires de France, 1971, p. 7.

5. Quoted by Busino in his introductory note to the COURS, loc. cit., p. xxv.

6. Quoted by Busino in his INTRODUCTION À UNE HISTOIRE, loc. cit., p. 27.

7. 'As rational mechanics are concerned with material points, so pure economics take into consideration *homo oeconomicus.*' (MANUAL, ch. 1, § 21.)

8. COURS, § 3.

9. Ibid., § 5.

10. Ibid., § 18.

11. Ibid., § 1.

12. Pareto, MARXISME ET ÉCONOMIE PURE, Geneva: Droz, 1966, pp. 107 and 109. It was published as Vol. IX of OEUVRES COMPLÈTES.

13. Ibid., p. 168.

14. Ibid., p. 127.

15. Ibid., p. 116.

16. Ibid., p. 17.

17. Ibid., p. 1.

18. Ibid., p. 164.

19. Ibid., p. 164.

20. Ibid., p. 166.

21. Ibid., p. 28.

22. Ibid., p. 4. See also MANUAL, ch. 3, § 3.

23. MARXISME, loc. cit., p. 2.

24. COURS, § 605.

25. Ibid., § 608.

26. MANUAL, ch. 3, § 22.

27. MARXISME, p. 167.

28. Ibid., p. 72.

29. Perrin, op. cit., pp. 28-30, 136-137, 179.

30. See in particular MARXISME, p. 109.

31. COURS, § 949.

32. Perroux, op. cit., p. 8.

33. Ibid., pp. 342 and 346.

34. MANUAL, ch. 3, § 14.

35. Ibid., ch. 3, § 3.

36. COURS, § 592.

37. See the long footnote to § 592 of the COURS.

38. Ibid., § 609.

39. Ibid., § 620.

40. Ibid., § 692.

41. Sorokin, Pitirim, 'Le Concept d'équilibre est-ilnécéssaire aux sciences sociales?' in REVUE INTERNATIONALE DE SOCIOLOGIE, Year 39 (1936), pp. 509 and 524, note 1.

42. TREATISE, § 2073

43. Pareto offered his own clarifications on the validity of interpolations in statistics in his STATISTIQUE ET ÉCONOMIE MATHÉMATIQUE, reprinted as Vol. VIII of his OEUVRES COMPLÈTES in 1966. See in particular pp.76ff.

44. The original paper is included in Vol.III of OEUVRES COMPLÈTES, published in 1965 under the general title of ÉCRITS SUR LA COURBE DE LA RÉPARTITION DE LA RICHESSE.

45. Davis, Harold Thayer, POLITICAL STATISTICS, Evanston, Il.: Principa Press, 1954.

46. Hayakawa, Miyoyi, 'The Application of Pareto's Law of Income to Japanese Data' in ECONOMETRICA, Vol. 19, No. 2, April 1951, pp. 174-183.

47. MYTHES ET IDÉOLOGIES DE LA POLITIQUE, a collection of articles by Pareto, published as Vol. VI of OEUVRES COMPLÈTES in 1966, pp. 141-142.

48. COURS, vol. 2, p. 408.

49. Ibid., § 957.

50. Ibid., § 957.

51. Ibid., § 1068.

52. SYSTÈMES, vol. 1, p. 125.

53. Perrin, op. cit., pp. 31, 41, and 63.

54. JUBILÉ PARETO, 1917, with a preface by J.C. Biaudet, reprinted as Vol. XX of OEUVRES COMPLÈTES in 1975, pp. 67, and 69-70. For the original text of Pareto's speech see also pp. 291-299 in the monograph by Homans and Curtis, listed in the Select Bibliography.

55. It was reprinted as Vol. XI of OEUVRES COMPLÈTES in 1967.

That volume also includes fragments of Pareto's diary for part of the year 1918, known as MON JOURNAL.

56. MANUAL, ch. 1, §1.

57. Ibid., ch. 2, §108.

58. TREATISE, §2013.

59. Ibid., §2011.

60. MANUAL, ch. 1, § 26.

61. TREATISE, §2079.

62. See in particular MANUAL, ch. 3, §§ 1-14.

63. TREATISE, § 69.

64. MANUAL, ch. 1, § 35.

65. Ibid., ch. 2, § 1.

66. Perrin, op. cit., p. 63.

67. TREATISE, §2219.

<h2 style="text-align:center">CHAPTER THREE</h2>

1.   See respectively Croce, Benedetto, 'Trattato di sociologia di Vilfredo Pareto' in CRITICA, Vol. 22 (1924), pp. 172-173. Aron's article quoted above in note 4, Chapter One. Halbwachs, Maurice, 'Le Traité de sociologie générale de M. Vilfredo Pareto' in REVUE D'ÉCONOMIE POLITIQUE, Year 32 (1918), pp.578-585, and finally Bousquest, G.-H., PRÉCIS DE SOCIOLOGIE D'APRÈS VILFREDO PARETO, 2nd ed., Paris: Dalloz, 1971, p. 9.

2. SYSTÈMES, vol. 1, p. 2.

3. The full title is INTRODUCTION À L'ÉTUDE DE LA MÉDICINE EXPÉRIMENTALE, first published in Paris by Baillière in 1865. An American edition was published in 1927 by Macmillan of New York, with an introduction by Lawrence J. Henderson who eight years later was to publish his own study of Pareto's general sociology.

4.   JUBILÉ PARETO, 1917, loc. cit., pp. 65-66.

5. TREATISE, § 81.

6. Quoted by Busino, op. cit., p. 73.

7. TREATISE, §73.

8. SYSTÈMES, vol. 1, p. 2.

9. Ibid., vol. 1, p. 3.

10. Pareto, Vilfredo, LETTERE A MAFFEO PANTALEONI, Gabriele de Rosa ed., Rome: Banca Nazionale del Lavoro, 1960, vol. 1, p. 428.

11. TREATISE, §106.

12. MYTHES ET IDÉOLOGIES, p. 240.

13. MANUAL, ch. 1, §32.

14. TREATISE, § 80n.

15. MANUAL, ch. 1, §1.

16. TREATISE, § 46.

17. MANUAL, ch. 1, § 9.

18. TREATISE, § 44.

19. Bousquet, PRÉCIS, loc. cit., p. 31.

20. Quoted by Busino, op. cit., p. 144.

21. Quoted by Busino, op. cit., p. 42.

22. Schumpeter, Joseph, CAPITALISM, SOCIALISM AND DEMOCRACY, 3rd ed., New York: Harper Torchbooks, 1962, pp. 256-259.

23. Aron, Raymond, MAIN CURRENTS IN SOCIOLOGICAL THOUGHT, Garden City: Doubleday Anchor Books, 1970, vol. 1, pp. 132-133.

24. Busino, op. cit., p. 54.

25. TREATISE, § 148.

26. MYTHES ET IDÉOLOGIES, pp. 113-114.

27. 'In the abstract, we may distinguish between: 1. the non-logical actions and 2. the logical actions. We say "in the abstract," because in the case of concrete actions the two types always merge, and so an action may be non-logical to a

greater extent and logical to a lesser extent, or the other way round.' (MANUAL, ch. 2,§ 3.)

28. TREATISE, §150.

29. In any case, the affinity between the logical-experimental method and the logical experimental action was the transition point from the preoccupation with economics to the reflection on social action and sociology. Pareto's article entitled 'Comment se pose le problème de l'économie pure?' is relevant to this matter. It has been included in MARXISME ET ÉCONOMIE PURE, loc. cit., pp. 102ff.

30. TREATISE, §161.

31.   MANUAL., ch. 2,§ 3.

32.   This is not to say that he sang the praises of the irrational because in the same way as the logical cannot be confused with the rational, the non-logical is not the equivalent of the irrational. More exactly, Pareto did not think in the terms provided by Max Weber's or Schumpeter's categories of the rational and the irrational.

33. SYSTÈMES, vol. 1, p. 5. See also MYTHES ET IDÉOLOGIES, pp. 263-264.

34. TREATISE, §154.

35. Ibid., §155.

36. See Aron's preface to the French reprint of the TREATISE, loc. cit., pp. xiv-xv, and his MAIN CURRENTS, loc. cit., vol. 2, p. 122.

37. SYSTÈMES, vol. 1, p. 25.

38. Ibid., vol. 1, p. 27.

39. Ibid., vol. 1, p. 21.

40. Ibid., vol. 1, p. 26.

41. TREATISE, §798.

42. Ibid., §818.

43. Ibid. §§ 850 and 851.

44. Ibid., § 875.

45. Ibid., § 852.

46. Ibid., § 870.

47. Ibid., § 879.

48. Ibid., § 883. See also § 158.

49. Aron, MAIN CURRENTS, loc. cit., pp. 165-166.

50. TREATISE, § 889. See also § 896.

51. Ibid., § 910. One recognizes here the student of John Stuart Mill.

52. Ibid., § 967.

53. Ibid., § 991.

54. Ibid., § 992.

55. Ibid., § 1066.

56. Ibid., § 1071.

57. Ibid., § 1077.

58. Ibid., § 1089.

59. Ibid., § 1133.

60. Ibid., § 1134.

61. Ibid., § 1144.

62. Ibid., § 1146.

63. Ibid., § 1152.

64. Ibid., § 1153.

65. Ibid., § 1156.

66. Ibid., § 1160.

67. Ibid., § 1166.

68. Ibid., § 1167.

69. Ibid., § 1206.

70. Ibid., § 1207.

71. Ibid., § 1207.

72. Ibid., § 1211.

73. Ibid., § 1227.

74. Ibid., § 1312.

75. Ibid., § 1388.

76. Ibid., § 995.

77. Aron, op. cit., p. 158.

78. TREATISE, § 1397.

79. Ibid., § 1431.

80. Ibid., § 1401.

81. Ibid., § 1400.

82. Ibid., § 1401.

83. Ibid., § 1415.

84. MYTHES ET IDÉOLOGIES, p. 310.

85. TREATISE, § 1450.

86. Ibid., § 1454. See also §2410.

87. Ibid., § 1402.

88. Ibid., § 1411.

89. Ibid., § 1420.

90. Ibid., § 1425.

91. Ibid., § 1426.

92. Ibid., § 1464.

93. Ibid., § 1479.

94. Ibid., § 1498.

95. Ibid., § 1543.

96. Ibid., § 1786.

97. Ibid., § 1759.

98. Ibid., §1859.

99. Ibid., §1722.

100. Ibid., §1690.

101. Ibid., §1702.

102. Ibid., §1698.

103. Ibid., §1712.

104. Ibid., §1727.

105. Ibid., §1732.

106. Ibid., §1732.

107. Ibid., §1735.

108. Ibid., §1746.

109. Ibid., §1747.

110. Ibid., §1748.

111. Ibid., §1750.

112. Ibid., §1768.

113. Ibid., §§1769 and 1771.

114. Ibid., §2079. See also §2219.

115. Ibid., §2073.

116. Ibid., §2066.

117. Ibid., §2067.

118. 'The social order is never in a state of perfect rest; rather it is in a state of perpetual transformation; the movement however may be slower or faster.' (TRANSFORMATION, p. 5.)

119. TREATISE, §1218.

120. MANUAL, ch. 2, §102.

121. Ibid., ch. 2, §102. Pareto also posed the problem of social heterogeneity in the COURS (§654). There, however, he gave it the Spencerian meaning of the transition from an

indeterminate homogeneity to a coherent heterogeneity.

122. TREATISE, §2060.

123. Sorokin, Pitirim, CONTEMPORARY SOCIOLOGICAL THEORIES, New York: Harper & Brothers, 1928, ch. 1, p. 61.

124. Perrin, op. cit., p. 39.

125. See TRANSFORMATION, loc. cit., p. 4.

126. TREATISE, §875.

127. MYTHES ET IDÉOLOGIES, p. 222.

128. TREATISE, §2250.

129. Ibid., §851.

130. Ibid., §2009.

131. Ibid., §1207.

132. Ibid., §2146.

133. MANUAL, ch. 2, §108.

134. TRANSFORMATION, p. 7.

135. TREATISE, §2115.

136. Ibid., §2131.

137. Ibid., §2110.

138. Ibid., §§2126 and 2127.

139. Ibid., §2137.

140. SYSTÈMES, vol. 1, p. 71.

141. TREATISE, §2143.

142. Ibid., §2393.

143. COURS, §927.

144. MANUAL, ch. 9, §75.

145. SYSTÈMES, vol. 1, p. 30.

146. TREATISE, §2329.

147. TRANSFORMATION, p. 6.

148. TREATISE, § 2338.

149. Ibid., § 2322.

150. TRANSFORMATION, p. 15.

151. COURS, § 152.

152. TREATISE, § 2079.

153. MANUAL, ch. 2, § 79.

154. TREATISE, § §2171 and 2172.

155. Ibid., § 2173.

156. MANUAL, ch. 2, § 83.

157. This paper was reprinted in MYTHES ET IDÉOLOGIES, pp. 259-265. An English translation appears as Appendix A to this present study.

158. Ibid., p. 259.

159. Ibid., p. 259.

160. Ibid., p. 260.

161. SYSTÈMES, vol. 1, pp. 80-81.

CHAPTER FOUR

1.   TRANSFORMATION, pp. 6-7.

2.   Ibid., p. 8.

3.   Ibid., p. 10.

4.   Ibid., pp. 12-13.

5.   See note 55, Chapter Two.

6.   TREATISE, § 2047.

7.   MANUAL, ch. 7, § 97.

8.   Ibid., ch. 7, § 103.

9.   SYSTÈMES, vol. 1, pp. 7-8.

10. Ibid., vol. 1, p. 56. TREATISE, § 2033, and MANUAL, ch. 2, § 102.

11.   SYSTÈMES, vol. 2, p. 423.

12.   Ibid., vol. 1, p. 9.

13.   TREATISE, §2301.

14.   MANUAL, ch. 7, §98.

15.   TREATISE, §2041.

16.   See SYSTEMÈS, vol. 1, pp. 41-51.

17.   MYTHES ET IDÉOLOGIES, pp. 271-272. See also TREATISE, §2048 and MANUAL, ch. 7, §§104-108.

18.   SYSTÈMES, vol. 1, p. 55.

19.   Ibid., vol. 1, p. 37.

20.   Ibid., vol. 1, p. 40.

21.   Ibid., vol. 1, p. 73.

22.   TREATISE, §2053.

23.   Ibid., §2032.

24.   Ibid., §2268.

25.   Ibid., §2268.

26.   Ibid., §2254.

27.   Ibid., §2235.

28.   MYTHES ET IDÉOLOGIES, pp. 273-274.

29.   TREATISE, §2313.

30.   Ibid., §2235.

31.   MYTHES ET IDÉOLOGIES, p. 275.

32.   TREATISE, §2257.

33.   Ibid., §2262.

34.   SYSTÈMES, vol. 1, p. 58.

35.   Ibid., vol. 1, pp. 60-61.

36.   COURS, §1051.

37.   SYSTÈMES, vol. 1, pp. 148-149.

38. TREATISE, § 2231.

39. Ibid., § 2025.

40. SYSTÈMES, vol. 1, p. 71.

41. Ibid., vol. 1, p. 134.

42. Ibid., vol. 1, pp. 117-118.

43. Ibid., vol. 2, p. 396.

44. Ibid., vol. 2, pp. 454-455.

45. Ibid., vol. 1, p. 39.

46. TREATISE, § 2183.

47. Ibid., § 2174.

48. SYSTÈMES, vol. 1, p. 38.

49. Ibid., vol. 1, p. 54n.

50. TREATISE, § 2180.

51. Ibid., §§ 2179 and 2178.

52. SYSTÈMES, vol. 2, p. 437.

53. TREATISE, § 2176.

54. Ibid., § 2185.

55. Ibid., § 2177.

56. SYSTÈMES, vol. 1, p. 37. See also vol. 2, p. 412.

57. MANUAL, ch. 2, § 107.

58. TREATISE, § 2181.

59. Ibid., § 2194.

60. SYSTÈMES, vol. 2, p. 399.

61. TREATISE, § 2189.

62. Ibid., § 2251.

63. Ibid., § 2244.

64. Ibid., § 2246.

65. Ibid., § 2178.

66. Ibid., § 2179.

67. Ibid., § 2190.

68. See ibid., § 2455 for the combination of the residues of the first and the second classes.

69. SYSTÈMES, vol. 1, p. 86.

70. Ibid., vol. 1, p. 27.

71. Ibid., vol.1, p. 93.

72. Ibid., vol. 1, p. 83.

73. Busino's preface to the French version of the TRANSFORMA-TION, loc. cit., p. IX.

74. SYSTÈMES, vol. 1, p. 71.

75. TRANSFORMATION, p. 36.

76. Ibid., p. 74. See also MON JOURNAL, loc. cit., p. 32.

77. SYSTÈMES, vol. 1, p. 119.

78. Ibid., vol. 1, p. 116.

79. Ibid., vol. 1, p. 132.

80. Ibid., vol. 1, p. 318.

81. Ibid., vol. 2, pp. 401-402.

82. MYTHES ET IDÉOLOGIES, p. 158.

83. Ibid., p. 117.

84. Ibid., p. 117.

85. MON JOURNAL, p. 42.

86. Ibid., p. 63.

87. MYTHES ET IDÉOLOGIES, p. 292.

88. MON JOURNAL, p. 33.

89. TREATISE, § 2454.

90. MYTHES ET IDÉOLOGIES, p. 142.

91.   TREATISE, § 2239.

92.   SYSTÈMES, vol. 2, p. 215.

93.   TREATISE, § 2390.

94.   Ibid., § 2553. See also TRANSFORMATION, p. 95.

95.   TREATISE, § 2612.

CHAPTER FIVE

1.   TREATISE, § 64.

2.   Perrin, op. cit., pp. 170 and 211.

3.   In Gerth, H.H. and C. Wright Mills, eds., FROM MAX WEBER, New York: Oxford University Press, 1972, p. 148.

4.   Ibid., p. 122.

5.   TREATISE, § 249.

6.   Ibid., § 1682.

7.   Ibid., § 219.

8.   Gerth and Mills, op. cit., p. 148.

9.   MON JOURNAL, p. 82.

10.   TREATISE, §§ 1891 and 1081.

11.   SYSTÈMES, vol. 1, p. 66.

12.   TREATISE, § 454.

13.   SYSTÈMES, vol. 1, p. 138.

14.   Ibid., vol. 2, p. 456.

15.   TREATISE, § 2330.

16.   Ibid., § 2330.

17.   TRANSFORMATION, p. 22.

18.   Pareto, Vilfredo, FATTI E TEORIE, Florence: Vallechi, 1920, p. 225. Meanwhile a French translation of the same work has been published as Vol. XXI of OEUVRES COMPLÈTES. No English translation is yet available.

19.   TREATISE, § 2344.

20.   Ibid., §2553.

21.   Ibid., § 1720.

22.   Ibid., § 2393.

23.   RIVISTA ITALIANA DI SOCIOLOGIA, Year XIV, May-August 1910, pp. 340 and 350.

24.   SYSTÈMES, vol. 1, p. 296.

25.   MYTHES ET IDÉOLOGIES, p. 316.

26.   SYSTÈMES. vol. 1, p. 319.

SELECT BIBLIOGRAPHY

1. PARETO'S WORKS, AS WELL AS SELECTIONS AND COMPENDIA

COMPENDIUM OF GENERAL SOCIOLOGY, trans. by Giulio Farina and Elizabeth Abbot, Minneapolis: University of Minnesota Press, 1980.

MANUAL OF POLITICAL ECONOMY, trans. by Ann Schweir and ed. by Ann Schweir and Alfred N. Page, New York: A.M. Kelley, 1971, c. 1969.

MIND AND SOCIETY: A TREATISE ON GENERAL SOCIOLOGY, trans. by Andrew Bongiorno and Arthur Livingston; ed. by Arthur Livingston, 4 vols., New York: AMS Press, 1983, c. 1935.

OEUVRES COMPLÈTES DE VILFREDO PARETO, publiées sous la direction de Giovanni Busino, 29 vols. so far. Geneva: Droz, 1964-1987. (For individual volumes see the NOTES.)

THE RISE AND FALL OF THE ÉLITES: AN APPLICATION OF THEORETICAL SOCIOLOGY, ed. by Lewis Coser and Walter W. Powel, New York: Arno Press, 1979, c. 1968.

THE RULING CLASS IN ITALY BEFORE 1900, ed. by S.F. Vanni, New York: H. Fertig, 1974, c. 1950.

THE TRANSFORMATION OF DEMOCRACY, trans. by Renata Girola and ed. by C. Powers, New Brunswick: Transaction Books, 1984.

THE OTHER PARETO, ed. by Placido Bucolo, trans. by Placido and Gillian Bucolo, New York: St. Martin's Press, 1980.

PARETO AND MOSCA, ed. by James Hans Meisel, Englewood Cliffs, N.J.: Prentice-Hall, 1965.

VILFREDO PARETO: SELECTIONS FROM HIS TREATISE, with an introductory essay by Joseph Lopreato, New York: Thomas Crowell, 1965.

SOCIOLOGICAL WRITINGS, ed. by S.E. Finer, New York: Praeger, 1976, c. 1966.

2. WRITINGS ABOUT PARETO'S WORKS

Alexander, Franz, OUR AGE OF UNREASON, Chicago: Lippincot,

1942.

Aron, Raymond, 'La signification de l'oeuvre de Pareto,'
   in CAHIERS VILFREDO PARETO, vol. I, 1963, pp.7-26.

Berger, Brigitte M., VILFREDO PARETO'S SOCIOLOGY AS A CONTRI-
   BUTION TO THE SOCIOLOGY OF KNOWLEDGE, New York: New School
   for Social Research, Graduate Faculty, 1964. Unpublished PhD
   dissertation.

Bobbio, Norberto, ON PARETO AND MOSCA, trans. by Giulio Pie-
   tranera, Geneva: Droz, 1972.

Borkenau, Franz, PARETO, Westport, CT.: Hyperion Press, 1979,
   c. 1936.

Bottomore, T.B., ÉLITES AND SOCIETY, London: Watts & Co.,1964.

Bousquet, G.-H., PARETO, LE SAVANT ET L'HOMME, Lausanne:
   Payot, 1960.

Brinton, Crane, 'The Future in Retrospect, the Residue of
   Pareto,' in FOREIGN AFFAIRS, vol. XXXII, No. 4, July 1954,
   pp. 640-650.

Burnham, James, THE MACHIAVELLIANS, DEFENDERS OF FREEDOM,
   Chicago: Henry Regnery, 1970, c. 1943.

Chipham, John S., THE PARETIAN HERITAGE, Stanford: Center for
   Advanced Studies, 1973. Unpublished.

Cirillo, Renato, THE ECONOMICS OF VILFREDO PARETO, Totowa,
   N.J.: Cass, 1979.

Ginsberg, Morris, REASON AND UNREASON IN SOCIETY, London:
   Longmans, Green & Co., 1947.

Handman, M.S., 'The Sociological Method of V. Pareto,' in
   METHODS IN SOCIAL SCIENCES, ed. by Stuart Arthur Rice,
   Chicago: University of Chicago Press, 1931.

Hecker, Andrew, 'The Use and Abuse of Pareto in Industrial
   Sociology,' in AMERICAN JOURNAL OF ECONOMICS AND SOCIOLOGY,
   vol. XIV, No. 4, 1955, pp. 321-333.

Henderson, Lawrence J., PARETO'S GENERAL SOCIOLOGY, A PHYSIOL-
   OGIST'S INTERPRETATION, New York: Russel & Russel, 1967,

c. 1935.

Homans, George Caspar and Charles Pelham Curtis Jr., AN INTRO-
    DUCTION TO PARETO, HIS SOCIOLOGY, New York: H. Fertig, 1970,
    c. 1934.

Hughes, Henry Stuart, CONSCIOUSNESS AND SOCIETY: THE REORIEN-
    TATION OF EUROPEAN SOCIAL THOUGHT 1890-1930, New York:
    Octagon Books, 1976, c. 1958.

Keller, Suzanne, BEYOND THE RULING CLASS: STRATEGIC ÉLITES IN
    MODERN SOCIETY, New York: Random House, 1963.

Madge, Charles, SOCIETY IN THE MIND, New York: Free Press of
    Glengoe, 1964.

Meisel, James H., THE MYTH OF THE RULING CLASS; GAETANO MOSCA
    AND THE 'ÉLITE', Westport, CT.: Greenwood Press, 1980, c.
    1958.

Millikan, Max, 'Pareto's Sociology,' in ECONOMETRICA, vol.
IV, No. 1, December 1936, pp. 323-337.

Piepe, Anthony, KNOWLEDGE AND SOCIAL ORDER, London: Heinemann,
    1971.

Samuels, Warren P., PARETO ON POLICY, Amsterdam and New York:
    Elsevier, 1974.

Schumpeter, Joseph A., TEN GREAT ECONOMISTS: FROM MARX TO
    KEYNES, New York: Oxford University Press, 1965, c. 1949.

Stark, Werner, 'In Search of True Pareto,' in BRITISH JOURNAL
    OF SOCIOLOGY, vol. XIV, No. 2, June 1963, pp. 103-112.

Tarascio, Vincent Joseph, PARETO'S METHODOLOGICAL APPROACH TO
    ECONOMICS, Chapel Hill: University of North Carolina Press,
    1968.

INDEX

APPENDICES

APPENDIX A

THE INDIVIDUAL AND THE SOCIAL

The meaning of each of these terms seems obvious; yet, a little reflection suffices to make one realize that they lack in precision, at least in certain cases. There is nothing exceptional about it, because this imprecision may be found in most of the vocabulary of the social sciences. More often than not, this terminology corresponds to the sentiments which it evokes rather than to objective realities. Whence the need of a twofold inquiry whenever the terms used by these sciences are concerned. On the one hand, one should find out to what objective realities they might correspond, and on the other, one should identify those sentiments which they serve to convey.

The term 'individual' is precise; it serves to indicate living beings considered in isolation. The term 'society' is rather vague: generally it designates an aggregate of these individuals taken together; yet additional conditions need to be known. First of all, the scope of the aggregate in space; it is seldom that by 'society' it is meant the ensemble of all the living human beings extant on earth at a given moment; rather one is more likely to mean the ensemble of human beings constituting a given political State, but without saying it in so many words. Then one must become aware of the extension in time; it is necessary to make clear whether one is talking about the ensemble of human beings extant at a given moment, or of those who existed, exist, or will exist in a determined interval of time.

The adjectives 'individual' and 'social' are vaguer still than the corresponding nouns. It may be said that since man lives in society, all his characteristic features are individual from a particular point of view, whereas from another, that they are all social. After all, there is no sure means by which to separate one type of features from the other. Whenever one thinks oneself capable of achieving this separation, one allows oneself to be guided by considerations of an order that is altogether different.

It is a trivial though often repeated remark to say that society is not a simple juxtaposition of individuals and that the latter acquire new features merely by living in society. Were we able to observe isolated individuals as well as individuals living in society, then we would have got the means of knowing in what lies the difference between them, and been capable of separating the individual from the social. However, we lack the first term of this comparison altogether, and it is only the second term that alone is known to us.

From the standpoint of the sentiments which they arouse, the terms 'individual' and 'social' very often mark an opposition between two parts of the aggregate; the former allegedly being made up of individuals while the latter is identified with 'society.' The modern trend is to see society itself in a certain majority or pseudo-majority, represented in a specific manner. The opposition between the individual and the social then becomes the opposition between a certain minority and a particular representation of a more or less real majority.

Whenever the term 'society' is applied to people living in a given space at a given time, the opposition between all the individuals who form that society, on the one hand, and that society itself, on the other, is an impossibility. Nevertheless, if the term 'society' is extended in time in order to designate those individuals, too, who are still to be born, then under this aspect, an opposition of interests may emerge between all the individuals living in a particular period of time, on the one side, and the individuals to come, on the other.

Any animal species may prosper, meaning by this statement that the number of individuals belonging to that species increases and their living space expands in two, quite different, ways. They may register a low birth-rate and an even lower death-rate; or they may show a very high mortality rate and an even higher natality rate. Indeed, this latter alternative is obviously less favourable than the former to the individuals living in a certain given interval of time. It is owing to the second alternative that several kinds of insects emerge victorious in their struggle against man, and with them in mind, one could say that often enough the individual is sacrificed for the sake of the species. Likewise, in the case of the human race, there are things in regard to which the interests of the present generations are in agreement with those of the future generations, and others, the related interests of which are in opposition. In this sense, one may come across conflicts between the interests of individuals living at a certain moment in time and those of society in general.

If one assumes the first meaning given to the term 'society' then the possibility is not excluded of an opposition between the interests of one part of this society and those of another part. This would occur ordinarily; the individuals making up a society have some interests in common and others that are in conflict.

Let us suppose, for instance, that a given society owns a specific amount of wealth distributed in a particular way. Likewise that the principle of distribution does not change while the total wealth increases. In that case each individual would receive more than before, and all of them would be interested in the augmentation of total wealth. However, as soon as the rule of distribution changes, two different phenomena may occur: 1. each individual will receive more than he had in the past; this alternative resembles the preceding, and so all the individuals will be interested in the presupposed increase of overall wealth; 2. some receive more, and the others less than they had in the past. In this case, there is obviously an opposition of interests relative to the growth in total wealth.

Not only is wealth far from being the only interest which people might have, but even if we consider wealth alone, the absolute sum in the possession of each individual does not represent all his interests; one must take into consideration the relative importance of the wealth owned by each individual. Thus an opposition of interests may obtain even when each individual, who is part of society, sees his wealth grow. On being granted a minimal percentage of the growth, some individuals might prefer to forgo it, provided others, too, are deprived of the considerable proportion of the growth in wealth which they would receive in turn.

By and large those people who make up a society have certain interests that are in conflict. It is a true fact whatever its causes; the slightest observation suffices to make one aware of it. It is only whenever sentiment pushes us to take our desires for the real thing that we can deny this fact.

It is assumed hypothetically that the individuals' identity of interests is achieved in the societies of insects, which provides that each individual finds its pleasure in contributing to the welfare of all by its own performance. It is not absurd to suppose that such a situation, or at least one that approximates it might also obtain in the case of human societies; our ignorance of their physiological laws expands considerably the field of what we consider possible; nonetheless, one must take note that neither the human societies of the past nor those of the present display instances of this kind of identity.

There have always been theoreticians attempting to deny, sweep under the carpet, or at least attenuate the opposition of interests shown by the various parts of the social aggregate. Generally speaking, these attempts are grounded in tautological reasoning. One starts from the premise of the existence of what is actually in question by affirming that the individual's genuine well-being consists in doing what is useful to 'society.' On that basis, one goes on to state that those individuals who act otherwise are looking for a 'false well-being' and that they have to be discouraged from harming the others and themselves. Since Plato, such arguments have been offered under every possible form. A modern doctrine of so-called 'solidarity' does nothing but bring them in again, in a rather unskilful way.

There are people who maintain that the moral, intellectual and religious 'unity' of society is a highly desirable thing; but these same persons doggedly imply that this uniformity is attained through the adoption of their ideas. Thus the proposition which they put forth is but an euphemism expressing the idea that the whole world should be forced to think as they do.

The opposition between one part of the individuals that form an aggregate and the other part is often described as the opposition between individuals and 'society.' Thus those persons who want to achieve the moral, religious and intellectual 'unity' of society humbly pose as the representatives of that society and affirm that those who oppose them are but 'disruptive elements.' Nonetheless, among the latter there are some who pay them in their own coin as they, too, look forward to achieving social unity by imposing their own ideas upon 'disruptive individuals' who do not accept them of their free will.

Thus part of the aggregate gets the name 'individuals' and the rest is called 'society.' It is necessary to draw a distinction between the two. At present it is enough to take into consideration the number of people on each side. The minority of the aggregate has to be content with the name, rather disparaged nowadays, of 'individuals,' whereas the majority has the right to the honourable title of 'society.' This majority, which often makes itself felt by more or less indirect and complicated means only, may well be just a pseudo-majority. It is not true that a parliamentary majority represents the majority of the electorate. Thus in Switzerland, for instance, a law passed by the National Council with only one vote against was rejected by a substantial majority of votes when submitted to the popular referendum.

In our time, it is generally admitted that the interests of the few should be sacrificed to the interests of the many, and this proposition tends to become an article of faith which one will not be able to deny without risk; a divine right of the crowds is replacing the divine right of kings; both have their origin in sentiment and are without any scientific foundation.

It is worth noting that the propositions mentioned here and similar others do apply only in the case of societies that constitute political entities; they are irrelevant in the context of international relations, without knowing precisely why. Such contradictions are peculiar to propositions originating in sentiment. One must also remember that the propositions in question are valid only within certain limits; one does not admit, for instance, the idea that the majority might reduce the minority to slavery. Such limits remain indeterminate and quite vague.

Attempts have been made to get rid of this indetermination. Thus one has come to accept the idea that the 'individual' has innate, natural rights which 'society' should not infringe. It is useless to add that the difficulty which one wanted to overcome reappears in full as soon as one tries to set down those rights. All the theories worked out on this subject-matter have resulted into sheer logomachy. The concept of right, born in society and varying with the constitution of each society, is utterly helpless in separating the individual from the social.

A theory which at one time used to enjoy a certain vogue but which nowadays is out of fashion is that of the social con-tract on which presumably human societies have been founded. Accordingly, at a given moment, society was formed by the unanimous adhesion of the individuals that constituted it. Their descendants are regarded as their heirs by analogy with certain concepts which, in our societies, are related to inheritance. These descendants are supposed to have inherited debts and credits from the founders, or in other words: part of their duties and their rights towards 'society.' On the pattern of commercial enterprises, a certain majority is represented as society itself. However, the analogy stops short at the way of counting the votes, and that without knowing the reason why. It seems that in human societies they should be counted per caput, whereas in commerical institutions they are counted by the share of interest one holds in the enterprise.

The mutual dependence of the individuals in society is noticed to be on the increase while the individuals are seen specializing their functions ever more and so enhancing their efficiency. These are two different ways of describing one and the same phenomenon. In the light of the former, one may say that the social tends to prevail over the individual; under the latter aspect, one may say that the individual tends to get stronger in relation to the social. Yet, if one wishes to reason with precision, then one should avoid talking like that and instead, try to use terms that would correspond to well defined empirical realities and which would leave no room

for ambiguity. Instead of seeking means to act upon the sentiments, one should try to discover the uniformities displayed
by the social facts and to enunciate these uniformities or
laws as rigorously as possible.

> (Paper delivered at the Second
> Session of the International Con-
> gress of Philosophy, Geneva, 4-
> 8 September, 1904.)

APPENDIX B

THE FUTURE OF EUROPE:

THE POINT OF VIEW OF AN ITALIAN

Forecasts of events are generally a synthesis of different
and varying elements. Some are more the product of the instincts of practical individuals rather than the result of the
reasoning done by theoreticians. The forecasts which refer to
particular cases are not the least certain because of that.
Others, relevant especially whenever evolutionary trends are
queried, originate mainly in theoretical considerations. All
in all, with few exceptions, one comes upon sentiments which
lead us easily to foresee what we desire or what agrees with
our beliefs, principles and prejudices. The experimental or
often the pseudo-experimental elements are almost never lacking, unless sheer prophecies are tha matter, and they are
little in use nowadays. Here, though, it is on experience alone
that I shall ground my exposition.

As far as forecasts are concerned, the deductions inferred
with the help of the experimental method may be divided into
two big classes. The first class has its origin in the analogies with past events; they inform us of the possibility rather
than the probability of future events. The second class results
from the research on the intrinsic nature of social facts; it
acquaints us with the higher or lower probability of future
facts analogous to those which the first class showed as

possible, and also with other facts, entirely new.

Let us examine some applications of these principles.

Under certain aspects, our societies present striking analogies with the Roman society at the end of its Republican era. One of these aspects may be described, though only approximately, as the domination of a demagogic plutocracy.

In the assemblies of the People, the Roman plutocrats were buying the right to milk the provinces; and those very exactions were enabling them to afford the expenses that bought them power. Our plutocrats are not loath to scatter money in order to secure a legislation favouring their interests. The expenses involved in the elections in the United States have nothing to grudge to those that went on in Rome. Certain exactions brought about by trade protection and by etatism are more regular, less arbitrary and less contrary to the law, though not less momentous than the sums exacted by the Roman proconsuls.

When Rome embarked upon the wars which in the aftermath of the conquest of the Mediterranean basin were to mark the triumph of the demagogic plutocracy, the People was reluctant to follow suit. Livy tells us that in 200 B.C. the proposal to wage war against Macedonia was rejected by almost all the centuries at the first assemblies. It was a spontaneous act of men grown weary of a long and painful war, who loathed the dangers and the exhaustion. The tribune G. Baebius accused the senators of provoking war after war in order to prevent the people from enjoying the sweets of peace. At the second assemblies, the Senate managed to prevail upon the People (XXXI, 6). In our times, the rivalries between the plutocrats were not without effect in the waging of the Great War and its prolongation. At present one may fear that they are preparing new conflicts.

One comes upon analogies even in particular cases. Thus, for instance, many of our modern speculators quite successfully reproduce the type of the Roman consul M. Aemilius Scaurus.

For intrinsic reasons which would take too long to discuss here (I have dealt with them in my TREATISE OF GENERAL SOCI-

OLOGY), the cycle of demagogic plutocracy cannot be much extended in time. Sooner or later the circulation of the élites will put an end to it, and one is permitted to believe that we are reaching the term of its power. Although we are with a high degree of probability in the know about this point, we are by far less knowledgeable of the form which the future transformation will assume. At Rome, it was the military élite that inherited the power of the assemblies of the People. However, the social and political conditions of those times were too different from ours to enable us to draw a lesson from them. The field remains open to hypotheses. Some authors, perhaps under the influence of the Bolshevist revolution, foresee some new middle ages. This hypothesis should not be discarded but its materalization is a very distant prospect.

Meanwhile it is certain that democracy is in full process of transformation. The phenomenon is more or less evident, depending on the country under scrutiny. It is less obvious in France, and more so in England, and above all in Italy, while setting aside the exceptional case of Russia.

Towards the end of the nineteenth century one could believe that the rule of our society was to be that of the greatest number, and that was to be achieved by universal suffrage and the parliamentary system. Nowadays one begins to notice that this power of the greatest number is more nominal than real, and that it is on the point of going under in the same way as the power of the constitutional monarchs. Even if it were admitted that the greatest number are capable of having a will of their own, and there are authors who contest it, experience shows that this will, seemingly all-powerful, is nothing of the kind in reality, and that it is cancelled through devices used by the rulers; possibly it reigns but certainly it does not rule. The war made the governments lay down the law. There is nothing exceptional about this and nothing in it to serve as an index of the future change. Not the same thing may be said about the fact that the war once over, the dictatorship of governments did not come to an end. The *salus populi* which had justified it when the supreme interests of the nation were at risk is far less apparent when it comes to secondary questions such as unemployment, or the interests of certain manufacturers and their auxiliaries, or even the general interests of the Treasury. At all times, laws have had to cope with exceptions, that is to say, one has had to bow to circumstances. The question is one of degree: more represents the arbitrariness of dictatorship, of that kind of régime which the Greeks used to call tyranny, or the disorder of anarchy; less means the rule of what the Greeks worshipped under the name of *nomos*, the Romans, under the name of *lex*, and what we call 'law.' Nonetheless, it would not be wrong to say that this kind of rule is breaking down and that we are approaching a state of things where the regard for law is becoming the exception. It Italy, for instance, the very great number of decrees tends to transform the preventive power of the Parliament into a repressive power, its law-making function into the simple licensing of the edicts decreed by the executive power. Not only the cabinet ministers but also the prefects place themselves above the fundamental Statutes of the Kingdom, the codes, and the law; sometimes these edicts have a retroactive effect. The Court of Cassation with all its desirable discretion could not help remarking the anti-juridical nature of some of them. Similar facts can be observed in other countries, too. In order to justify these measures, the urgent needs of the moment are invoked alongside the technical incapacity of parliaments. Whether these justifications are grounded or not, they leave unchanged the fact that the legislative function tends to evade parliaments and as a result the greatest number of which they are or seem to be the emanation.

Whenever the legal power fulfills its function badly, that is, the function to secure the authority of the law, to defend the citizens and their rights, then forces outside the law replace it. It was one of the causes for the establishment of the secret tribunals in old Germany. Nowadays it is the main cause of Fascism in Italy. This phenomenon is the index of a frame of mind which, although more evident in Italy, is to be found elsewhere, too, and may help bring about considerable changes.

If we direct our eyes towards a less distant future, a fact strikes us: the little change in the forces that act upon society. After the Great War, one used to hope that it would be different: one was expecting to see the causes of hatred and war among peoples disappear and an era of peace and prosperity set in.

Unfortunately, most of those hopes have been belied. Sr Nitti has been able to write a book entitled EUROPE WITHOUT PEACE, and Mr Lloyd George brandishes Athena's shield before the prostrated peoples. The state of unstable equilibrium experienced by Germany, the Russian enigma, the threatening rise of Islam, without taking into account the less important facts such as Austria's collapse, weigh heavily upon the world. The economic prosperity seems quite slow in coming. It is true that very fine speeches are made about the 'reconstruction' of Europe, but even the tiniest millet seed, that is to say, the smallest practical relief would do more good to the peoples.

One must confess that among the hastily conceived hopes there were some without any solid base at all. For instance, how could one sensibly believe that the enormous destruction of wealth brought about by the war expenditures would result in the greatest number working less and consuming more? The clauses of the Treaty of Versailles alone were supposed to help achieve this result which would have been as miraculous as the multiplication of the fishes and the loaves of bread.

Nothing comes out of the impossible; but by not being able to enjoy the real thing, one at least wanted to make do with appearances, and it is thus that wages have been set, as well as fees and mortages; by being expressed in phoney money they were higher than those which would have been worked out in terms of goods. That is one of the causes of the currency depreciation in many countries. Others may be found in the advantage which certain governments take by paying in depreciated currency the interest on their debts, to dissmulate the transfer of wealth between different social classes and thus to obtain for their countries a fictitious prosperity destined, it is true, to disappear, but which while it lasts contributes to the preservation of social and political stability. At present, there are already precursory signs of a change in the state of things. The workday of eight hours is under hard debate, and when it cannot be attacked head on,

one tries to turn its flank; wages get lower almost everywhere; the workers themselves acknowledge that they cannot be
maintained at the exaggerated level to which they have been
raised. The transfer of wealth seems to reach its end by
mere exhaustion if for no other cause. Thus, for instance, in
Russia and in Austria the depreciation of the currency has
yielded everything likely to be got out of it, while it also
has had considerable effects in Germany.

These facts and similar others allow for the belief that
the economic equilibrium would not be too slow in redressing
itself from that standpoint.

One is less inclined to say the same thing about the exchange of goods and the means of transportation. It is a well-
established fact that the prosperity of the nineteenth century
was largely due to the enormous increase in internal and
external trade, favoured by relatively cheap means of transportation. It is not enough to produce cheaply; one must also
obtain raw materials easily and sell the finished product.
However, as soon as all this is admitted, one must also reach
the conclusion that the measures that nowadays raise the
cost of transportation and set countless obstacles in the way
of the exchange of goods have the reduction of that prosperity
as a necessary result.

There are certain facts which at first sight seem puzzling.
Thus it is quite certain that a nation cannot make payments
abroad for long whenever it is prevented to export its goods.
That seems to be forgotten when in order to meet her obliga-
tions Germany is required to pay huge amounts of money while,
on the other hand, barriers are raised against her exports,
to prevent her from 'flooding' the foreign markets with her
goods. It is true that each and every country dreams only of
protecting its own market against this 'flooding.' As all of
them agree on this matter, it looks like a general measure to
protect one's exports.

Another thing. There are European nations which think that
the opening of the Russian market is a matter of life and
death for their economies, and which at the same time give
up more considerable markets of their own free will. They
renounce more lucrative operations which are within their

reach and aspire to settle for less which so far has been eluding them. One may also notice that certain nations go by the general rule of rejecting the goods of the countries with 'damaged currencies,' while all too easily they overlook it in particular instances, such as Russia's. In the latter's case, the resumption of trade with her is considered of the highest interest, though quite rightly Russia may be given as the typical example of a nation with an extremely impaired currency. Furthermore, such an exchange cannot obviously take place unless Russia's exports are accepted in turn. The distinction which one tries to draw in this matter between manufactured goods, on the one side, and raw materials, on the other, is far-fetched, because Russia's agricultural exports belong mostly to that category of goods against which one tries to defend one's markets. A good many economists are quite wrong when they think that their science suffices to resolve most of the practical problems that are called 'economic.' Wrong, too, are those who believe that they can solve these problems by means of formulae that are ethical, juridical, political and the like.

Not at all. The mutual dependence of social phenomena makes it impossible to resolve most of the problems, not to say all of them, in any other way than by making use of several social sciences simultaneously. The practical measures which governments adopt need to take into consideration the state of the economy and the frame of mind, the sentiments and the ideas. Thus it is in vain to hope to cure the present ills of Europe either by simple economic measures or by others of an exclusively moral, juridical, political or such like nature. In order to be efficacious, these two kinds of measures need to be brought to bear together. Pure historical materialism and unadulterated idealism each contain a part of truth and a part of error.

Quite often economics point to certain limits that cannot be exceeded; other sciences inform us of the movements that occur within these limits.

Thus, as we have seen, economics provide us with certain gauges, determined by the effects of wealth-destruction and the barriers raised against international exchange. Furthermore, one must ask sociology how and why the effects of those phenomena become manifest within those boundaries. It is only by putting all these different viewpoints together that we are able to explain the past and acquire an idea of the future.

Let us try to learn the causes which give rise to the contradictions that we have just noted. Let us not stop at the appearances of things. Looking closer we see that as soon as a distinction is drawn between the general interest, on one side, and certain particular interests, on the other, the contradiction diminishes. Plutocrats and their ancillaries, as well as those who revolve round them, the politicians included, may find their advantages in the application of these various measures which instead of contradicting each other converge towards one and the same goal. Referring to the Russian market, Mr Lloyd George has been talking about the 'hunters of concessions.' He could have directed his attention upon countries closer to home, and talked instead of the very many individuals who make their profits from the differences in the fluctuation of customs tariffs, from its 'coefficients,' from import restrictions and from a variety of subsidies which the ingenious greed of those concerned discovers every day of the week. That is an almost constant force the effects of which would not be slow to materialize when the circumstances become favourable.

We should not stop at this result in our research but rather find it more convenient to go on and ask ourselves about those circumstances. An exhaustive reply to this question will take us too far, as it will involve the full explanation of the cycle of the demagogic plutocracy. For our subject-matter here it would suffice to signal one of the circumstances only.

After long and extensive wars, one notices a recrudescence of the 'protective spirit.' That is what Herbert Spencer noticed in connection with the French-Prussian war of 1870-1871. Nowadays it makes itself manifest on a far larger scale: each nation tends to isolate itself not only economically but also intellectually, it becomes xenophobic. That being the case, individuals and organizations crop forth by necessity and do their utmost to exploit the prevailing frame of mind.

As this state changes very slowly, one may predict that until the cycle of the demagogic plutocracy comes to a halt, great changes in the present situation are less likely.

This also applies to the political conditions, without as much as a trace of doubt, because in that field one deals with even more general facts. A generous illusion made one believe that: *magnus ab integro soeculorum nascitur ordo*, in the aftermath of the Great War which was concluded through the Treaty of Versailles.

Unfortunately it had to be reconsidered because one came eventually to witness the same divergencies of interest reappear among the nations, the same rivalries as in the past. In many of its aspects, the Genoa Conference was reproducing the Congress of Vienna of 1815 or that of Verona of 1822. There are remarkable coincidences. Likewise, the present animus between England and France about the recognition of the Soviet government seems a genuine copy of the friction about the recognition of the governments of the Spanish colonies of America as soon as they proclaimed their independence; they are reproduced nowadays even in regard to such details as the debate round the recognition *de jure* and the recognition *de facto*.

The coincidence is not accidental. It is due to the fact that the same forces that are active nowadays were at work then, and also to their different impact in England, on the one hand, and in France, on the other, which gives rise to the disagreement between the two countries. The former nation is more trade-oriented, more industrial, speculative and more responsive to the influence exerted by the plutocrats than the latter nation. Previously, the former had been anticipating considerable advantages from the opening of the American markets. France, on the other hand, had had no intention to get too involved in such an enterprise. That is exactly what happens nowadays, only this time it refers to the Russian market.

At present, the confidence which the Soviets might inspire is weakening among the Socialists, whereas it looks like growing stronger among certain plutocrats. The reason for the difference in attitude is easy to get by, it has all to do with the plutocratic watchword: 'business is business.'

By lengthy discussions one tries to make out whether Germany wants but cannot, or can but does not want to pay the sums of money she is due in accordance with the Treaty of Versailles. That is important from the ethical, juridical and political points of view, but leaves out the probability that for one reason or another these payments might not be made in full and that the expense incurred to induce her to do so may quite well reduce the net product to a considerable degree. It is very difficult to foresee the consequences of this situation; one only can say that the consequences will be very grave in all likelihood.

Not only the expectations of economic prosperity were belied, but unfortunately, others, too, shared the same fate. The mirage of an era of universal harmony grows ever more distant. The horizon towards the East is dim. One has been forced to give up the hypothesis of a repenting Germany that would keep reciting '*mea culpa*'; no human force would be able to induce her to give up the prospect of revenge. The attempts to attract Russia into the orbit of the Western bourgeois states have not been too successful so far. Sooner or later, common political interests will bring about an alliance between Germany and Russia. An invasion by the forces of these two nations is not to be feared for the time being, but should not be dismissed for a more distant future.

History displays quite remarkable uniformities. For example, the Rhine would deserve to be called the river of blood. Since times immemorial various races and civilizations have clashed on its banks and gored its waters. It is quite unlikely that in our very times the course of history would change.

Talking about the peoples living beyond the Rhine, Tacitus wished that the intestine hatreds would stay and last with those peoples in the absence of any affection for the Romans; because as pressed as the Romans were by the problems of the Empire, fortune could not have offered them anything better than the discord of their enemies. That is what the citizens of the first French Revolution seem to have forgotten as did the governments of Napoleon I and Napoleon III, when willy nilly they helped bring about Germany's unification.

That is also what the governments of the Western nations seem to have forgotten when by the Treaty of Versailles they consolidated this unity which they could have undermined. At present, without wanting it, they push Germany and Russia to come to terms with one another, whereas they could at least delay this alliance.

Similar facts may often be observed within the cycle of the demagogic plutocracy and also outside it. One's prospects are compromised for the sake of an immediate advantage or simply in order to avoid exerting oneself at a time when it is likely to pay. Thus Athens had allowed Macedonia to increase its power and become dominant; and the peoples of the Mediterranean basin had permitted the Roman power to grow and consolidate at the expense of their own enslavement.

Such facts affect differently the individual fate of nations and the general progress of civilization: the latter might have profited by what had been the ruin of Athens or the destruction of Carthage. If one chooses this point of view, then it becomes quite difficult, not to say impossible, to foresee the distant effects of what is cooking up now, and if one tries to guess them, then one steps out of the domain of the empirical sciences.

(Printed in LA REVUE DE GENÈVE,
July-December, 1922, pp.438-448.)

APPENDIX C

THE FASCIST PHENOMENON

The study of Fascism, like that of most social phenomena, meets with difficulties related to their complexity, as well as with others of an altogether different nature. Among the latter the most remarkable difficulty derives from the fact that one and the same name is used to designate two obviously distinct situations.

On the surface, Fascism appears very different when looked at as it was before or after the 'march on Rome' and the revolution which brought it to power. After all, its leader has stressed this difference quite well in an article printed in GERARCHIA, by calling the present state of things 'the second phase' of Fascism.

In its 'first phase.' Fascism seemed a spontaneous and somewhat anarchical reaction set up by a part of the population against the 'red tyranny' to which the Government had permitted every licence, leaving it to the private citizens to defend themselves. At that time Fascism did not bother about theories; many of its adherents used to claim publicly that it was an 'action' and not an 'ideology.' From this point of view, its formation and its role are part of a well-known order of things. One of the main objectives of any government is to protect persons and assets; whenever it overlooks that, forces from the midst of the population are likely to emerge in order to compensate for its failures. As manifestations of this trend one may recall the secret tribunals in Germany in the Middle Ages...

Such a situation is essentially transitory among the most civilized peoples in particular,for which order is absolutely necessary; sooner or later the old government, or by default, a new government resume the function temporarily surrendered to private initiative.

Thus one could have foreseen that early Fascism might not have lasted long, that it would have disappeared in order to make room for a new arrangement of things. The latter could have been the work of the ruling class still in power, or of a new ruling class: either the adversaries of Fascism or Fascism itself, transformed, grown into an organic doctrine of the State, reaffirming government authority and public order. It is the latter alternative that has materialized. We have to trace the reasons for such an occurrence. This is also suggested to us by another proposition which may be added to the one just stated. Governments also have among their objectives the function to manage the finances of the State and the economy of the nation. It may be repeated that in the case of failure, those particular governments end by being replaced by others. One could witness that happening at the time of the fall of the ancien régime in France.

The Italian ruling class was not doing its job any better than its forerunner. It was aware of that, and the feeling of its own impotence was depressing it. In vain did it try to react. Among other things, Sr. Giolitti came to power on account of the programme to 'restore' State authority and the finances. He had to step down without attaining either objective. His successors were not more successful; on the contrary, the ills were growing worse with every passing day, the boat of the State was drifting at the mercy of the winds. The Lower House dismissed the Facta Cabinet and then, failing to find anybody to take his place as prime-minister, resigned itself to recalling him to form the government once more.

The members of this new cabinet did not listen to him. As a matter of fact, the State was left without any power. Consequently, the choice of a new régime was narrowed down to the Fascists or their adversaries. The former got it; why?

A first difference between the Fascists and their opponents can be perceived instantly. The latter were looking for immediate results which would have satisfied their appetites and provided them with material advantages at the earliest; they had been striving to grab assets and positions freely, without bothering too much about the day after. In 1919 and 1920 the Socialists and their allies were on the verge of seizing power; a slight effort on their part would have rendered them masters of the situation. They did not make it. Instead, they scattered their forces by occupying lands and factories, by simply demanding more gain and less work, and various sinecures. The conquest of municipalities appeared to them an opportunity to plunder them only, to share the product of taxes increased beyond measure, and to despoil the endowments of charitable institutions and of hospitals. At one moment, Milan and Bologna became little States almost independent of the central power. It could have been a first stage towards the conquest of the latter. Instead, it proved rather to be the finish for all those who had profited by the changed situation.

The contrast with the Fascists is striking. Indeed, there are black sheep in every flock, and among the Fascists, too, there were some seeking their personal and immediate interests, but their number was very small. The great majority were following a line that led to a more or less mythical ideal: the exaltation of the national sentiment and of the power of the State, the reaction against democratic, pseudo-liberal, pacifist and humanitarian ideologies. Most of them were probably experiencing nothing more than a vague and indistinct sentiment that was egging them on to action, but they were led skilfully and unfalteringly by their chiefs, or perhaps one should say their chief, towards a lofty goal of great importance: the conquest of the central power. At the time when they came within reach of that goal, one tried to stop them by offering them a large part to play in a par-liamentary cabinet. Sr Mussolini turned down the offer. He wanted everything or nothing. This is another application of the law drawn from a great many facts and which has been mentioned in the TREATISE OF SOCIOLOGY, namely that given a number of social groups, the upper hand is got by that group the leaders of which have the instinct of combinations de-veloped to a high degree while the rest are imbued with firm, ideal sentiments. Sr Mussolini could claim that his support-ers were inspired with the 'mysticism of obedience.' There is much truth in this assertion. After the revolution which brought Fascism to power, the Fascists' individual and some-what disorderly action was replaced with little protest by a rigorous discipline allowing only for the rule of the central power.

Another difference between the Fascists and their adver-saries is made clear by the examination of the economic or financial conditions. Any problem related to them may be solved in two ways: one, which secures the maximum economic utility, and the other, the greatest satisfaction of certain sentiments and particular interests. The weak governments, those which have to cope with the greed and the prejudices of their supporters, favour the second solution. Only the strong governments, relying on the armed forces and on strong sentiments of ideality, are in the position of adopting the first solution.

As long as society is rich and prosperous, the first solu-tion may be overlooked in favour of the second; yet as soon as the wealth is exhausted and crises occur, to persist stub-bornly in sacrificing the economy for the sake of prejudices and particular interests may lead to the the worst disasters.

One finds an example of that kind of occurrence in the revolution that led to the fall of the ancien régime in France.

Nowadays all Europe finds itself in the same plight, and
its ruling classes cannot find adquate solutions to the trou-
blesome problems facing them. In Italy, Fascism has come
to sketch out one of these solutions by substituting a new
ruling class to that which proved itself incapable of governing. Wherever the power of the State lay abandoned, Fascism
has tried to raise it to its feet. It is left to the future
to tell us whether a new era has dawned or whether one is
going back to the old ways which seem very likely to lead to
an anarchy similar to that which the world experienced during
the Middle Ages.

Somehow everywhere, and in Italy in particular, the sentiments of the people after the war reveal a strange anomaly.
The living conditions of the working class have known a considerable improvement; the workday of eight hours and the
wage increases, which sometimes are enormous, are clear indices of that. On the other hand, the material situation of
the petty bourgeoisie, the rentiers and above all of those
who are called the 'intellectuals' has generally worsened,
and in particular cases has become wholly abject. As a result,
it seems that the former should bless warfare and the latter
should curse it. What happens is just the other way round.

The explanation of this fact is not hard to come by. The
working masses accept as their due the benefits brought to
them by the war. They put forth new 'claims,' demand further
benefits which their rather simplistic notion of social phenomena makes them see in the appropriation of the assets
of the other social classes.

The others, with few exceptions and the plutocrats are the
main one, are to a high degree imbued with the religion of
patriotism and nationalism. Like most believers, these classes put up with the sufferings imposed by faith and rock in
the illusion that their misfortunes are transient.

In Italy, Fascism has come in part to amend this error of
logic in the sentiments of the social classes. It has known
how to lend to the nationalist religion a goal to act upon:

the defence of the State, the social renovation. The essence of the 'Fascist revolution' lies mainly in this.

The contingent, occasional causes should be added to the general causes. Among them one of the most remarkable is the fact that Fascism has found a first-class politician in its leader.

To use his power with firmness but also with moderation, to avoid any weakness but also any excess are among the most difficult conditions for a dictator to fulfill. It was precisely because he met those conditions that Octavian Augustus could lay the foundations of a lasting empire. It was by disregarding them, particularly in the area of foreign policy, that Napoleon III was led to his own ruin.

The dictatorship established in the aftermath of a revolution often has an easy start, only to meet with growing difficulties as it goes on. Momentarily constrained and reduced to silence, the hostile forces eventually recover and find their voice, and undermine the power. In Italy, one may already see the signs of this process, though very feint at this time.

One of the problems hardest to solve is that of freedom. In order to set up a dictatorship, freedom has to be considerably restricted. On the other hand, in order to set up a long-lasting régime one has to grant a certain amount of freedom. It is quite difficult to distinguish between the dangerous opponent and the inoffensive adversary, yet it is indispensable to treat each of them differently. Salvation is available at this price only.

Sr Mussolini has brought a firm and quite remarkable moderration to foreign policy. One had had the impression that he was going to break all the windowpanes; however, he showed himself capable of distinguishing what was possible from what was not, and of working out quite a realistic line of action.

As for his home policies, any final judgment at this stage would be premature. One may only say that the beginnings are good and open to the prospect of a happy future. But one steers with frightening rocks in sight. Sooner or later one must come out of the provisional and solve some very serious constitutional problems, and that perhaps may not be possible without a stroke of genius. It is there that lies one of the greatest dangers that threaten the new régime and the new order in general.

(Printed in the Genevan weekly LA SE-
MAINE LITTÉRAIRE, 1st September, 1923,
pp. 419-420.)

JULIEN FREUND, Professor of Sociology at the University of Strasbourg, is the eldest son of a numerous working-class family from Lorraine. In 1940 he managed to escape through the fingers of the German occupants and travelled south to the area of the Massif Central, known at the time as the Free Territory. It was there during his student years that he became an active member of the French Resistance, was arrested and imprisoned, but eventually managed to escape again. After the war, he had Raymond Aron as the supervisor of his doctoral dissertation which under the title of ESSENCE DU POLITIQUE is now in print in its third edition. Part of his complementary thesis on Max Weber was translated into English as THE SOCI-OLOGY OF MAX WEBER. A tireless lecturer and author of numerous articles and books, he is also a partisan of the choucroute and co-author of a cookbook. Recently he has published a massive and very impressive study entitled LA DÉCADENCE. In rest, Professor Freund likes to call himself 'a conservative of the left.' He is married and has two grown-up sons.

SIMONA DRAGHICI, an European-American scholar, holds among other things a PhD degree in sociology from the University of Texas at Austin. Her interests have to do with problems of conceptualization and the historical analysis of social in-stitutions.